W9-BVD-552

The Impeachment and Trial
of Andrew Johnson

THE NORTON ESSAYS IN AMERICAN HISTORY

Under the general editorship of

HAROLD M. HYMAN

William P. Hobby Professor of American History
Rice University

E666
B46
1973

The Impeachment
and Trial
of Andrew Johnson

Michael Les Benedict

New York W · W · NORTON & COMPANY · INC ·

OCT 25 1974

184718

FIRST EDITION

Copyright © 1973 by Michael Les Benedict. All right reserved. Published simultaneously in Canada by George J. McLeod Limited, Toronto. Printed in the United States of America.

Library of Congress Cataloging in Publication Data

Benedict, Michael Les.

    The impeachment and trial of Andrew Johnson.

    Bibliography: p.

    1. Johnson, Andrew, Pres. U.S., 1808–1875—

Impeachment.   I. Title.

E666.B46   1973   973.8′1′0924 [B]   72–10883

ISBN 0–393–05473–X

ISBN 0–393–09418–9 (pbk)

2 3 4 5 6 7 8 9 0

For Brenda

Contents

Preface

~~~~~~

IN PERHAPS NO FIELD of American history has scholarly opinion shifted so completely as in the assessment during the past decade and a half of Reconstruction after the Civil War. Instead of describing vindictive radicals seething with vengeance or cynical capitalists using emotions fostered by the war to fasten their economic control upon the nation, historians now speak in terms of well-meaning efforts of conscientious Republicans to establish national security on the basis of racial equality before the law. If anything, the criticism is that the so-called radicals did not go far enough.[1] Only one event has resisted this historical reversal—the impeachment and trial of President Andrew Johnson. Even to those who sympathize with Republican purposes and programs during Reconstruction, "the impeachment was a great act of ill-directed passion, and was supported by little else."[2] The two full-length works that center upon the impeachment, both apathetic if not hostile to Republican concerns, offer even less friendly judgments.[3]

To some extent, these conclusions are based upon the mature reconsiderations of some of the most respected participants. As James G. Blaine wrote nearly twenty years after he voted in favor

1. A brief discussion of the historiography of reconstruction may be found in the bibliographical essay, pp. 191–96.
2. Eric L. McKitrick, *Andrew Johnson and Reconstruction* (Chicago, 1960), 506.
3. David Miller DeWitt, *The Impeachment and Trial of Andrew Johnson, Seventh President of the United States: A History* (New York and London, 1903), and Milton Lomask, *Andrew Johnson: President on Trial* (New York, 1960).

of the impeachment resolution, "The sober reflection of after years has persuaded many who favored Impeachment that it was not justifiable on the charges made, and that its success would have resulted in greater injury to free institutions than Andrew Johnson in his utmost endeavor was able to inflict." John Sherman, while defending his vote to convict on the evidence presented, concluded that on the substantive issues that precipitated the crisis, Johnson had been right all along.[4] But these were the opinions of conservative men who had never really been committed to impeachment and who had exercised a strong, moderating influence on the course of Reconstruction itself. They wrote in the 1880s and 1890s, when the spirit of crisis that permeated the 1860s had faded into shadowy memory, and their conclusions cannot convey the urgency, passions, or necessities that in the opinion of so many Americans justified perhaps the most remarkable event in the history of American government, the trial of the Chief Executive of the United States. That is the goal of this study.

The research necessary for this project was made possible in large part by financial support from the Center for Research in Social Change and Economic Development, of Houston, Texas, and the Woodrow Wilson Foundation. For their help in completing this study, I want to thank the librarians and clerical employees of the Fondren Library at Rice University and of the many manuscript repositories I visited in the course of my research; my friend, Rick Jones, who developed the computer programs I used; my wife, Karen, whose patience, support, and criticisms sustained me unfailingly; and especially Professor Harold M. Hyman, my mentor, who is primarily responsible both for developing any good professional qualities I have acquired and for minimizing the bad ones.

MICHAEL LES BENEDICT

March, 1972

4. Blaine, *Twenty Years of Congres* . . . , 2 vols. (Norwich, Conn., 1884–86), II, 376; Sherman, *Recollections of Forty Years in the House, Senate, and Cabinet: An Autobiography,* 2 vols. (New York, 1895), I, 361–64, 346–76, 431–32.

The Impeachment and Trial
of Andrew Johnson

1

Andrew Johnson, the Republicans, and Reconstruction

~~~~~~

Andrew Johnson and the Problem of Reconstruction

At the heart of the only impeachment of a president of the United States lay the crisis of American Reconstruction after the Civil War.[1] In the dry pages of history books, the reality of that crisis sometimes fades. The danger through which the Union had just passed seems to pale. The Union victory appears foreordained, secure reunion certain. But the generation of Northerners who shed their blood or watched loved ones and friends spill theirs had no such assurance. The danger of national disintegration had been all too real, the sacrifices to prevent it great. When the war ended, loyal Americans faced real traitors, people who had fought gallantly and bitterly to rend the fabric of the nation. To understand the spirit of the Reconstruction crisis, one must grasp the reality of civil war,

1. This discussion of Reconstruction is not intended to be exhaustive, but merely to outline the problem and the issues that formed the background of the impeachment of Andrew Johnson. The reader who desires a more thorough discussion should consult the works cited in the Bibliographical Review upon which this discussion is based. My interpretation of the development of the Reconstruction struggle does not correspond at all points with those offered in these studies; the differences are based upon my work, "The Right Way: Congressional Republicans and Reconstruction, 1863–1869" (unpublished Ph.D dissertation, Rice University, 1971), to be published by W. W. Norton.

1

recognize that the generation of Americans caught up in the web of Reconstruction actually lived, actually confronted a situation, today totally alien to us, where countrymen killed countrymen, where political power involved more than the simple control of administration. In that charged milieu, political differences inevitably transcended mere questions of policy in which well-spirited, restrained disagreement was possible. In the crisis of Reconstruction the future of the nation hung in the balance.

But with all that depended upon a secure Reconstruction, Americans were singularly ill equipped to cope with the problem effectively. By 1865 most Northerners, especially Republicans, had come to identify security for the Union with tangible, fundamental change in southern society, particularly in black-white relations. Most important, Republicans insisted upon protection for former slaves in their new freedom.[2] Yet these same Northerners, including Republicans, displayed a remarkable reluctance to force these changes on the South through the power of the national government. On the part of those who had adhered to a Jacksonian philosophy of limited government before the war, this hesitation is not surprising. But the reluctance to alter fundamentally the relations between the state and national governments also affected former Whigs. At first many Republicans hoped Southerners themselves would inaugurate the necessary changes voluntarily, but it quickly became apparent that even modest change in southern society (beyond the mere abolition of slavery) would require the national action so many Northerners wanted to avoid. So Republicans in 1865 were faced with an intimidatingly difficult problem, even without further complications. But further complications arose—in the person of the seventeenth president of the United States, Andrew Johnson. If the critical importance of

2. During the war, Republicans had ostensibly submerged their party organization in a broader Union party. Although many former Democrats did join this new, expanded organization, it clearly retained its Republican character, and by 1865 the term "Republican" was in general use again.

Reconstruction for the security of the nation provided the kindling for the impeachment crisis, it was the torch of Andrew Johnson's personal character that ignited the flame.

Raised in poverty in North Carolina, his father dead, his stepfather unwilling and probably unable to improve the family fortunes, Johnson had acquired no formal schooling. But he was remarkably and overpoweringly ambitious. His life, wrote his old enemy, Oliver P. Temple, "was one intense, unceasing, desperate, upward struggle," and the grinding poverty of his youth appears to have been a torment to him not only because of financial hardship but also because of the constant social humiliation he felt he endured.[3] Johnson was embarrassed by the deficiencies of his education all his life, but he overcame them as much as possible by force of his incredible will. Apprenticed to a tailor at the age of fourteen, he taught himself, to read with the aid of the foreman of the shop; he was over twenty when his wife taught him to write. But he never acquired the breadth and suppleness of mind that formal training might have developed. Complex problems frustrated him, and he sought refuge from them in general rules to govern all situations. "There is nothing like starting out on principle," he told a confidant while he was president. "When you start out right with principles clearly defined you can hardly go astray." [4] "His mind had one compartment for right and one for wrong, but no middle chamber where the two could commingle," concluded the sympathetic historian, Howard K. Beale. Having gone through the agony of decision-making, Johnson's narrow mind snapped shut. In Beale's words, "He could bear insult, personal danger, obloquy; but he could not yield his point." [5] Instead, he would fight to sustain his position with every weapon at hand.

3. Temple, *Notable Men of Tennessee from 1833 to 1875: Their Times and Their Contemporaries* (New York, 1912), 466.

4. Notes of William A. Moore, private secretary to President Johnson, in the Johnson Mss., October 26, 1866, Library of Congress, Washington, D.C.

5. Beale, *The Critical Year: A Study of Andrew Johnson and Reconstruction* (New York, 1930), 26.

By 1827, when Johnson opened his own tailor shop in Greeneville, Tennessee, his thirst for recognition and his talent for debate were already developed. Once a week he pitted his powers against those of the other members of the Greeneville College debating society. At the same time, he played host to a budding political club at his shop. In 1829 the young political organization sponsored and elected a slate of candidates for the city council. By the 1830s it was the dominant element in Greeneville politics, and by force of his personality Andrew Johnson had emerged as its leader. Elected mayor of Greeneville, state representative, congressman, governor of Tennessee, and senator, the former tailor's apprentice became the most powerful politician of his state. Allied to the Democratic party, he appealed to its radical wing, espousing its most egalitarian, democratic tenets.

As the only southern senator who had remained loyal to the Union in 1861, Johnson was appointed military governor of Tennessee by Lincoln, who then encouraged the Union-Republican party to make him its candidate for vice-president. When Lincoln died, Andrew Johnson, self-educated poor boy from North Carolina and tailor from Tennessee, became president of the United States.

In politics and government, the rules Johnson applied to difficult questions were those he had developed as a strict-constructionist, economizing, Locofoco Jacksonian Democrat. His Jacksonian devotion to limited government and his tight-fistedness with the people's money were so closely interwoven that they defied separation. Johnson's first term in the Tennessee legislature ended in disastrous defeat because he so rigidly opposed state-supported improvements for his region. In Congress, he waged resolute warfare against appropriations for the Smithsonian Institution, tried to reduce the salaries of government white-collar workers, fought to limit the number of clerks in the House, and voted against increasing pay for soldiers during the Mexican War. He spoke against appropriating money to help famine-stricken Ireland and opposed increases in the size of the standing army. On both constitutional and financial grounds, Johnson even opposed a congressional appropriation to pave the streets of the District of Columbia. Johnson set his direction on any public question by his twin guideposts—opposition to governmental "extravagance" and rigid adherence to his own strict interpretation of the Constitution. "I have, during all of my political life, been guided by certain fixed political principles," he once remarked. "I am guided by them still. They are the principles of the early founders of the Republic, and I cannot certainly go far wrong if I adhere to them, as I intend to." [6]

Having taken a position on any issue, Johnson interpreted every attack upon that position as an attack upon himself. Rarely has a politician evidenced such personal involvement in his policies. Ill at ease in Washington society, lonely, with few warm friends even in Tennessee, Johnson sought affection from the public at large. "[M]ost of his speeches, no matter what else they dealt with," Eric L. McKitrick has noted, "may be read as demands for personal vindication and personal approval." [7] When that approval was not forthcoming, when he or his policies were attacked, Johnson's response was bitter.

It was that kind of personal repudiation that engendered his well-known hostility to the southern slaveholding aristocracy. Scorned by his social "betters" both in Tennessee and in Washington, Johnson manifested an exaggerated pride in his "plebeian" origins. Subject to venomous attacks from that quarter all his life, he developed a capacity for answering his opponents with an invective that was dazzling in its intensity. "If Andy Johnson was a snake," Tennessee's Confederate governor, Isham G. Harris, said caustically, "he would hide in the grass and bite the heels of rich men's children." [8] Demolishing local opponents with sledge-hammer blows, Johnson earned a reputation as the finest stump speaker in Tennessee. But a talent so often

6. Moore notes, October 26, 1866, Johnson Mss.
7. McKitrick, *Andrew Johnson and Reconstruction* (Chicago, 1960), 89.
8. Lately Thomas, *The First President Johnson: The Three Lives of the Seventeenth President of the United States of America* (New York, 1968), 229.

and so successfully employed is not easily discarded, and Johnson aimed his raking fire at slaveholding aristocrats, "Black
Republicans," southern secessionists, and postwar Republicans
in turn, igniting in each group a burning resentment that nearly
led to his lynching before the Civil War and fueled the impeachment movement after it.

Lincoln's death elevated Johnson to the presidency at a time
of crisis. Immediately, the new president faced the complexities
of Reconstruction, and his background and principles led him
to set a policy that most Republicans eventually repudiated. In
following his program, Johnson would ignore some congressional
enactments and violate the spirit of others.

Johnson shared with other border-state Unionists a conception of the "fruits of victory" that differed markedly from
that of northern Republicans. Concerned only tangentially, if at
all, with the well-being of black Southerners, Johnson took victory to mean the return of the southern white masses to loyalty
and the humiliation of the southern aristocracy that had misled
them into treason. Inheriting from Lincoln the bare outlines of
a Reconstruction policy that seemed to pursue a similar goal,
Johnson fixed on a program of amnesty for all Southerners
who would swear future loyalty to the Union, with the exception
of the southern political and economic elite. Those "aristocrats," the men who had attacked him all his life, and most
bitterly when he alone of southern senators remained loyal to
the Union, would have to petition him personally for pardon.

Beyond a return to loyalty, Johnson demanded what must
have appeared to him—as a Southerner—to be significant
concessions. In state constitutional conventions, delegates
elected by all whites who had received amnesty would have
to amend their constitutions to abolish slavery, ratify the Thir-
teenth Amendment to the United States Constitution, repudiate
all debts contracted by the Confederate governments, and nullify
the secession ordinances. Having done that, Southerners could
organize elections to establish regular civil governments. To
Johnson, the abolition of slavery itself must have seemed a radical step, one that overturned the social and economic system

of generations. His later actions indicated that he found it almost inconceivable to require more.

As reports came in of renewed southern loyalty and of mass participation in the state elections held in much of the South in the fall of 1865, and as applications for pardons flooded his offices, the President became more and more convinced of the basic success of his policy. As military governor of Tennessee, he had only with the greatest difficulty persuaded enough Tennesseans to take the amnesty oath to establish a creditable civil government. Now Southerners flocked to swear loyalty. Progress had been so rapid, Johnson told a visitor, "that I sometimes cannot realize it. It appears like a dream." [9] A few problems did arise here and there—a reluctance to repudiate the Rebel debt, or Mississippi's hesitation in ratifying the constitutional amendment abolishing slavery. Most disquieting must have been the election in several states of Rebel-backed officials to administer the restored civil governments. But Andrew Johnson had committed himself to his policy. Republicans who hoped that that policy was merely experimental did not know the character of their president. Johnson had fixed on a course; he would accept almost any southern rebuff rather than abandon it.

When the 39th Congress of the United States assembled in December 1865, therefore, Johnson believed the process of restoration nearly over. Apathetic to the desires of northern Republicans to protect blacks in their liberty, he felt no need for further interference in the internal political and economic structure of the southern states.

The Republicans

Historians have had a great deal of trouble in trying to understand the nature of the so-called "Radical Republicans," who opposed Andrew Johnson's Reconstruction policy and ultimately replaced it with one of their own. Until recently, they were believed to represent the opinions of only a minority of

9. Thomas, *The First President Johnson,* 361.

Republicans, and historians had difficulty explaining how these "radicals" could exercise enough power to take control of the party from the President or maintain the two-thirds majority required in Congress to pass legislation over presidential vetoes and propose constitutional amendments to the states. In general, historians credited this feat to Johnson's ineptness, the strength of personality of the leading Radicals, and the power of the party "lash" and caucus system in Congress.

But in the past decade scholars have revised their interpretations. It has become apparent that the term "radical" has been poorly defined and that the concept needs reassessment. The denomination "radical Republican" was used by contemporaries during the Civil War to denote those Republicans who favored a more active antislavery policy than that followed by President Lincoln. Even after Lincoln promulgated the Emancipation Proclamation, those differences remained, as "radicals" pressed for a Reconstruction policy that would guarantee the permanence of abolition and minimize the danger of continued Rebel political dominance in the South. But when Andrew Johnson vetoed key legislation in 1866, he broke not with these "radicals" alone but with nearly the entire Republican party, radical and nonradical. Johnson and his primarily Democratic allies called all these Republicans "Radicals" in an attempt to discredit their opponents, and perhaps also because they were too single-minded to recognize the real differences among them. In turn, most Republicans defiantly accepted the appellation, but the differences between what one Republican senator called "radical radicalism" and "conservative radicalism" remained.[10]

Among the leading radicals in the House of Representatives were the intense, strong-willed Thaddeus Stevens, recognized leader of the Republican majority; the distinguished, "practical" representatives George S. Boutwell and Samuel

10. Senator Charles D. Drake in the *Congressional Globe*, 40th Congress, 1st Session, 100–101 (March 14, 1867). My study, "The Right Way," chronicles the tensions between radical and nonradical Republicans from 1863 to 1869.

Shellabarger; and the "impractical," idealistic reformers, James M. Ashley and George W. Julian. Soon to join them, in the 40th Congress, was Benjamin F. Butler, self-seeking and powerful, with an earthy appeal to the masses that his enemies called demagoguery. In the Senate, radicals held less power and appeared to follow no leader. The great Charles Sumner, vain, disliked by many of his colleagues, but a national symbol of moral rectitude with tremendous influence on reformers and intellectuals outside Congress, fought lonely battles for principles other senators could not understand. Blunt, partisan Benjamin F. Wade and Zachariah Chandler also earned the hostility of more conservative colleagues for their steam-roller pursuit of national security at the expense of national conciliation. Henry Wilson shared Sumner's principles but possessed a temperament similar to more conservative allies.

More conservative Republicans in the House found their spokesmen in John A. Bingham, whose vapid eyes and slight frame concealed a devastating talent for obstruction and a contempt for radical "impracticables." Many of the rising young men of the party—Henry L. Dawes, James G. Blaine, and James A. Garfield—shared Bingham's intolerance for idealistic colleagues "who live among the eagles on the highest mountain peaks, beyond the line of perpetual frost" and who denounced every practical effort to secure freedom as "poor and mean and a surrender of liberty." [11]

In the Senate, conservatives carried the weight of prestige and influence. William Pitt Fessenden, the Senate's most respected member and chairman of its most important committees; Lyman Trumbull, the stiff, cold chairman of the Judiciary Committee, which embodied the Senate's legal and constitutional expertise; John Sherman, the influential young expert on finances; and James W. Grimes, Fessenden's acerbic friend and a power in his own right, all shared not only a fundamentally conservative approach to government but a smoldering dislike for their more radical allies.

11. Garfield in the *Congressional Globe,* 39th Congress, 2nd Session, 1320 (February 18, 1867).

In both houses there was a large group of Republican "swing" votes, legislators who occupied a position midway between radicals and conservatives. Often these "centrists" would form a cohesive group, forcing compromises between the two more extreme wings of the party. On other occasions the centrists would divide, some supporting more conservative and others more radical propositions. (In the following pages, the term "nonradical" will denote conservative Republicans and those centrists who were generally allied with them when centrists divided.)

A few Republicans shifted positions between 1865 and 1868. Representative James F. Wilson, chairman of the House Judiciary Committee, who at first favored a radical Reconstruction policy, joined conservative ranks as the issue of impeachment came to the foreground. Elihu B. Washburne, the senior Republican in the House and Ulysses S. Grant's close friend and political mentor, moved in the same direction. The influential Robert C. Schenck and John A. Logan followed the opposite course.

As the 39th Congress convened in December 1865, most Republicans felt that President Johnson had effectively precluded any fundamental alteration of the structure of southern society by his Reconstruction policy. Most Republicans, radical and nonradical, would have preferred at least the enfranchisement of black Southerners in an effort to enable them to protect their newly won freedom; all of them were unhappy that former Rebels were emerging as the strongest political force in most of the governments created by Johnson's authority. Few of those governments displayed any concern for the protection of black rights, and most of them openly limited blacks to a legally sanctioned second-class citizenship. But the President had committed himself to the restoration of these states, and although many Republicans believed that Johnson had exceeded his authority, usurping the functions of Congress in Reconstruction, they knew that to proceed against his clear wishes meant dividing the party and probably restoring the Democrats to power. Most Republicans simply refused to risk it.

To be sure, some radicals, like Sumner and Boutwell, urged fellow Republicans to ignore political expediency and at least impose black suffrage on the southern governments. Stevens, Julian, Ashley, and a few others still openly hoped that Congress would repudiate Johnson's work and reorganize the South as United States territories. But as a whole, Republicans concluded that it was politically impossible to force fundamental change by reordering power within the southern states, even by the rather limited mode of imposing black suffrage. Led by more conservative men who intended to conciliate the President whether radicals approved or not—Senators Fessenden and Trumbull, Representative Bingham, and others—Republicans instead reluctantly decided to offer national protection for the rights of southern loyalists against their own state governments. This inevitably meant expanding the powers and jurisdiction of the national government beyond the bounds pre–Civil War statesmen thought appropriate, but only in this way did it appear possible both eventually to accept Johnson's governments and to avoid completely abandoning southern Unionists—particularly blacks—to the mercies of Johnson's ex-Rebel-dominated organizations. Unable to persuade their colleagues to stand on principle, most radicals acquiesced in the course dictated by the nonradicals. Even Stevens, meeting his responsibility as House Republican leader, swallowed his preferences and worked for the politically more conservative program.

The practical efforts to translate this policy into legislation centered in two congressional committees. A Joint Committee on Reconstruction—of which Fessenden and Stevens, respectively, were the senior Senate and House members—struggled to develop a constitutional amendment that would give the national government new powers to protect rights. At the same time, Trumbull's Senate Judiciary Committee reported legislation designed for the same end. Careful to consult the President, Trumbull told senators that Johnson did not object to this mode of guaranteeing freedmen's liberties. Republicans, confident that a rupture with their president had been avoided, passed the Freedmen's Bureau and Civil Rights bills by overwhelming margins, only two Republicans voting against the first and nine against the second in both houses of Congress.[12]

But Trumbull and the other nonradical Republicans had misplaced their confidence in Johnson. Sharing Republican reluctance to expand permanently the powers of the national government, he did not share their committment to black rights that made that distasteful expansion appear necessary. Even if he had, it is questionable, given the rigidity of his mind, whether he could have deviated from principles to which he had adhered so firmly. Johnson, a strict-constructionist, economy-minded Jacksonian, judged the two bills by the general principles he had so painstakingly developed decades earlier: the Freedmen's Bureau bill would require a prodigious appropriation, "more than the entire sum expended in any one year under the Administration of the second Adams." [13] Both propositions violated the Constitution, repudiating the proper role of the national government in the federal system. "In all our history," the President wrote of the Civil Rights bill, ". . . no such system as that contemplated by the details of this bill has ever before been proposed or adopted. . . . It is another step, or rather stride, toward centralization and the concentration of all legislative powers in the National Government." [14] Resolutely, he vetoed both measures.

Republicans reacted with frustrated outrage. The President had left them no avenue at all to protect southern loyalists. He had exercised questionable powers in the first place. He had scorned Republican attempts at conciliation. He had misled them as to his intentions, indicating his approval of the legislation he had vetoed. Their denunciations were bitter.

12. *Congressional Globe*, 39th Congress, 1st Session, 421 (January 25, 1866), 606 (February 2), 668 (February 6), 1367 (March 13), 1413 (March 15, 1866). The Civil Rights bill did not pass the House until after the President vetoed the Freedmen's Bureau bill. Despite that, few of the Republicans who had supported the veto opposed it.

13. James D. Richardson, ed., *A Compilation of the Messages and Papers of the Presidents, 1789–1897*, 10 vols. (Washington, 1896–97), VI, 401.

14. *Ibid.*, 412–13.

The intensity of the reaction shocked Johnson at first. Painfully, he appeared to hesitate and reconsider. Rumors spread that compromise was possible. For Johnson this must have been a difficult process. His narrow mind was accustomed to acting directly upon general principles; reevaluation was foreign to his nature. He must have suffered anguishing self-doubt. Was his unusual reflectiveness a statesmanlike attempt to discover light to illumine a murky problem of constitutional principle or merely a cowardly flinching from duty in the face of surprisingly strong pressure? "Courage" was Johnson's watchword, and these questions must have troubled him.

When he made his final decision, it came with all the force of that tremendous will: he could not bend his long-held convictions. "Sir," he exploded to his secretary, William A. Moore, "I am right. I know I am right and I am damned if I do not adhere to it."[15] Inflexibly, without doubts, Johnson proceeded to carry out his determination, launching a series of biting attacks upon the party that had elected him, rising to the occasion as if he were still on the hustings in Greeneville, Tennessee. The sizzling personal hostility Johnson always directed against opponents now scorched Republicans as it had southern aristocrats before them. Charging that they had threatened his life, he compared Republicans to the traitors who had fought for the Rebellion. Both the Southerners and the Republicans, who refused to recognize the restoration of his southern governments, were disunionists and deserved equal disapprobation. Indeed, the Republicans had always been as bad as the secessionists: one stood "for destroying the Government to preserve slavery, and the other to break up the Government to destroy slavery." His former political allies were "a common gang of cormorants and blood-suckers, who have been fattening upon the country . . . ."[16]

15. Moore notes, October 26, 1866, Johnson Mss.
16. The quotes are from Johnson's speech in Washington on February 22, 1866, in Lillian Foster, *Andrew Johnson, President of the United States: His Life and Speeches* (New York, 1866), 246, and his speech in Cleveland on September 3, 1866, as reported in the Cleveland

Such unbounded personal vindictiveness stunned Republicans. Perhaps appropriate on the stump in Tennessee, Johnson's fierce attack humiliated and outraged them. One of the articles of impeachment would charge him with attempting "to excite the odium and resentment of all the good people of the United States against Congress . . . [through his] intemperate, inflammatory, and scandalous harangues," conduct that was "particularly indecent and unbecoming in the Chief Magistrate of the United States . . . ." [17]

Many radicals had hoped that Republicans would adopt more extreme measures when it became clear that it was impossible to conciliate the President with conservative legislation; they were sorely disappointed. With congressional elections pending and Johnson going over to the opposition, most Republicans became even more committed to a fundamentally conservative course. They dared not risk alienating the conservative elements who might follow the President out of the party. In essence, Republicans decided to continue the policy they had evolved in their efforts to satisfy Johnson. They still refused to impose black suffrage or to force change in southern society in other ways. Instead, they persevered in their development of measures to enable the national government to protect citizens' rights. Adhering to the Civil Rights bill and passing a new Freedmen's Bureau bill over a presidential veto, Republicans completed their program by proposing a constitutional amendment, which forbade state action that denied citizens' fundamental rights or subjected them to discriminatory laws.[18] The

---

Herald and quoted in U. S. Senate, *The Trial of Andrew Johnson, President of the United States, Before the Senate of the United States, on Impeachment by the House of Representatives, for High Crimes and Misdemeanors,* 3 vols. (Washington, 1868), I, 335. The wording differed slightly in other reports, *ibid.,* 327, 332.

17. Article X of impeachment, Richardson, ed., *Messages and Papers of the Presidents,* VI, 714–18.

18. For many years historians and lawyers believed that the Fourteenth Amendment prohibited only overt state action that denied rights. Recently, they have concluded that Congress also intended to give the national government power to protect citizens when states would not or

southern state governments erected under Johnson's authority need only ratify that amendment and repeal their discriminatory laws. Upon doing so, they would be restored to normal relations in the Union.

The manifest conservatism of the Republican program blunted Johnson's appeal to the conservative elements of the Republican party. Wavering Republicans, like Governor Jacob D. Cox of Ohio and the editor of the New York *Evening Post,* William Cullen Bryant, returned to the fold. Johnson's own cabinet split over his determination to form a coalition with Democrats to oppose Republicans in the 1866 congressional elections. Three of the department heads resigned. Only Secretary of State William Henry Seward, Secretary of the Treasury Hugh McCulloch, and Secretary of the Navy Gideon Welles remained firmly in the President's camp. Secretary of War Edwin M. Stanton, torn between conflicting loyalties but disagreeing with Johnson's policies, was persuaded to remain by Republicans and Army officers, who urged him to serve as a buffer between the President and the armed forces.[19]

The decisions of leading Republican conservatives reflected the decision of Republican voters as a whole. With Republican campaigners emphasizing the moderation of their Reconstruction program, the party's candidates overwhelmingly defeated

---

could not do so. See Alfred Avins, "The Ku Klux Klan Act of 1871: Some Reflected Light on the Fourteenth Amendment," *St. Louis University Law Journal,* XI (Spring 1967), 331–81; Laurent B. Frantz, "Congressional Power to Enforce the Fourteenth Amendment Against Private Acts," *Yale Law Journal,* LXXIII (July 1964), 1353–84; Robert J. Harris, *The Quest for Equality: The Constitution and the Supreme Court* (Baton Rouge, 1960), 44–53; John Silard, "A Constitutional Forecast: Demise of the 'State Action' Limit on the Equal Protection Guarantee," *California Law Review,* LXVI (May 1966), 855–72.

19. Traditionally, historians interpreted Stanton's position as hypocritical, but his latest biographers argue cogently that in fact Stanton was making a significant sacrifice to stay where he, leading military men, and Republicans felt duty required him to remain. Benjamin P. Thomas and Harold M. Hyman, *Stanton: The Life and Times of Lincoln's Secretary of War* (New York, 1962), 471–94.

the opponents put forward by the Democratic-Johnsonian coalition.

In the face of such a decisive repudiation, another man might have acquiesced in the Republicans' policy of restoration. Had Johnson done so, at least some of the southern governments might have accepted Congress's terms and returned to normal federal relations. Tennessee had already followed this course in July 1866. Movements to "accept the situation" as a distasteful necessity developed in Alabama and Virginia, but Johnson aborted them with private and public exhortations to remain firm.[20] As a result, every southern state but Tennessee rejected the amendment. Throughout his term, Johnson would use his prestige and power to stiffen southern resistance to Republican construction. This was merely the first example.

The Reconstruction Act

Republicans gathered in Washington, D.C. for the second session of the 39th Congress in December 1866, just as the southern states, encouraged by the President, one after another rejected the Fourteenth Amendment. Reassured by their campaign victories, they responded to southern intransigence by formulating a new Reconstruction policy, embodied in the Reconstruction Acts of 1867.

Traditionally, historians interpreted this legislation as proof of radical ascendancy in the Republican party in 1867, but once again recent scholarship has challenged established interpretations. In fact, the first Reconstruction Act, which set the new policy, passed only after a long and bitter struggle between radical and nonradical Republicans, and it seriously compromised the radical position.[21]

When Republicans first began discussing how to react to

20. McKitrick, *Johnson and Reconstruction*, 454–55.
21. The discussion that follows again differs in some ways from the interpretations offered in most of the works discussed in the Bibliographical Review. It is based upon my work in "The Right Way," 274–339.

the southern refusal to acquiesce in the conservative Reconstruction policy embodied in the Fourteenth Amendment, radicals hoped to enforce the program of fundamental change for which they had been pressing unsuccessfully for so long. At best, most of them favored an indeterminate period of territorial status for the South, with Southerners governing themselves through territorial legislatures to be elected by both whites and blacks. (Some plans called also for the election of governors; others for their appointment.) Since territories were subject to the direct control of Congress, Congress could intervene to set aside legislation of which it did not approve. Many radicals also favored guarantees for black education, confiscation and land redistribution, and a fairly broad disfranchisement of Rebel leaders. As a minimum, these radicals demanded that Congress finally disperse completely the Rebel-dominated governments that Johnson had created. To replace them, radicals insisted upon provisional civil governments administered by men who had never aided the Rebellion. Most radicals no doubt hoped that these provisional governments would turn into the territorial governments they desired, but here they knew they would meet nonradical opposition.

But instead of cooperating with this program, nonradical Republicans checked its advocates and substituted a new scheme of their own. The Reconstruction Act of 1867 still provided for the restoration of southern states upon their ratification of the Fourteenth Amendment, but added to that condition was a new one—a requirement that Southerners extend the right of suffrage to blacks on the same terms as whites. Until Southerners agreed to meet these conditions for restoration, the rights of southern loyalists, especially blacks, would be protected by the United States Army. (The Rebel states were divided into five military districts, each with a commander appointed by the President.) The nonradicals refused to dissolve the Johnsonian governments, but when radicals threatened to join Democrats to defeat the entire measure, they agreed to make clear that the authority of the military was paramount over the provisional governments and to authorize the removal of state officials who obstructed the military in the performance of its duty.[22]

At first more conservative Republicans hoped that President Johnson might acquiesce in their new policy, and even endorse it, but when that hope dissipated, making it unlikely that the southern governments would agree to the new conditions, they completed their program with a Supplementary Reconstruction Act. This enactment passed quickly through the 40th Congress, which organized immediately upon the dissolution of the 39th Congress, in March 1867. The law instructed the military commanders to supervise the election of delegates to constitutional conventions. These conventions were charged to establish new state governments that would finally meet the requirements Congress had set for restoration. The Supplementary Reconstruction Act went further toward replacing the Johnsonian southern governments than any previous congressional legislation, but Johnson had eliminated other alternatives. Without his cooperation, the likelihood was that his southern governments would continue their intransigence indefinitely, rendering the Republican political position in the North ever more precarious.

Although this program, especially the black-suffrage requirement, might have seemed outrageously radical to southern whites, to Andrew Johnson, and to later generations of historians, it was in fact no more than most Republicans had been ready to demand in the summer of 1865, before Johnson's policy had become settled and his opposition to imposing impartial suffrage in the South manifest.[23] It certainly did not

22. The more conservative Republicans also agreed to forbid men disqualified from officeholding by the Fourteenth Amendment from serving in the provisional governments, but the military commanders interpreted that ban to apply only to *new* officials, not those already in office, rendering the effect of the provision nugatory.

23. This conclusion may surprise readers familiar with traditional interpretations of the developments of 1865. It is not within the scope of this essay to defend it. I will point out, however, that even the referenda on black suffrage in northern states in 1865, so often cited to prove

satisfy the radicals. Sumner publicly announced that he voted for it "not because it is what I desire, but because it is all that Congress is disposed to enact at the present time." Stevens expressed similar sentiments, and Ben Perley Poore, the knowledgeable Washington correspondent of the Boston *Evening Journal,* wrote that other radicals felt the same way.[24]

Frustrated by their inability to carry their own Reconstruction program, many radicals were dismayed at the mode in which their more conservative allies had decided to secure theirs. Recognizing the force of Andrew Johnson's indomitable will and the single-minded doggedness with which he would sustain his principles and prejudices, radicals had urged throughout the struggle that the President's influence in any new Reconstruction program be kept at a minimum. In their proposed legislation, radicals had tried to free the temporary authorities in the South as much as possible from Johnson's control. One radical bill, for example, authorized Chief Justice Salmon P. Chase to appoint these officials from the ranks of Southerners untainted by treason.[25] Another dispersed Johnson's governments and required Senate consent for both the President's replacements and any future removals.[26] Stevens, in his first Reconstruction plan, had proposed to empower Congress itself to appoint loyal civilians temporarily to govern the

---

northern opposition to that measure, indicate that at least half of all Republicans favored it in their own states. It is likely that even more favored it in the South, where it was clearly more necessary to preserve the fruits of Union victory. For a fuller discussion, see Benedict, "The Right Way," 117–50.

24. Sumner in the *Congressional Globe,* 40th Congress, 1st Session, 165 (March 16, 1867); Stevens in the New York *Herald,* July 8, 1867, p. 6; Poore (writing as "Perley") in the Boston *Evening Journal,* March 20, 1867, p. 4; Benedict, "The Right Way," 332–35.

25. House Resolution No. 856, resubmitted as H.R. No. 5 in the 40th Congress, in the House bill file, 40th Congress, Record Group 233, National Archives, Washington, D.C.

26. This bill, the Louisiana Reconstruction bill, actually passed the House but withered in the Senate. *Congressional Globe,* 39th Congress, 2nd Session, 1128–29 (February 11, 1867); Charles Fairman, *Reconstruction and Reunion, 1864–1888* (New York and London, 1971), 285–91; Benedict, "The Right Way," 303–11, 315–21.

South. Later, he had turned to the Supreme Court of the District of Columbia.[27]

The Republican majority had refused to adopt the radicals' alternatives. Instead, they had placed the task of enforcing the Reconstruction Acts in the hands of the Army. And the Constitution recognized Andrew Johnson as commander in chief of the armed forces for as long as he remained in office. Trying to avoid the obvious consequences, House Republicans had decided to authorize General of the Army Grant, rather than Johnson, to appoint military commanders under the new bill. But the whole unprecedented effort to bypass presidential authority in Reconstruction left many of them uneasy. "[M]y opinion is that we cannot long carry on the government in that way . . . ," worried the conservative congressman Nathaniel P. Banks, "that we must have laws in which the Executive will cooperate, in order to make those laws effective." [28] Agreeing with Banks, conservative Republican senators repudiated the House provision, and in its final version the Reconstruction Act left the appointment power with the President. "As well commission a lunatic to superintend a lunatic asylum, or a thief to govern a penitentiary!" exclaimed the New York *National Anti-Slavery Standard,* organ of the radical abolitionists. It was "an act of folly which no language can fitly describe." [29]

Republicans had proved unwilling to take Reconstruction completely out of the hands of the President. Rather than turn the administration of the southern states over to loyalists, they had left it in the hands of governments created under Andrew Johnson's authority. They had subordinated those governments to the armed forces of which he was commander in chief. They had decided against giving General Grant the responsibility for appointing district commanders under the law and left that power to the President also. Although many his-

27. *Congressional Globe,* 39th Congress, 2nd Session, 250 (January 3, 1867). The Supreme Court of the District should not be confused with the Supreme Court of the United States.

28. *Ibid.,* 1105 (February 8, 1867).

29. New York *National Anti-Slavery Standard,* March 2, 1867, p. 2.

torians have argued the contrary, Republicans were surprisingly sensitive to the proper functions of the President and most reluctant to tamper with them. Many of them now believed that Johnson had usurped the rightful legislative powers of Congress by inaugurating his own system of Reconstruction and then denying them any power in the premises. They would not now usurp his powers. They had fulfilled their duty by framing a Reconstruction law. The President would fulfill his by administering it. The government could operate in no other way under the rather rigid concept of separation of powers to which most Americans adhered at mid-century.

It was because so many Republicans could not envision legislative despotism that the impeachment question arose. "[W]e must have laws in which the executive will cooperate, in order to make those laws effective," Banks had insisted. But he had added, "And if, after we . . . have agreed as to what laws are necessary to secure the peace of the country and to maintain the existence of the Government, . . . the President then refuses cooperation, it is our duty to lay aside the question of reconstruction for a time and proceed to a consideration of the position and purposes of the President himself." [30] Because Republicans respected the presidency, they would if necessary remove the President.

The Impeachment Movement

The reluctance of nonradical Republicans to abandon traditional reliance upon the presidency for the enforcement of laws led directly to the impeachment movement. While more conservative Republicans hoped for Johnson's cooperation, radicals shared no such illusions. In their opinion, the President had already demonstrated his capacity for destructiveness. His mild restoration policy had reawakened southern belligerence after Lee's surrender and was responsible for all the suffering that implied for southern loyalists. Republicans laid directly at his feet responsibility for the brutal New Orleans massacre

30. *Congressional Globe,* 39th Congress, 2nd Session, 1105 (February 8, 1867).

of the summer of 1866, in which the city police killed 40 mainly black Republicans and injured 160 more in dispersing a peaceful convention of doubtful legality. They were equally convinced that the general mood of hostility to Union soldiers and blacks could be traced to the President's lenience.[31]

Moreover, Johnson had already shown his willingness to nullify congressional legislation. Where it suited him, he had ignored the Senate's right to confirm government appointments, disregarded the Test Oath law, and emasculated the Freedmen's Bureau and Confiscation Acts (this will be discussed in Chapter 2). He now proclaimed the Reconstruction Act "without precedent and without authority, in palpable conflict with the plainest provisions of the Constitution, and utterly destructive to those great principles of liberty and humanity for which our ancestors on both sides of the Atlantic have shed so much blood and expended so much treasure." [32] Anyone who understood the President's character, radicals insisted, must recognize what lay ahead.

Fearing the worst, radicals had launched a movement to impeach Johnson during the second session of the 39th Congress, as the new congressional Reconstruction program took shape. Outside of Congress, the radical newspapers, Benjamin F. Butler, George Wilkes, editor of the radical *Wilkes' Spirit of the Times,* and Ebon B. Ward, president of the pro-soft-money, high-tariff Iron and Steel Association, led the movement. Inside Congress, Boutwell, Stevens, and Ashley spearheaded efforts.

Bingham and Representative Rufus P. Spalding led the op-

31. Hans L. Trefousse has edited a compilation of testimony given before several congressional committees in 1866 and 1867 relating to conditions in the South and the effect of Johnson's policy: *Background for Radical Reconstruction* (Boston, 1970). For accounts of the New Orleans massacre, see *ibid.,* 168–80; McKitrick, *Johnson and Reconstruction,* 422–27; Willie Malvin Caskey, *Secession and Restoration in Louisiana* (Baton Rouge, 1938), 165–204; Emily Hazen Reed, *Life of A. P. Dostie; or, the Conflict in New Orleans* (New York, 1868), 286–330.

32. Veto of the Reconstruction bill, March 2, 1867, in Richardson, ed., *Messages and Papers of the Presidents,* VI, 500.

position. Moving quickly after Ashley announced his intention to present resolutions calling for an investigation of Johnson's activities, Spalding called a caucus of House Republicans. To check Ashley's designs, Spalding moved that no measure of impeachment be presented in the House unless first approved by the caucus. Elihu B. Washburne proposed to add the further requirement that the caucus itself not approve any actual impeachment unless sanctioned by the House Judiciary Committee. Over the objections of Stevens and Ashley, the Republicans agreed overwhelmingly to the proposals. But Ashley refused to be bound by the caucus decision and offered his resolution anyway. Two Missouri Republicans moved similar resolutions, which, despite the efforts of Bingham and Speaker Schuyler Colfax, came to the floor. However, although this handful of radicals had thwarted the will of the Republican majority, the Republicans acted on the second branch of their caucus decision and referred the resolutions to the Judiciary Committee, which began the long and tedious job of collecting evidence and taking testimony.[33]

After the passage of the unsatisfactory Reconstruction bill, radicals concluded that the President's removal was a necessity. Impatient with the Judiciary Committee's slow progress, Butler called a secret caucus of radicals to prepare a resolution appointing a special committee to investigate Johnson in place of the Judiciary Committee. Advocated by Butler, John A. Logan (both just entering Congress), and Schenck, the resolution was defeated in caucus on March 6 through the efforts of Bingham, Blaine, and Judiciary Committee chairman Wilson, who promised all possible dispatch in his committee's investigation.[34]

33. New York *Times,* January 6, 1867, p. 1; January 7, 1867, p. 5; Boston *Evening Journal,* January 7, 1867, p. 4; New York *National Anti-Slavery Standard,* January 19, 1867, p. 2; *Congressional Globe,* 39th Congress, 2nd Session, 319–21 (January 7, 1867), 443–46 (January 14, 1867), 807–8 (January 28, 1867), 991 (February 14, 1867).
34. New York *Times,* March 7, 1867, p. 4; Boston *Evening Journal,* March 6, 1867, p. 4; March 7, 1867, p. 4.

Now radicals determined to prevent the customary adjournment to the following December, fearing what Johnson might do during a long congressional recess and hoping to force the Judiciary Committee into an early report on the impeachment resolutions. Over both radical and conservative objections, centrist Republicans in the same caucus carried resolutions to adjourn, but only until May 8.[35]

Most senators, however, were becoming more confirmed in the conviction that impeachment was not a viable possibility. In the Senate Republican caucus, only Chandler endorsed the measure. Grimes wrote home, "We have very successfully and thoroughly tied his [Johnson's] hands, and, if we had not, we had better submit to two years of misrule . . . than subject the country, its institutions, and its credit, to the shock of an impeachment. I have always thought so, and everybody is now apparently coming to my conclusion." [36]

A hard-fought struggle ensued. Radicals, led by Stevens, Butler, Ashley, Schenck, and Ignatius Donnelly in the House and Sumner and Charles D. Drake in the Senate, fought for a short adjournment to be followed by a reconvened session to settle the impeachment question. Conservatives, led by Representatives Bingham and Blaine and Senators Trumbull and Fessenden, tried to force an adjournment to November or December. After these rival forces battled to a stalemate, conservatives joined centrists to pass an adjournment resolution providing that Congress might reconvene on the first Wednesday in July if a quorum was present. If no quorum could be found, Congress would reconvene on the first Wednesday of November. Behind the scenes, radical Representative Schenck and conservative Senator Edwin D. Morgan, the co-chairman of the Congressional Campaign Committee, were delegated the responsibility of deciding whether it would be necessary to meet.

35. New York *Times,* March 7, 1867, p. 4; Boston *Evening Journal,* March 7, 1867, p. 4.

36. Grimes to Mrs. Grimes, March 12, 1867, quoted in William Salter, *The Life of James W. Grimes, Governor of Iowa, 1854–1858; Senator of the United States, 1859–1869* (New York, 1876), 323; New York *Times*, March 8, 1867, p. 1.

All agreed a July meeting was unlikely; the radicals had received another setback.[37]

A correspondent of the New York *Times* had gauged the sentiment in Congress correctly in February. Impeachment was dead, he wrote. But "there is one qualification to be made. . . . If the President persistently stands in the way . . . ; if he fails to execute the laws in their spirit as well as in their letter, if he will forget nothing, if he will learn nothing; if, holding the South in his hand, either by direct advice or personal example he shall encourage them to such resistance to progress as may tend to defeat the public will—in such event . . . the President may, after all, come to be regarded as an 'obstacle' which must be 'deposed.' " [38]

37. John W. Forney to Sumner, July 10, 1867. Sumner Mss., Houghton Library, Harvard University (Forney, the secretary of the Senate, was so certain that there would be no July session—he received "the assurances of experienced Senators" to this effect—that he left for Europe); Zachariah Chandler, speaking at Ashtabula, Ohio, in The Edward M. McPherson scrapbook: Campaign of 1867, III, 135–36, McPherson Mss., Library of Congress; *Congressional Globe,* 40th Congress, 1st Session, 16 (March 7, 1867), 303–8, 315–20 (March 23, 1867), 321–22, 331, 334 (March 25, 1867), 352–60 (March 26, 1867), 387–91 (March 27, 1867), 401–8, 419–20, 425–27 (March 28, 1867), 438–41, 446–54 (March 29, 1867).

38. "B" in the New York *Times,* February 13, 1867, p. 2.

2

Presidential Obstruction and the Law of Impeachment

AS AMERICANS FOR THE first time seriously discussed the possibility of impeaching a president, they arrived at two opposing concepts of the law of impeachment. These differing opinions were expounded and developed primarily through three discussions: first, an indirect exchange in the *American Law Register* in March and September 1867 between Professor Theodore W. Dwight of Columbia College Law School and Representative (formerly Judge) William Lawrence of Ohio, a member of the House Judiciary Committee; second, in the majority and minority reports on impeachment delivered by the House Judiciary Committee in November; and third, in the speeches George S. Boutwell and James F. Wilson delivered on the floor of the House on December 5 and 6 in defense of the majority and minority reports, respectively.[1]

1. Dwight, "Trial by Impeachment," *American Law Register,* XV, o.s. (March 1867), 257–83; Lawrence, "The Law of Impeachment," *ibid.* (September 1867), 641–80; *House Report No. 7,* 40th Congress, 1st Session, 1–59 (majority), 59–105 (Republican minority), 105–11 (Democratic minority); *Congressional Globe,* 40th Congress, 2nd Session, appendix, 54–62 (December 5, 6, 1867; Boutwell), 62–65 (December 6, 1867; Wilson). Charles Mayo Ellis wrote a less influential article, endorsing what would become the radical position. Ellis, "The Causes for Which a President Can Be Impeached," *Atlantic Monthly,* XIX (January 1867), 88–92.

Democrats, Republicans who opposed impeachment, and most lawyers argued that a government officer could be impeached only for an act actually criminal, a violation of a criminal statute. Many historians have accepted this view as embodying the proper law of impeachment, accusing those who insisted on a broader interpretation of using impeachment wrongly in a purely political vendetta.[2] But those who espoused the narrow view had an extremely difficult task in sustaining it, because in fact it was a novel argument, running counter to precedent, the overwhelming weight of American legal authority, and logic.

The first problem conservatives faced involved the precedents. To bolster their arguments, proponents of the restrictive theory of impeachment turned to English law. Impeachment, they argued, was merely an alternative form of charging a man with a crime. The usual form was indictment, which was followed by a common-law trial. Impeachment was for criminals so powerful that they might overawe the ordinary courts. Since one could be indicted only for a violation of law, they averred, the same rule must apply to impeachments. Yet, as the conservatives conceded, the House of Lords had convicted offenders impeached by the House of Commons for acts that did not constitute indictable crimes, although the supposed rule had been followed in most cases.[3] These embarrassing

2. The scholar who has most recently asserted something akin to this proposition is Irving Brant, in *Impeachment: Trials and Errors* (New York, 1972). Although totally hostile to the Johnson impeachment proceedings, David Miller DeWitt, who wrote the only monographic study of the Johnson impeachment, did conclude that the conservative view was "altogether too narrow." DeWitt, *The Impeachment and Trial of Andrew Johnson, Seventeenth President of the United States: A History* (New York and London, 1903), 295. Raoul Berger has recently published a full, thoroughly documented analysis of the constitutional grounds for impeachment, also concluding that the House of Representatives can impeach government officers for noncriminal conduct. Berger, "Impeachment for 'High Crimes and Misdemeanors,'" *Southern California Law Review,* XLIV (1971), 395–460.

3. Dwight, "Trial by Impeachment," 264. See also the report of the Judiciary Committee minority, *House Report No. 7,* 40th Congress, 1st Session, 69–70, 71–72, where Chairman Wilson and his fellow dis-

inconsistencies were attacked by conservatives as "extreme cases" tried on "frivolous charges."[4] But the conservatives' definition was self-serving. They insisted that impeachment lay only for indictable offenses and then charged that convictions based on nonindictable acts were frivolous and not entitled to consideration as precedents. Dwight even suggested that many of these cases were probably based on violations of statutes after all, but that the laws involved had been lost or forgotten.[5]

The best English precedent conservatives found was the impeachment of Viscount Melville, in which Parliament's House of Lords asked its legal experts whether the defendant's acts were indictable. When the experts said they were not, Melville was acquitted. But the precedent was weakened because Melville's trial took place in 1806, nearly twenty years after the power of impeachment had been incorporated in the United States Constitution. The case could not explain the intention of the framers of the Constitution except insofar as it illustrated the English concept of impeachment before 1789.[6]

Recognizing the weakness of the conservative case under English precedent, the Judiciary Committee minority expressly denied the validity of those precedents in determining the scope of impeachment in America, arguing, "The power of Parliament over the subject is far greater than that which . . . Congress can exercise over the citizen."[7] Instead, they turned

---

senter, Frederick E. Woodbridge, listed English impeachments brought for partisan purposes, negating their own argument that impeachment lay for indictable offenses alone, and then denied the authority of the precedents because they were partisan.

4. The conservatives also omitted to mention that the House of Commons had regularly impeached royal officials for noncriminal conduct, whether the Lords convicted them or not. For obvious reasons, they preferred to concentrate on the action of the House of Lords, which offered more support for their position. See Berger's list of impeachments in his "Impeachment," 408–10.

5. Dwight, "Trial by Impeachment," 267–68.

6. *House Report No. 7,* 40th Congress, 1st Session, 74–75.

7. *Ibid.,* 68. That, however, did not prevent the minority from citing English precedents supporting its case for whatever value they might be, and especially the Melville case.

to American precedents, but they treated these much as they had the English.

Americans studying impeachment in the United States had two distinct lines of precedents from which to draw. On one hand, an investigator might argue that the true precedents for impeachment were those set by the House of Representatives in presenting impeachments to the Senate. On the other, he might insist that the true precedents lay in how the Senate decided the cases. Since the House of Representatives had limited its accusations to indictable crimes in at most one of the five impeachments it had presented to the Senate before 1867, conservatives turned to the decisions in the Senate.[8]

Senate proceedings on impeachment offered two strong precedents for the conservatives. In the impeachment trial of Supreme Court Justice Samuel Chase in 1805, the managers of the impeachment were unable to muster the two-thirds majority of the Senate necessary to convict on any of the articles, none of which was indictable. The Senate reached a similar result in the trial of Judge James H. Peck in 1830. In Peck's case, the Senate's decision may not have turned upon the indictability of the judge's conduct, there being substantive doubt as to the facts, but in the Chase trial there could be no doubt that the question was important. Yet politics clouded the issue; every Federalist senator voted against convicting a political ally. Moreover, a majority of senators—although not the two-thirds required for conviction—voted to convict on three of the eight articles. Advocates of a broad power of impeachment could claim that actually the Chase precedent supported their arguments. On one of the articles, nineteen of thirty-four senators found Chase guilty, although no indictable crime had been charged. Peck escaped conviction with twenty-

8. The one case where an indictable crime was alleged was the impeachment of West H. Humphries in 1862. Humphries, a United States district judge, had joined the Rebellion. Wilson suggested that the essential charge against Humphries was treason. But at least one article charged only that he had not held court during his assigned term. *Congressional Globe*, 37th Congress, 2nd Session, 2247–48, 2777–78 (May 22, 1862), 2943–53 (July 26, 1862).

two senators pronouncing him removable for his nonindictable conduct and twenty-one holding the other way.[9]

To the further discomfort of those who favored a narrow limit to the impeachment power, the Senate had on at least one occasion removed a judge on impeachment for conduct not indictable at law. The offender was Judge John Pickering, accused of drunkenness and profanity on the bench (in fact, his son had notified the Senate that Pickering was insane). In that case the Senate had gone so far as to imply that its role was limited to determining only whether defendants had committed the acts of which they were accused. Reluctant to pronounce an insane man guilty of "high crimes and misdemeanors," senators had conceded to the House the full right of deciding whether his acts were impeachable. Instead of voting on the question "Is John Pickering . . . guilty of high crimes and misdemeanors upon the charges . . . , or not guilty?" the Senate had voted on the question "Is John Pickering . . . guilty *as charged* . . . by the House of Representatives?" (italics mine). The conservatives denied the value of this case as a precedent; they called it "a disgrace to the court that tried it." But its primary offense seems to have been that it contradicted their argument.[10]

Since legal authorities had almost unanimously adopted the broad view of impeachment, conservatives proceeded to the lawyerlike task of citing their testimony on questions not quite in point. They argued that the power of impeachment should be determined primarily by the words of the Constitution. The

9. U.S. Senate, *Trial of Samuel Chase, an Associate Justice of the Supreme Court of the United States, Impeached by the House of Representatives, for High Crimes and Misdemeanors, Before the Senate of the United States,* 2 vols. (Washington, 1805); U. S. Senate, *Report of the Trial of James H. Peck, Judge of the United States District Court for the District of Missouri, before the Senate of the United States, on an Impeachment Preferred by the House of Representatives Against Him for Misdemeanors in Office* (Boston, 1833).

10. U.S. Senate, *Record of Proceedings in the Case of William Blount; Trial of John Pickering, Judge of New Hampshire District; Trial of Samuel Chase, One of the Associate Justices of the Supreme Court* (Washington, 1805).

framers had authorized the House of Representatives to impeach government officers for "treason, bribery, or other high crimes and misdemeanors." [11] Arguing that the language raised the presumption that impeachment lay only for actual crimes, despite the number of impeachments that seemed to imply the opposite, conservatives cited the great English constitutional commentators Blackstone, Wooddeson, and Hale to the effect that a crime was a violation of law and that laws must be known to the people.[12]

To bolster this contention, those favoring the narrow view pointed to other provisions of the Constitution relating to impeachment. They emphasized that the Constitution required senators to try cases of impeachment upon an oath or affirmation. This indicated that they "were as much restrained by law as any other criminal court," conservatives argued. An impeached officer was still liable for his offense before the civil courts after removal. This also indicated that impeachment was proper only in the case of indictable offenses. Article III, section 2, of the Constitution required that all crimes be tried by jury, *except those tried on impeachment.* Article II, section 2, empowered the president to pardon men for all "offences against the United States, except in cases of impeachment." The language in both constitutional provisions, conservatives insisted, linked impeachment to crimes indictable before civil courts.[13]

Surprisingly, the advocates of a broad power of impeachment did not reply to the fallacies perpetrated in these arguments, and their failure to do so materially weakened their case before the nation, the legal community, and Congress. The oath of affirmation required of senators, for instance, was not necessarily connected with the issue of proper grounds for impeachment at all. It might just as logically mean only that senators must be on oath to judge the evidence impartially in determining whether a defendant was guilty of conduct alleged by the House, whether that conduct constituted an indictable offense or

11. U.S. Constitution, Article II, section 4.
12. *House Report No. 7,* 40th Congress, 1st Session, 61–62.
13. *Ibid.,* 62–64.

not. The other conservative arguments contained specific logical fallacies. That an impeached official can be tried in criminal court after his trial on impeachment does not imply that only those who can be tried in a criminal court may be impeached. It means, rather, that when an officer *is* impeached for an offense that happens to be indictable, the impeachment does not preclude a later indictment. The framers of the Constitution wished to prevent officials guilty of criminal conduct from pleading that their impeachment rendered them immune from the jurisdiction of criminal courts under common-law doctrines forbidding double jeopardy. In fact, this constitutional provision should have bolstered the contention of the radicals that the framers of the Constitution considered impeachment something other than a criminal process: if it were a criminal process, a new trial *would* have constituted double jeopardy.

The provision requiring jury trial for all crimes except those for which the House instituted impeachment proceedings does not necessarily mean, as conservatives insisted, that impeachment lay only for crimes that otherwise would have to be tried by jury. Logically, it may as well mean that impeachment is proper for both criminal and noncriminal offenses perpetrated by government officials, but that if the offense for which impeachment proceedings are instituted happens to be criminal, the defendant cannot raise constitutional objections to the absence of a jury trial. The same holds true of the president's power to pardon men for all federal offenses, except those tried by impeachment. This does not necessarily mean, as conservatives argued, that impeachment lay only for offenses that might otherwise be pardoned, that is, indictable, criminal offenses. All it logically means is that when an officer has been impeached for an offense that happens to be indictable, the president cannot pardon him. The clear implication is that the framers feared that the president might negate the impeachment power by pardoning officers congress might impeach, that they feared he might seek to save from removal men to whom he was politically obligated or who were politically obligated to him. Once again, this provision indicated that the authors of the Constitution were as much concerned with the political as with the criminal implications of impeachment.

Radicals argued that the "misdemeanors" the Constitution referred to as grounds for impeachment included misfeasance and malfeasance in office as well as crimes indictable before criminal courts. In defending this position, those who argued that impeachment was a power of broad scope could not decide how to treat the English precedents. Lawrence, in his "Law of Impeachment," and Boutwell, in his speech before the House favoring impeachment, emphasized the essential differences between impeachment in England and in America, differences they believed explained why Englishmen may have circumscribed the impeachment power more narrowly than Americans had in the 1787 Constitution. In England, impeachment was directed at the punishment of crime. A defendant found guilty upon an impeachment could be sentenced even to death by the House of Lords. In the United States, impeachment was only a mode of removing officeholders and disqualifying them from holding government positions. Furthermore, in England any subject might be impeached, tried, and punished. In the United States, the already more limited impeachment power could be used only against those who held public trust. Because of these basic differences, Boutwell and Lawrence minimized the importance of English precedents.[14] In contrast, the Judiciary Committee's majority report in favor of impeachment, written by Representative Thomas Williams, emphasized the English precedents to prove that impeachment was usually instituted there to punish acts detrimental to the welfare of the state.[15] But all advocates of a broad impeachment power agreed that

14. Lawrence, "Law of Impeachment," 642–45; Boutwell in the *Congressional Globe,* 40th Congress, 2nd Session, appendix, 55 (December 5, 1867).

15. *House Report No. 7,* 40th Congress, 1st Session, 47–49. Lawrence, trying to have his precedents both ways, also offered such English precedents as supported his arguments. Lawrence, "Law of Impeachment," *passim.*

the place of impeachment in American constitutional law should be determined primarily by examining American precedents and American legal authorities.

Naturally, those who favored the broad conception of Congress's power to impeach turned to the line of precendents established by the House in presenting impeachments rather than to those established by the Senate in deciding them.[16] In every impeachment the House had presented to the Senate, at least some of the articles had alleged nonindictable offenses. Of course, the radicals also cited with special emphasis the convictions of Pickering and Judge West H. Humphries by the Senate.

But the radicals' greatest strength resided in the unanimity with which the great American constitutional commentators had upheld the broad view of the impeachment power. Those eminent legal writers had recognized that both English and American precedents were mixed. They had eschewed legal authority, therefore, and had appealed to reason instead. In an age accustomed to analyzing government primarily in terms of its theoretical and legal foundations rather than its practical workings, such "appeals to reason" offered scholars an opportunity for assessments based on the actual relationships between the various institutions of government. In short, the great constitutionalists for a moment left the realm of law and entered what is now called political science.

As a practical matter, American constitutional commentators—Story, Duer, Kent, Rawle, and the authors of *The Federalist*—recognized that the maintenance of proper checks and balances in government, which they believed guaranteed liberty, depended upon the good faith and restraint of those entrusted with power. They recognized that the danger to liberty and the efficient workings of government lay not in the possibility that the president or lesser executive officers might act illegally, but rather that they might abuse the powers the Con-

16. *Ibid.*, 667–73. Lawrence also pointed to impeachment cases in the states. *Ibid.*, 674–77; Boutwell in the *Congressional Globe*, 40th Congress, 2nd Session, appendix, 58–60 (December 6, 1867).

stitution *had* delegated to them. Although earlier constitutional analysts had arrived at the same conclusion, this consideration was stated most succinctly by the great nationalist legal scholar John Norton Pomeroy, perhaps because he was writing at the very time impeachment became a topic of popular discussion.

The importance of the impeaching power consists, not in its effects upon subordinate ministerial officers, but in the check which it places upon the President and the judges. They must be clothed with an ample discretion; the danger to be apprehended is from an abuse of this discretion. But at this very point where the danger exists, and where the protection should be certain, the President and the judiciary are beyond the reach of Congressional legislation. Congress cannot, by any laws penal or otherwise, interfere with the exercise of a discretion conferred by the Constitution. . . . If the offense for which the proceeding may be instituted must be made indictable by statute, impeachment thus becomes absolutely nugatory against those officers in those cases where it is most needed as a restraint upon violations of public duty.[17]

The abuses commentators feared were precisely those "too artful to be anticipated by positive law, and sometimes too subtle and mysterious to be fully detected in the limited period of an ordinary investigation." That the rules of evidence required for indictment and conviction were too rigid to serve in an area so dangerous to society worried William Rawle. Incriminating facts might be uncovered "which may be properly connected with others already known, but [which] would not form sufficient subjects of separate prosecution. Of these accounts a peculiar tribunal seems both useful and necessary," he reasoned, "a tribunal of a liberal and comprehensive character, confined as little as possible to strict forms, enabled to continue its session as long as the nature of the case may require, qualified to view the charge in all its bearings and dependencies, and to appreciate on sound principles of public policy the defense of the accused . . . ." Without dissent, although often with less

17. Pomeroy, *An Introduction to the Constitutional Law of the United States* (New York, 1870), 491–92. Although first published in 1870, Pomeroy had completed the text by 1868, when he had it copyrighted.

clarity and succinctness, the other major American constitutionalists echoed these opinions.[18]

Had Republicans acted upon these doctrines, there can be no doubt that Andrew Johnson could have been impeached, tried, convicted, and removed at any time after December 1865, for his activities fitted precisely into the pattern Pomeroy, Rawle, and others had outlined.

Republican congressmen had not passed a Reconstruction law before the Rebel armies laid down their arms, in April and May 1865, but they had passed a series of measures that should have had a great impact on the reorganization of southern political, social, and economic institutions after the war. The "ironclad" test oath, required of all elected and appointed officers in the public service of the United States, effectually barred former Rebels from national office. The Confiscation Act

18. Rawle's essay on impeachment is in his *A View of the Constitution of the United States of America*, 2nd ed. (Philadelphia, 1829), 209–19. The quoted material is at pp. 211–12. Pomeroy's entire discussion is in his *Constitutional Law of the United States*, 440–45, 482–92. See also Alexander Hamilton, *The Federalist*, Nos. 65, 66, and 81, in Hamilton, James Madison, and John Jay, *The Federalist on the New Constitution, Written in the Year 1788 . . .* (Washington, 1818), 407–13, 413–19, and 501–11, respectively (the last particularly at p. 505); William A. Duer, *Outlines of Constitutional Jurisprudence of the United States* (New York, 1833), 89–91; Duer, *A Course of Lectures on Constitutional Jurisprudence*, 76–78; Joseph Story, *Commentaries on the Constitution*, 2 vols. (Boston, 1851), I, 553–58; James Kent, *Commentaries on American Law*, ed. George F. Comstock, 11th ed., 3 vols. (Boston, 1867), I, 302, 367n; Timothy Farrar, *The Manual of the Constitution of the United States* (Boston, 1867), 436–37. The great constitutional commentators and historians who wrote after the President's acquittal in 1868 have continued to endorse the broad view of the impeachment power, despite historians' evident belief to the contrary. See, for instance, Thomas McIntyre Cooley, *The General Principles of Constitutional Law in the United States of America*, ed. Alexis C. Angell, 2nd ed. (Boston, 1891), 165–66; H. von Holst, *The Constitutional Law of the United States of America*, trans. Alfred Bishop Mason (Chicago, 1887), 158–61; Andrew C. McLaughlin, *A Constitutional History of the United States* (New York, 1935), 320–24; Samuel P. Weaver, *Constitutional Law and Its Administration* (Chicago, 1946), 167; Edward S. Corwin, *The Constitution of the United States of America: Analysis and Interpretation* (Washington, 1952), 502–4.

of July 17, 1862, made this prohibition explicit but was less effective than the law requiring the oath, because its disqualification provision referred only to those *convicted* of treasonable activities.[19]

The Confiscation Act provided for the seizure of all the real and personal property of major Rebel officeholders and all Rebels who did not return to their allegiance within sixty days of a presidential warning proclamation. Title would be secured to the government through proceedings *in rem* before federal courts, and the property would be used in prosecuting the war or the proceeds of its disposal would be paid into the United States Treasury.[20] An explanatory resolution limited the forfeiture to the life of the Rebel, minimizing the law's utility.[21]

The concept of confiscation had been fundamentally altered when Republicans passed the Freedmen's Bureau bill during the second session of the 38th Congress, early in 1865. By that act, southern lands abandoned by their owners, which were subject to confiscation under the Confiscation Act, were put under the administration of a new Bureau of Refugees, Freedmen, and Abandoned Lands. The commissioner of the Bureau was to use the abandoned land to aid black men in the transition from slavery to freedom. He was specifically empowered, under the direction of the president, to set aside for the use of freedmen and refugees abandoned land and land to which the government had acquired title through confiscation proceedings. The land was to be divided into forty-acre plots or less and rented to individual freedmen and refugees for three years. At the end of the three years, or any time earlier, the occupants could purchase the

19. *U.S. Statutes at Large,* XII, 502–3 (the Test Oath Law), 589–92 (the Confiscation Act; the disqualification provision, section 3, on p. 590).

20. *Ibid. In rem* proceedings lie against property rather than persons. That is, if the property were tainted by ownership by someone adhering to the Rebellion, the court would find against it and transfer title to the government.

21. The development and passage of the Confiscation bill and supplementary resolution is discussed in Leonard Curry, *Blueprint for Modern America: Nonmilitary Legislation of the First Civil War Congress* (Nashville, 1968), 75–100.

land they were working, receiving from the government "such title thereto as the United States can convey." [22]

The peculiar limitation Congress set upon the title freedmen could purchase indicates one of the problems the bill raised. Because federal courts were not yet operating in most areas conquered from the Rebels, the national government had secured title to hardly any land at all through confiscation proceedings. Of course, land liable to confiscation lying behind Rebel lines remained untouched. Most Rebel land in government hands, therefore, was classified as "seized" or "abandoned." When Congress passed the Freedmen's Bureau bill, it evidently intended that government officers should institute confiscation proceedings while freedmen worked the land. But the bill required no one to do so. Under the Confiscation Act, Treasury agents had spurred the small number of confiscation proceedings instituted, since it was the Treasury Department that gained from them. With that spur removed, it was not clear who would accept the burden of litigation.

Nonetheless, the landholding provisions of the Freedmen's Bureau bill clearly demonstrated a desire on the part of Republicans to provide an economic foundation for black men's new freedom. Republicans further evidenced their intentions when each house of Congress passed legislation repealing the resolution limiting forfeiture under the Confiscation Act to the lifetime of the Rebel. Since no single resolution to this effect passed both houses, however, the limiting resolution remained law.[23]

22. *U.S. Statutes at Large,* XIII, 507–9.
23. A large literature has accumulated recently indicating how close Republicans came during the war to inaugurating a real land reform in the South. See LaWanda Cox, "The Promise of Land to the Freedmen," *Mississippi Valley Historical Review,* XLV (December 1958), 413–40; Paul W. Gates, "Federal Land Policy in the South, 1866–1888," *Journal of Southern History,* VI (August 1940), 303–30; John A. Carpenter, *The Sword and the Olive Branch: Oliver Otis Howard* (Pittsburgh, 1964), 106–7. For experimental land reforms and the pressure leading to the creation of the Freedmen's Bureau with its land-reform potential, see John G. Sproat, "Blueprint for Radical Reconstruction," *Journal of Southern History,* XXIII (February 1957), 25–44; Willie Lee Rose, *Re-*

Congress, therefore, had set rather specific parameters to the Reconstruction process when the 38th Congress adjourned. If Lincoln, and later Johnson, intended to continue the policy of administering conquered areas through provisional governors, those provisional governors, as officers of the United States, would have to take the "ironclad" test oath. They would be thoroughly loyal men who had never endorsed or encouraged secession or resistance to national authority. Moreover, although former Rebels could take part in the reorganization after taking the amnesty oath, national patronage could go only to those who could take the test oath. Republicans believed that the best security for a loyal Reconstruction would be a government politically allied to the Republican party, even if former Rebels served in it. With national patronage required by law to be put in the hands of loyalists, with the all-important provisional governors required always to have been loyal Union men, Republicans could expect that their allies would control the Reconstruction process in the South. This had been the case in Tennessee, Arkansas, and Louisiana, where Reconstruction had begun before the war ended.

Furthermore, a strong start had been made in solving the problem of transition from slave to free labor. The Freedmen's Bureau, funded by the income of abandoned, seized, and confiscated lands, would cooperate with missionary organizations in educating black people, guard freedmen's interests in the unaccustomed process of contracting for wages, and begin the process of distributing land to establish black homesteads.

But within a year of Andrew Johnson's elevation to the presidency, the preliminary Reconstruction program enacted by Congress lay in utter ruin. In pursuing his own policy, Johnson had destroyed it, without violating a law, using only his constitutional powers as president of the United States. Ignoring

---

hearsal for Reconstruction: The Port Royal Experiment (New York, 1964), 3–345; George R. Bentley, *A History of the Freedmen's Bureau* (Philadelphia, 1955), 16–49; William S. McFeely, *Yankee Stepfather: General O. O. Howard and the Freedmen* (New Haven and London, 1968), 45–64.

the Test Oath Act of Congress, he appointed former Rebels provisional governors in several southern states. He had excepted leading Confederates from his Amnesty Proclamation, but he willingly pardoned virtually any Rebel upon the recommendation of his provisional governors. The provisional governors were politicians, interested in political power, and they knew that their political futures would be more promising if they conciliated white southern leaders. When Johnson made it obvious that he would support such a policy by pardoning Rebel leaders, and when he made alternatives impossible by opposing black suffrage, most of the provisional governors began to work with former Confederates and to proscribe former Unionists who refused to cooperate. By December 1865, nearly every southern state had returned to Confederate leadership.

The Johnson administration had also ignored the congressional oath requirement in making ordinary appointments to the national civil service in the South. Postmaster General William Dennison and Attorney General James Speed found it possible to obey the law (although with difficulty), but Treasury Secretary McCulloch, encouraged by Secretary of the Navy Welles, had abandoned the oath requirement in August 1865, staffing the southern Treasury Department network with former Rebels. After the Post Office Department, the Treasury Department was the largest single source of national patronage within the states, and its positions were far more lucrative and sought after. In ignoring the oath requirement enacted by Congress, McCulloch abetted the pro-Rebel policy established at the state level by most of Johnson's provisional governors.[24]

Johnson's decisions had been as disastrous to the race and labor policy of the Republicans as to their protean Reconstruction program. These decisions centered on enforcement of the

---

24. The most intensive study of the problem of loyalty oaths during the Civil War and Reconstruction is Harold M. Hyman's *The Era of the Oath: Northern Loyalty Tests During the Civil War and Reconstruction* (Philadelphia, 1954). Jonathan Truman Dorris studied the pardon and amnesty question exhaustively in *Pardon and Amnesty Under Lincoln and Johnson: The Restoration of the Confederates to Their Rights and Privileges, 1861–1898* (Chapel Hill, N.C., 1953).

Confiscation Act and the President's absolute right to pardon under the Constitution.

By late July 1865, Attorney General Speed began to restrict the enforcement of the Confiscation law. It is not clear that he did so at the direct order of the President, but there can be no doubt that the decision was part of a uniform administration program to restore the Union by conciliating white Southerners. At the urging of the provisional governor of Florida, Speed ordered the United States Attorney for the Northern District of Florida to halt proceedings for the sale of confiscated lands there and to cease proceedings to confiscate railroads. The officer protested the individual case, but agreed that no new confiscation proceedings should be instituted, lest such a course "make desperadoes of ninety-nine in every hundred of the property holders of this country." [25] In September, Speed ordered the cessation of all confiscation proceedings in Virginia and ruled that the law could not be invoked to seize corporate property.[26] From September 1865 to December 1867, the Attorney General's office repeatedly ordered local officers to cease or suspend confiscation proceedings, bringing to a standstill nearly all the activity in this area.[27] By fall and

25. J. Hubley Ashton (acting Attorney General) to Nathaniel Usher (U.S. Attorney, Northern District, Florida), July 25, 27, 1865; Ashton to William Marvin (provisional governor, Florida), July 27, 1865. Attorney General's Letterbooks, General Correspondence, Record Group 60, National Archives, Washington, D.C. Usher to Speed, August 17, 1865, Attorney General's Office, Letters Received, R.G. 60, N.A.

26. Speed to Lucius H. Chandler (U.S. Attorney, Virginia), September 5, 1865; Ashton to James Q. Smith (U.S. Attorney, Alabama), September 2, 1865. Attorney General's Letterbooks, General Correspondence, R.G. 60, N.A.

27. William Stewart (clerk) to Perkins Bass (U.S. Attorney, Northern District, Illinois), September 1, 1865; Ashton to Usher, September 1, 1865; H. F. Pleasants (clerk) to Chandler, September 2, 1865; Ashton to William A. Grover (U.S. Attorney, Missouri), September 2, 1865; Ashton to William J. Jones (U.S. Attorney, Maryland), September 2, 1865; Speed to Benjamin F. Smith (U.S. Attorney West Virginia), September 6, 1865; Speed to William N. Glover [?], September 6, 1865; Speed to James Q. Smith [?], September 22, 1865; Speed to Horace H. Harrison (U.S. Attorney, Middle District, Tennessee), September 27, October 20, 1865; Speed to Isaac Murphy (governor of Arkansas),

winter of 1865, Speed was informing his subordinates "that it is not the wish of the Government to harass or impoverish any of the citizens who desire in good faith to return to their allegiance and duty." Confiscation proceedings should be carried out only against "those who are still rebellious and contumacious . . . ." [28] Both Speed and his successor, Henry Stanbery, finally decided that confiscation was illegal in peacetime. In June 1866, Speed ordered a complete end to all proceedings.[29]

At the same time the Attorney General acted to minimize enforcement of the Confiscation law, Johnson effectively destroyed the capacity of the Freedmen's Bureau to fulfill its congressional mandate. Former Confederates pardoned under the Amnesty Proclamation or by special presidential action immediately began to demand the return of their abandoned and seized property. When Bureau officials refused to accede to their demands, the pardoned Rebels appealed to the President.

November 28, 29, 1865; Speed to Harrison, November 30, 1865; Speed to [?] Jennings, April 11, 1866; Speed to Bennet Pike (U.S. Attorney, Western District, Missouri), April 11, June 15, 1866; Stanbery to Pike, June 23, 1866; Pleasants (acting chief clerk) to John L. Williamson (U.S. Attorney, Tennessee), August 20, 1866 (halting confiscation proceedings against Confederate General P. G. T. Beauregard); Ashton to C. C. Carrington (U.S. Attorney, Washington, D.C.), November 10, 1866; Stanbery to James Q. Smith, January 16, 1867 (halting proceedings against Cassius C. Clay); Ashton to the district attorney and U.S. marshal, Georgia, March 27, 1867; Stanbery to L. V. B. Martin (U.S. Attorney, Alabama), March 29, 1867; Pleasants to Henry A. Fitch (U.S. Attorney, Georgia), April 15, 1867; F. U. Still (acting chief clerk) to Francis Bugbee (U.S. Attorney, Northern District, Florida), November 4, 1867; Binckley (Assistant Attorney General) to Usher, November 29, 1867; Binckley to Bugbee, December 6, 1867. Attorney General's Letterbooks, General Correspondence, R.G. 60, N.A.
28. Speed to Usher, December 9, 1865. See also Speed to Daniel R. Goodloe (U.S. Attorney, Louisiana), November 27, 1865; Speed to Crawford W. Hall, January 11, 1866. Attorney General's Letterbooks, General Correspondence, R.G. 60, N.A. Also the testimony of D. H. Starbuck before the Judiciary Committee on impeachment, *House Report No. 7,* 40th Congress, 1st Session, appendix, 154–55.
29. Speed to Pike, June 15, August 14, 1866, Attorney General's Letterbooks, General Correspondence, R.G. 60, N.A.; Stanbery's testimony before the House Judiciary Committee on impeachment, *House Report No. 7,* 40th Congress, 1st Session, appendix, 420.

Commissioner Oliver Otis Howard argued that acquiescence in the Rebels' demands would completely disrupt the Bureau's activities and urged Johnson to consider property already condemned by the government to be beyond the reach of pardon. Instead, the President held that only confiscated land *already sold to third parties* should remain unreturned. Even land to which the government had received title under the Confiscation law would be restored to its former owners. Since little land had been subject to confiscation proceedings before the war's end because of the absence of courts, and since even land to which the government had received title had been turned over to the Freedmen's Bureau rather than sold, Johnson's order effectually nullified both the Confiscation and the Freedmen's Bureau laws. Howard then asked Johnson to add a stipulation to the pardons he was granting former Confederates to require them to transfer five to ten acres of land to the head of each slave family living on their property. The President did not act on the proposal.[30] After the fall of 1865, one of the Freedmen's Bureau's primary functions was to administer the restoration of seized and abandoned property to pardoned Rebels. The Freedmen's Bureau held roughly 800,000 acres of land in September 1865. It never gained control of any more. By April 1866, 414,652 acres had been restored to former owners, including almost 15,000 acres that had already been turned over to freedmen.[31]

Bad as the effect of these acts was on the Freedmen's Bureau, the real tragedy lay in their effect on the lives of individual men and women. Commissioner Howard recalled with anguish the meeting at which he informed black men who had been pro-

30. Howard to Stanton, September 4, 1865, Johnson Mss.; Howard's testimony on impeachment, *House Report No. 7*, 40th Congress, 1st Session, appendix, 89.
31. Message from the President Relative to Pardons and Abandoned Property, *House Executive Document No. 99*, 39th Congress, 1st Session; *House Report No. 30*, 40th Congress, 2nd Session; McFeely, *Yankee Stepfather*, 111–17; Oliver Otis Howard, *Autobiography of Oliver Otis Howard*, 2 vols. (New York, 1908), II, 234–36; Dorris, *Pardon and Amnesty*, 227–33; Carpenter, *Sword and the Olive Branch*, 106–9.

mised ownership of the soil they worked in the Sea Islands that they had to restore the land to their former owners. "Why . . . do you take away our lands?" one of the freedmen had asked. "You take them from us who are true, always true to the Government! You give them to our all-time enemies!" Silently agreeing, Howard could give no answer.[32]

As the conflict between Johnson and Congress grew in intensity, the President became progressively more hostile to the Freedmen's Bureau, its agents, and its commissioner. After May 1866, he began a program of harassment, authorizing political allies to "investigate" operations, removing and reassigning key Bureau personnel, and holding the threat of dismissal over Howard.[33]

Johnson used his presidential powers to moderate Reconstruction in other ways also. One of the principal objects of his attacks was the Army's use of military tribunals to punish wrongdoers in the South when state courts would take no action. One type of military tribunal, the Freedmen's Bureau Court, was an integral part of the Bureau's operation. Other military commissions were occasionally organized in the South because of the unwillingness of state courts to protect Union soldiers, loyal whites, or blacks. To put an end to the jurisdiction of such tribunals over civilians, Johnson had issued a proclamation on April 2, 1866, formally declaring an end to the insurrection and clearly intended to restore in all states the privilege of the writ of habeas corpus. The proclamation wrought chaos in the southern military establishment, as commanders urgently sought instructions. To circumvent the President's decree, Secretary of War Stanton and General Grant had been

32. Howard, *Autobiography*, II, 236–41; James M. McPherson, *The Struggle for Equality: Abolitionists and the Negro in the Civil War and Reconstruction* (Princeton, 1964), 407–10; Dorris, *Pardon and Amnesty*, 233–34; McFeely, *Yankee Stepfather*, 130–48; Saxton testimony on impeachment, *House Report No. 7, 40th Congress, 1st Session*, appendix, 111–26.

33. Howard, *Autobiography*, II, 280, 283–84; Carpenter, *Sword and the Olive Branch*, 118–20. McFeeley deals with Johnson's relations with Howard and the Bureau throughout his *Yankee Stepfather*.

forced to issue a secret circular reminding commanders in the South that military courts were authorized under the Freedmen's Bureau law, which continued in force during peace. In response to direct queries, Grant stolidly insisted that he did not interpret the Peace Proclamation as abrogating martial law.[34] But on May 1, 1866, Johnson had forced the circulation of an order pursuant to his Peace Proclamation. It required an end to all trials of civilians by military tribunal wherever civil courts were open. In July he had delivered yet another blow, ordering the release of all prisoners sentenced by military courts who had served six months, except those held for murder, rape, or arson, and those in the Tortugas.[35] On August 20, Johnson issued a second Peace Proclamation, this one applying specifically to Texas, which had been excluded from the first, and affirming that "peace, order, tranquillity, and civil authority now exist in and throughout the whole of the United States of America." But after some hesitation, Grant continued to insist that the proclamations did not abrogate martial law.[36]

By May 1866, Johnson's interference on behalf of the South had become so blatant that many Republicans feared the President might attempt a *coup d'état*. This apprehension, fanned by Johnson's intemperate language and by the open advocacy of such a course by southern and northern Democratic organs, continued until the impeachment.[37]

34. Richardson, ed., *Messages and Papers of the Presidents,* VI, 429–32; Thomas and Hyman, *Stanton,* 477–79; Grant to General George H. Thomas, April 10, 1866, Headquarters of the Army (hereafter cited as HQA), Letters Sent, R.G. 108, N.A.; Davis Tillson to O. O. Howard, April 7, 1866, and E. D. Townsend to Tillson, April 17, 1866, quoted in Edward McPherson, ed., *The Political History of the United States of America, During the Period of Reconstruction* . . . , 3rd ed. (Washington, 1880), 17*n*.

35. General Order No. 26, May 1, 1866, quoted in Richardson, ed., *Messages and Papers of the Presidents,* VI, 440–42; General Order No. 46, July 13, 1866, quoted in McPherson, ed., *Political History of Reconstruction,* 198–99.

36. Richardson, ed., *Messages and Papers of the Presidents,* VI, 434–38; Thomas and Hyman, *Stanton,* 498–99.

37. The only study of the fears of renewed strife during Reconstruction is William A. Russ, Jr., "Was There Danger of a Second Civil

Finally, Johnson exercised the presidential power of removal and appointment in an effort to influence officeholders —and through them the public—to endorse his Reconstruction policy. It is difficult to judge how much of the outcry against Johnson's partisan use of the patronage axe was inspired by the forcing out of Republican "ins." But a good part of the complaint was based on principle. The man who first proposed curbing the

---

War During Reconstruction?" *Mississippi Valley Historical Review,* XXV (June 1938), 39–58. Russ's study is suggestive but incomplete. A new look at this question would be most useful. For Republican fears as to Johnson's intentions from 1866 to 1867, see William Lloyd Garrison to James Miller McKim, March 3, 1866, McKim Mss., Margaret S. Maloney collection, New York Public Library; Justin S. Morrill to [?] Jewett, May 4, 1866, quoted in William Belmont Parker, *The Life and Public Services of Justin Smith Morrill* (Boston and New York, 1924), 229–30; Boutwell's speech in the secret Republican caucus of July 11, 1866, reported in the New York *Times,* July 16, 1866, pp. 4–5; John A. Krout, ed., "Henry J. Raymond on the Republican Caucuses of July, 1866," *American Historical Review,* XXXIII (July 1928), 837–39; Charles Sumner to John Bright, September 3, 1866, quoted in Edward L. Pierce, *Memoir and Letters of Charles Sumner,* 4 vols. (Boston, 1893), IV, 298–99; New York *Independent,* August 9, 1866, p. 4; Samuel F. Miller to David Davis, October 12, 1866, David Davis Mss., Illinois State Historical Society, Springfield, Ill.; George S. Boutwell, *Reminiscences of Sixty Years in Public Affairs* (New York, 1902), II, 107–8; Grant's testimony on impeachment, *House Report No. 7,* 40th Congress, 1st Session, appendix, 833–34; Adam Badeau, *Grant in Peace: From Appomattox to Mount McGregor—A Personal Memoir* (Hartford, 1887), 51; New York *Independent,* January 31, 1867, p. 1; Carl Schurz, *Reminiscences of Carl Schurz,* 3 vols. (New York, 1908–9), III, 252; speech of John Sherman in Cincinnati quoted in the McPherson scrapbook: Campaign of 1867, II, 111, McPherson Mss.; Schurz to Mrs. Margarethe Meyer Schurz, August 31, November 9, 1867, quoted in Schurz, *Intimate Letters of Carl Schurz, 1841–1869,* ed. Joseph Shafer (Madison, Wis., 1928), 392–93 and 412–16, respectively; John Binney to Schuyler Colfax, September 9, 1867, enclosed with Binney to John A. Andrew, September 12, 1867, Andrew Mss., Massachusetts Historical Society, Boston; Boston *Daily Advertiser,* August 29, 1867, p. 2; September 2, 1867, p. 2; New York *Times,* September 17, 1867, p. 4; Chicago *Tribune,* September 27, 1867, p. 2; October 1, 1867, p. 1; October 3, 1867, p. 1; October 11, 1867, p. 2; New York *National Anti-Slavery Standard,* October 27, 1866, p. 2; [anonymous], "The Conspiracy at Washington," *Atlantic Monthly,* XX (November 1867), 633–38. As can be seen, apprehensions were not limited to radical alarmists alone.

President's power of removal was Lyman Trumbull. The
Senate manager of the Tenure of Office Act was George F.
Edmunds. Both remained consistent and vociferous advocates
of civil-service reform after Republicans regained control of the
presidency. Trumbull's firm convictions in the matter ultimately
became an important factor in his adoption of Liberal Repub-
licanism.

There may have been a profoundly principled objection to
Johnson's use of patronage on the part even of those who did
not specifically repudiate the "spoils" system. There has been
no intensive study of how men viewed political parties and
their relationship to government in the critical mid-nineteenth
century, when so many concepts of politics changed fundamentally. But it is possible that Republicans, agreeing that "to
the victor belong the spoils," objected on principle to Johnson's
policy of delivering the spoils to the losers. So long as the people
freely elected an administration, patronage distribution remained
the result of democratic decision. Johnson was distributing
national offices in disregard of that decision. Furthermore, he
was not using patronage to bolster either of the political
parties, stable organizations whose primary purpose was to
reflect the public will accurately enough to win elections. His
freely admitted purpose was to organize a new party around
himself and his policy. No doubt he honestly believed in that
policy, but along with its enactment he sought personal power.
And in large measure he sought that power through his control
of the civil service of the nation.[38]

Beale argued in his *Critical Year* that Johnson did not make
adequate use of his control of patronage. McKitrick, comment-
ing on Beale's observation, has demonstrated how impotent the
patronage "whip" was in influencing voters in the 1866 election,
but the myth persists that the President never really used all his

38. For the process through which the collector of the Port of
New York—one of the most important positions in the nation both in
patronage and responsibility—was filled early in 1866, see LaWanda
and John H. Cox, *Politics, Principle, and Prejudice, 1865–1866: Dilemma
of Reconstruction America* (New York, 1963), 113–27.

power in this field.[39] In fact, Johnson and his supporters did crack the whip, and with great success, so far as the activities of Republican officeholders in 1866 were concerned. Beale's evidence to the contrary comes almost totally from letters written before May 1866 by men who had their own patronage axes to grind.[40]

From December 1865 through June 1866, Johnson removed only 52 postmasters. In July, after he signaled his opposition to the Fourteenth Amendment and girded for war, he removed 56. Especially hard hit were Wisconsin and New York, where the President had active and vigorous allies long involved in factional disputes who now evened scores with old enemies.[41] During the recess between the first and second sessions of the 39th Congress from July 28 to December 4, 1866, Johnson removed 1,664 postmasters, 1,283 of them for political reasons alone. Excluding the southern and border states, 1,352 of 12,836 postmasters were replaced—1,210, nearly 10 percent of the total, for political reasons only.[42] And in many of those states—New York, Wisconsin, and Connecticut, for example—factions allied with Johnson had already controlled large amounts of the patronage before he began his assault.

The effect of these removals cannot be judged by their number alone. Johnson never intended to replace every federal

39. Beale, *Critical Year*, 117–21; McKitrick, *Johnson and Reconstruction*, 377–94.

40. In his discussion, Beale cites only three letters written after May 1866. The others are dated from October 1865 to April 1866. Since Beale assumed that the confrontation between Johnson and the Republican party was inevitable, he concluded that Johnson had delayed nearly nine months before beginning to bring government officers into line. Actually, as has been noted, there were many conservative and center Republicans who hoped to cooperate with Johnson. Their hopes for harmony materially weakened the radicals. If Johnson had begun an attack through the patronage, the nonradicals would certainly have realized that their hopes were ephemeral.

41. In Wisconsin, where Doolittle wielded the axe, sixteen postmasters were decapitated. In New York, fourteen. This information was derived from a tedious search of the *Senate Executive Journal*, XVI. It is possible that a few more removals escaped my attention.

42. *House Executive Document No. 96*, 39th Congress, 2nd Session.

officeholder; he meant to force them to endorse his policy of Reconstruction. As they saw their colleagues fall, they began grudgingly to do so. As early as April, the pleased Senator James R. Doolittle wrote his wife that "the tone of the office holders [in Wisconsin] is changing. They are becoming very conservative." Rush R. Sloane, a Post Office agent in Ohio who supported Johnson until June 1866, told the impeachment investigators (with some exaggeration, perhaps) that he was the only national officeholder in Ohio who had not responded to the July 1866 call for a pro-Johnson convention in Philadelphia. He had been removed immediately.[43] Most patronage employees probably tried to remain strictly neutral between the contestants during the elections of 1866, but not until Congress passed the Tenure of Office Act, restricting Johnson's removal power, did some of them cautiously begin to speak out for their principles once more.

The President's course, none of the elements of which clearly violated law, had a staggering effect on the South. He converted a conquered people, bitter but ready to accept the consequences of defeat, into a hostile, aggressive, uncooperative unit. He restored to them political and economic power and through that power domination of the men and women they had recently held as slaves. He had set back the work of Reconstruction, as it turned out, two full years and had ensured that Southerners would resist the process instead of cooperating. To a large degree, the failure of Reconstruction could be blamed alone on President Johnson's abuse of his discretionary powers.[44]

43. Doolittle to Mrs. Mary Doolittle, April 9, 1866, Doolittle Mss., Wisconsin Historical Society, Madison, Wis.; *House Report No. 7,* 40th Congress, 1st Session, appendix, 270.

44. The correspondence of Republicans is filled with evidence of the change that came over Southerners when they realized the President's intentions. J. W. Sprague to John Sherman, March 29, April 4, 1866, Sherman Mss., Library of Congress; Jonathan Roberts to Lyman Trumbull, April 21, 1866; A. P. Field to Trumbull, May 17, 1866, Trumbull Mss., Library of Congress; William G. Brownlow to Salmon P. Chase, June 20, 1866, Chase Mss., Library of Congress; James Speed to Henry S. Lane, August 6, 1866, Lane Mss., Smith Library, Indiana

The Republicans' response to the President's activities was remarkably slow and unbelievably mild. In the attempt to conciliate Johnson before he vetoed the Freedmen's Bureau and Civil Rights bills, Republicans had virtually ratified his dismantling of their Reconstruction and race policies. In his Freedmen's Bureau bill, Lyman Trumbull had confirmed for only three years black men's rights to the land they had been promised in the Sea Islands. He had recognized the end to hopes of land reform based on confiscation by authorizing the Bureau to procure homesteads for black families in the public lands alone. Trumbull accepted Johnson's elimination of the Bureau's independent financial support, which was originally to have come from the income of confiscated and abandoned lands, by authorizing a specific appropriation. The Senate had passed the bill in this form. In the House, Republicans roundly defeated Thaddeus Stevens' attempt to restore the freedmen's rights to homestead on confiscated property.[45]

Moreover, Republicans had made no legal objections to the governments reorganized under Johnson's authority through provisional governors, none of whom had taken the test oath and several of whom could not have taken it, even though those governments had been controlled by the very elements Republicans had wanted to proscribe. On the contrary; Republicans had implicitly offered to recognize those governments should they ratify the mild Fourteenth Amendment. Even when enacting the Reconstruction law, Republicans did not disperse Johnson's governments, and only at the last minute acquiesced in radical demands to disqualify from office under them those classes of men disqualified by the Fourteenth Amendment.

Republicans were only slightly more insistent that the Test Oath law be complied with in the national civil service. They did

---

State Historical Society, Indianapolis; A. Warren Kelsey to Edward Atkinson, November 13, 1865, Atkinson Mss., Massachusetts Historical Society: William Smith to D. H. Bingham, March 31, 1866, Papers of the Joint Committee on Reconstruction, 39th Congress, R.G. 233, N.A.; McKitrick, *Johnson and Reconstruction,* 154–58, 186–213.

45. *Congressional Globe,* 39th Congress, 1st Session, 688 (February 8, 1866).

not accede to requests from Secretary of the Treasury McCulloch and the President to repeal or modify the Test Oath Act, but Charles Sumner's opposition to paying men who had accepted government positions contrary to the law failed to impress his Senate colleagues. Only resistance from the House prevented Congress from appropriating money to pay the former Rebels' salaries.[46]

Republicans responded most forcefully to the President's patronage offensive, but even here they had resisted the Senate Judiciary Committee's effort to prevent political removals in the Post Office Department in May 1866.[47] In December 1866, when Johnson's success in neutralizing Republican office-holders became apparent, such conservatives as Sherman, John B. Henderson, and George H. Williams proposed bills to regulate the tenure of offices. Republicans passed a Tenure of Office bill in February 1867 almost without dissent. It forbade the removal of appointed government officers when the Senate was in session until the Senate had confirmed the appointment of replacements. When the Senate was not in session, an officer might be suspended and a replacement named ad interim. When the Senate convened, the President was required to offer reasons for the removal, and if the Senate agreed, the removal would become permanent. If it refused, the suspended official would

46. *Ibid.,* 39th Congress, 2nd Session, 1903, 1911 (February 28, 1867); Hyman, *Era of the Oath,* 60–68.

47. The Judiciary Committee had agreed to the measure at the urging of its chairman, Trumbull, who represented a state (Illinois) with numerous local factional rivalries among Republicans. Timothy Otis Howe, of Wisconsin, also spoke for the measure. Both were beginning to feel the effect of the "axe," long before other Republican senators. Trumbull's papers were filled with complaints regarding the patronage at this time, as disappointed office-seekers and veterans, jealous of civilians' domination of Illinois offices, began to use the dispute between Johnson and congressional Republicans to urge the removal of their opponents from their positions. See also Howe to Horace Rublee, June 21, 1866. Although a dissenting member of the Judiciary Committee led Republicans opposing the patronage restriction, Howe blamed Fessenden for its defeat. Howe to Rublee, April 13, 1867, Howe Mss., Wisconsin Historical Society. The votes on the measure are in the *Congressional Globe,* 39th Congress, 1st Session, 2339 (May 2, 1866), 2423 (May 7, 1866), and 2559 (May 11, 1866).

resume his place. Even here, however, the Senate had refrained from tying the President's hands completely. Nonradical and Democratic senators insisted that department heads be exempted from the bill's operation, and the confusing compromise on this issue agreed upon by Senate and House conferees played a significant role in impeachment.[48]

Beyond this Republicans had not been willing to go. In July 1866, with officeholders pleading with their representatives not to adjourn (so long as the Senate sat, it could prevent removals by refusing to confirm replacements) and some congressmen fearing a *coup d'état,* radicals had proposed remaining in session through the summer and fall. "[T]he most absurd idea . . . that was ever cherished outside of a Lunatic Asylum," conservative Representative Henry L. Dawes fumed.[49] Confiding their fears to a secret Republican caucus, radicals succeeded in having a special, overwhelmingly radical, committee appointed to recommend a course of action. But at the next caucus, held three days later, conservatives and centrists had taken control. They repudiated the committee recommendation to remain in session,. and by a 64 to 40 vote Republicans had agreed to adjourn the session as usual.[50] The radicals then carried the fight to the floor of the House, only to lose once more. Furious at the radicals, Dawes had written, "If the republic doesn't die of the combined effect of Johnson's treachery and our madness then it is immortal." [51]

Given Johnson's history of disregard for congressional

48. *Ibid.,* 39th Congress, 2nd Session, 1739, 1966 (March 2, 1967). Williams's bill was the one that passed. Sherman's (Senate Bill No. 452) and Henderson's (S.B. No. 315) are in the Senate bill file, 39th Congress, R.G. 46, N.A. Sherman and Williams had opposed the 1866 version.

49. Dawes to Mrs. Electa Dawes, July 12, 1866, Dawes Mss., Library of Congress.

50. New York *Times,* July 16, 1866, pp. 4–5; July 18, 1866, p. 4; Krout, ed., "Raymond on the July Caucuses," 835–42.

51. *Congressional Globe,* 39th Congress, 1st Session, 3912–13 (July 18, 1866), 3933–34 (July 19, 1866), 3981–85 (July 20, 1866), 4009, 4017 (July 21, 1866), 4113–15, 4155–56 (July 25, 1866). Dawes to Mrs. Electa Dawes, July 17, 1866, Dawes Mss.

enactments that ran counter to his policy, the insistence of radicals in the spring of 1867 that his removal was an essential part of any new Reconstruction program was not unreasonable. But despite their strenuous efforts, the radicals had not convinced conservatives and centrists of the urgency, and Republicans had left Washington in April 1867, without impeaching the President and only grudgingly agreeing to even the barest possibility of meeting again in July should the necessity arise.

But once again Johnson determined to use his presidential powers to obstruct congressional Reconstruction. The occasion soon arose in Louisiana. Johnson had appointed General Philip H. Sheridan commander of the military district comprising Louisiana and Texas under the terms of the Reconstruction Act, and one of his first acts was to remove the state and local officials responsible for the bloody New Orleans massacre. Although Sheridan already had made complete reports that had incriminated the officials, Johnson demanded an explanation of the removals, making his displeasure manifest. Stung, Sheridan answered, "I did not deem it necessary to give any reason for the removal of these men, especially after the [earlier] investigations . . . ," but he sent the information.[52] Johnson then ordered Sheridan to defer the removals, asking his conservative attorney general, Henry Stanbery, for an opinion on Sheridan's power in the premises.[53]

When other commanders indicated that they too had decided it necessary to remove officials in the states under their command, Johnson and Stanbery hurried the opinion. Stanbery read it to the cabinet on May 14 and 21, and it appeared officially on June 12, 1867. Stanbery's interpretation virtually emasculated the Reconstruction Act. Holding that all new laws should be narrowly construed, the Attorney General insisted that the military commanders had power only to keep the peace and to punish criminal acts. The Johnsonian provisional governments and the United States courts retained all other jurisdictions,

52. Sheridan to Grant, April 19, 1867, HQA, Letters Received, R.G. 108, N.A.
53. Thomas and Hyman, *Stanton,* 534–35.

and therefore the military authorities could not intervene to protect the rights enumerated in the Civil Rights Act. They had no jurisdiction over crimes committed before Congress passed the Reconstruction Act and none over acts not in violation of state or national law. Commanders could not remove the officials of the provisional governments, Stanbery maintained. Registration boards had to accept Southerners' oaths that they were not disqualified by law from voting; they had no power to investigate whether the swearer had perjured himself. Finally, Stanbery affirmed that the President retained supervisory power over the enforcement of the Reconstruction Acts, "to see that all 'the laws are faithfully executed.' " [54]

Gideon Welles, Johnson's archconservative Secretary of the Navy, although despairing of the practical effect of the opinion, agreed that the Attorney General "had done more for popular rights, under a law which despotically deprived the people of their undoubted guaranteed rights, than I had supposed possible." But General Daniel Sickles, whose acts as military commander in the Carolinas Stanbery had specifically denounced as illegal, angrily requested to be relieved from duty so he could defend his conduct before a court of inquiry. "[T]he declaration of the Attorney General that Military authority has not superceded [the provisional governments] . . . prevents the execution of the Reconstruction acts, disarms me of means to protect life, property, or the rights of citizens and menaces all interests in these States with ruin." [55] Sheridan and General John Pope hurriedly asked General of the Army Grant if they must consider the circular notifying them of the Attorney General's opinion a direct order. Grant told them to enforce their own constructions of the law until ordered otherwise.[56]

As rumors circulated that Johnson would order the mili-

54. U. S. Department of Justice, *Opinions of the Attorneys General of the United States,* XII, 182–206.

55. Gideon Welles, *Diary of Gideon Welles—Secretary of the Navy Under Lincoln and Johnson,* 3 vols. (Boston and New York, 1911), III, 110 (June 20, 1867); Sickles to the Adjutant General, June 19, 1867, Edwin M. Stanton Mss., Library of Congress.

56. George C. Gorham, *Life and Public Services of Edwin M. Stanton,* 2 vols. (Boston and New York, 1899), 381.

tary commanders in the South to restore to office all officials they had removed, even conservative Republican congressmen recognized that a July session of Congress would be necessary after all. But they worried lest radicals use the occasion to press for a more stringent Reconstruction law or impeachment of the President. They determined to limit the business of the session to repairing the damage Johnson and his Attorney General had done to the Reconstruction Act, and assurances from Washington that Johnson did not intend to interfere further with the law's enforcement reinforced that determination. "I am disgusted with Johnson for giving [the radicals] such a pretense," Fessenden wrote Grimes. "God only knows what mischief will be done if we get together." [57]

When congressmen gathered in Washington, nonradicals seized control of the session. In caucus, senators agreed to Roscoe Conkling's proposed resolution to limit the business of the session to amendments of the Reconstruction Act. A similar resolution passed the House on July 5, with radicals making only ineffectual opposition.[58] In the Senate, Sumner opposed the resolution on the floor, despite the caucus decision, but only nine senators sustained him.[59]

By July 6 radicals realized they could not hope to persuade their reluctant allies to remain in Washington's summer heat to impeach the President. Instead, they decided to press

57. Fessenden to Grimes, June 18, 1867, quoted in Charles A. Jellison, *Fessenden of Maine: Civil War Senator* (Syracuse, N.Y., 1962), 221; New York *Times,* June 12, 1867, p. 4; Schenck to Rutherford B. Hayes (sent to all representatives), June 21, 1867, Hayes Mss., Rutherford B. Hayes Library, Fremont, Ohio; Edwin D. Morgan to Fessenden, June 22, 1867; Morgan to Roscoe Conkling, June 22, 1867; Conkling to Morgan, June 24, 1867, Morgan Mss., New York State Library, Albany; Boston *Daily Advertiser,* June 21, 1867, p. 2.

58. *Ibid.,* July 4, 1867, p. 1; *Congressional Globe,* 40th Congress, 1st Session, 480 (July 3, 1867).

59. The nine senators voted with Sumner either to amend the resolution to remove its restriction or against the resolution itself. They were Chandler, Drake, Fowler, Howe, Ross, Thayer, Tipton, and Wade among the Republicans and Buckalew among the Democrats. Ross, at least, was primarily interested in legislation to protect the frontier against Indian raids. *Ibid.,* 481–99 (July 5, 1867). The votes are at 487 and 498.

for an October session for the purpose. "They are determined to ruin the Republican party," Dawes complained. But, like Fessenden, he lamented, " [T]he President . . . *does* continue to do the most provoking things. If he isn't impeached it wont [*sic*] be his fault." [60]

On July 10, Boutwell proposed a resolution in the House to adjourn until October 16. In the course of the discussion, Judiciary Committee chairman Wilson announced that the committee at the moment opposed impeachment by a five to four margin. From the acrimonious debate, it became clear that Wilson himself led the opposition to impeachment, sustained by two Democrats and Representatives Frederick E. Woodbridge and John C. Churchill. Boutwell, William Lawrence, Thomas Williams, and Francis Thomas advocated the measure. As opposition to an October "impeachment" session continued to mount, radicals warned their colleagues of the effect of timidity. The people were becoming impatient. "We want peace and quiet," Illinois Representative Lewis Ross implored. "We want this disturbing element removed." [61] But despite the earnest entreaties of radicals and those centrists who agreed with them, a Republican-Democratic coalition succeeded in amending Boutwell's resolution to provide for reconvening Congress in mid-November.[62]

Even this was too much for Senate conservatives. Sherman amended the House resolution to provide for reassembly the first day of December, and again a conservative Republican-Democratic coalition passed this amended resolution over the radicals' objections.[63]

But Senate radicals had seen enough. On July 20, Zachariah Chandler, the tough, radical boss of the Michigan Republican party, launched a bitter attack on Fessenden, continually referring to him as "the Conservative Senator from Maine." He

60. Dawes to Mrs. Electa Dawes, July 9, 16, 1867, Dawes Mss.; Boston *Evening Journal,* July 5, 1867, p. 4; July 7, 1867, p. 4; July 8, 1867, p. 4.

61. *Congressional Globe,* 40th Congress, 1st Session, 589 (July 11, 1867).

62. *Ibid.,* 590 (July 11, 1867).

63. *Ibid.,* 732–35 (July 19, 1867).

and conservative allies had steadily opposed provisions for a July session. Now they were following the same course in regard to an October session. The President had for all practical purposes announced his intention not to execute the law, Chandler insisted. "[W]hen we first captured this monster there was one thing for us to do, and only one; but instead of doing that we undertook to surround him with nets, to hem him in, to bind him with nets of zephyr. The very moment we left he thrust his paw through. . . . Now we have met here and what have we done? We have patched up the net. It is the same net; but we have mended up the hole. . . . And now this Congress seems to hope that the same animal that thrust his paw through the net when it was new will not thrust it through again when it is merely a patched net. . . ." [64] As Fessenden defended himself, naming the senators who had voted with him, it was evident that the gap separating radicals from conservatives on the impeachment issue was widening.[65]

But the conservatives would not weaken. In the conference committee to iron out differences, the House was represented by conservatives who had forced adjournment until November 13, and the Senate by conservatives who had insisted on adjournment to December. They compromised on November 21. The radicals had been routed.[66]

While Congress debated the date to which it should adjourn, it also passed another Reconstruction measure. Both the Senate Judiciary Committee and the House Reconstruction Committee had reported bills patching, as Chandler said, the torn netting of the previous law. The bill as passed did no more than restore the authority of the military commanders and voting registration boards to what it had been when Congress

---

64. *Ibid.*, 749 (July 20, 1867).

65. The Chandler-Fessenden exchange, *ibid.*, 749–52 (July 20, 1867).

66. *Ibid.*, 757, 761, 764, for the House; 753, 753–54, 755, for the Senate (July 20, 1867). In the House, 47 Republican radicals and centrists opposed the conference report, which was carried by the united effort of 51 conservative and centrist Republicans and 10 Democrats and Johnsonians. In the Senate, 15 conservatives and centrists and 2 Democrats defeated 14 radicals and centrists.

passed the original Reconstruction Acts. Once again, Congress
had refused to take the steps radicals considered essential: the
dispersal of the Johnson governments and impeachment.
"This is the third bill of reconstruction on which we have been
called to act," Sumner lamented. "We ought never to have acted
on more than one; and if the Senate had been sufficiently radical, . . . there would have been no occasion for more than
one." [67]

As soon as Congress adjourned, Johnson proved that the
radicals had been right. Betraying the conservatives who had
believed his interference ended, on August 5 he asked for
Stanton's resignation. The Secretary of War, encouraged by
Republican friends, refused, and on August 12 the President
ordered his suspension and named Grant secretary of war ad
interim. Johnson followed this by ordering the removal of Sheridan from his southern command, against the advice of Grant
and his entire cabinet except the irrepressible Welles.[68] Republicans reacted with stunned outrage. Even Grant, who had not
yet publicly questioned Johnson's policy or motives, wrote
that Johnson's course would embolden Rebels to oppose the
Reconstruction laws and oppress loyal men. It would "be regarded as an effort to defeat the laws of Congress," he
warned.[69] The conservative publisher of the Boston *Daily
Advertiser* wrote Sumner, "Is the President crazy, or only
drunk? I am afraid his doings will make us all favor impeachment." The Chicago *Tribune*'s editor, Horace White, now decided impeachment was necessary. Congressional leaders Colfax, Elihu B. Washburne, and Henry Wilson reached the same
conclusion. Such conservative newspapers as the New York
Times, the Boston *Daily Advertiser,* the Boston *Evening Journal*, and the Providence *Journal* began to threaten impeach-

67. *Ibid.,* 625 (July 13, 1867). The text of the passed measure is
ibid., appendix, 39–40.

68. Grant to Johnson, August 1, 1867. Copy in Moore notes, Johnson Mss.; James G. Randall, ed., *Diary of Orville Hickman Browning,*
2 vols. (Springfield, Ill., 1938), II, 153–54 (August 2, 1867); Moore
notes, August 19, 1867, Johnson Mss.

69. Grant to Johnson, August 17, 1867, quoted in McPherson, ed.,
Political History of Reconstruction, 306–7.

ment, as did the Chicago *Tribune*, which had previously opposed it.[70]

But despite Republicans' violent reactions, Johnson continued the offensive, removing Sickles on August 27 and threatening the removal of General Pope from his command in Georgia, Alabama, and Florida.[71] As Johnson's rampage went on, Republicans began to fear more than ever that he might finally transcend the bounds of reason. "What does Johnson mean to do?" former Attorney General Speed begged Sumner. "Does he mean to have another rebellion on the question of Executive powers & duties?" The *Times* worried uneasily, "Mr. JOHNSON has said and done so much that is wild and wanton that people have ceased to judge of the probabilities of his action according to any received standard of right or duty." [72]

Radicals blamed conservatives for the destruction and the danger. "For every broken heart and desolate home in the South, for every murdered black there, we hold Fessenden, Wilson, Edmunds, Conklin [*sic*], and their clan, responsible," the *Anti-Slavery Standard* railed.[73]

One fact emerged clearly from the confusion: the conserva-

70. Peleg Chandler to Sumner, August 15, 1867, Sumner Mss., Houghton Library, Harvard University; Horace White to Zachariah Chandler, August 20, 1867, Chandler Mss., Library of Congress; Schuyler Colfax to James A. Garfield, September 11, 1867, Garfield Mss., Library of Congress; Willard H. Smith, *Schuyler Colfax: The Changing Fortunes of a Political Idol* (Indianapolis, 1952), 261; New York *Times*, August 26, 1867, p. 4 (for Washburne's views); New York *Times*, August 2, 1867, p. 4; Chicago *Tribune*, August 21,1867, p. 2; Boston *Daily Advertiser*, September 2, 1867, p. 2; September 3, 1867, p. 2; Schurz to Mrs. Margarethe Schurz, August 27, 1867, quoted in Schurz, *Intimate Letters*, 391–92; Burke Hinsdale to Garfield, September 30, 1867, quoted in Mary L. Hinsdale, ed., *Garfield-Hinsdale Letters: Correspondence Between James Abram Garfield and Burke Aaron Hinsdale* (Ann Arbor, Mich., 1949), 107–9.

71. Grant to Pope, September 9, 1867, HQA, Letters Sent, R.G. 108, N.A.; W. A. Swanberg, *Sickles the Incredible* (New York, 1956), 290–93.

72. Speed to Sumner, September 12, 1867, Sumner Mss.; New York *Times*, September 14, 1867, p. 4. For a full compilation of sources indicating that Republicans were seriously worried about the possibility of a *coup d'état*, see note 37, pp. 45–46, *supra*.

73. New York *National Anti-Slavery Standard*, August 17, 1867, p. 2.

tive Republican policy had failed. As the observant French correspondent and future statesman, Georges Clemenceau, explained to the readers of *Le Monde*:

> Congress may, when it pleases, take the President by the ear and lead him down from his high seat, and he can do nothing about it except to struggle and shout. But that is an extreme measure, and the radicals [i.e., the Republicans generally] are limiting themselves . . . to binding Andrew Johnson firmly with good brand-new laws. At each session they add a shackle to his bonds, tighten the bit in a different place, file a claw or draw a tooth, and then when he is well bound up, fastened, and caught in an inextricable net of laws and decrees, more or less contradicting each other, they tie him to the stake of the Constitution and take a good look at him, feeling quite sure he cannot move this time.
>
> But then . . . Samson summons all his strength, and bursts his cords and bonds with a mighty effort, and the Philistines (I mean the radicals) flee in disorder to the Capitol to set to work making new laws stronger than the old, which will break in their turn at the first test.[74]

Yet Johnson had broken no law; he had limited himself strictly to the exercise of his constitutional powers. Confused constituents turned to their congressmen: "Is it possible that there can be a wrong without a remedy . . . ," one asked Trumbull. "Must the great people who patriotically saved the Republic remain chained by an arbitrary rule until a usurper at Washington overthrows our liberties?" [75] Many congressional Republicans were finally prepared to answer the question by removing the obstacle to peace. But they could not do so until Congress reconvened on November 21. Then radicals and nonradicals would finally confront the great issue.

74. Georges Eugene Benjamin Clemenceau, *American Reconstruction,* ed. Fernand Baldensperger (New York and Toronto, 1926), 102–3 (September 10, 1867).
75. Logan Uriah Reavis to Trumbull, August 30, 1867, Trumbull Mss. Reavis was a well-known western nationalist, who among other things advocated moving the national capital to St. Louis. This was not then considered so outlandish a proposition as it seems today.

3

The Politics
of Impeachment

DESPITE President Johnson's growing belligerence and the resulting increase in the appeal of impeachment to angry, frustrated Republicans, opposition to the measure remained strong among party leaders. Several factors cooled the ardor of nonradicals for the President's removal during the summer and fall of 1867, despite the unmistakable damage he was going to their floundering Reconstruction program. Most important of these was the ever more bitter struggle that was developing between radical and nonradical Republicans for control of the party. The impeachment issue, more than any other, perhaps, began to appear to be the issue that would determine the future direction of the Republican party. And it is in this context that the battle over impeachment must be understood.

Ironically, the real issue that divided the radical and nonradical factions of the Republican party was not the nature of its obligation to southern loyalists or the desirability of a "thorough" Reconstruction. All Republicans hoped to institute racial equality before the law and to place loyal southerners, if possible, in power in the South. The divisive question was how far to go in securing those goals. Nonradical Republicans were convinced that the American people would not sustain a truly radical Republican party. They recoiled from radical proposals they were sure would alienate conservative Republican voters. Continually, the nonradicals urged moderation for the sake of political expediency. A radical Republican party, committed to the most extreme measures to protect black and white loyalists' rights, they warned, could accomplish nothing if the Democrats were restored to power through Republican excesses. "I have been taught since I have been in public life to consider it a matter of proper statesmanship, when we aim at an object which we think is desirable and important, if that object . . . is unattainable, to get as much of it and come as near it as we may be able to do," explained Fessenden, the conservative leader in the Senate.[1]

Radicals, on the other hand, chafed at the timidity of their "practical" allies. "Ample experience shows that [compromise] . . . is the least practical mode of settling questions involving moral principles," Sumner responded. "A moral principle cannot be compromised." [2] The public, radicals urged, was more advanced than the party and wanted only active, radical leadership.

Voters would have an opportunity to prove one side or the other right in twenty states that held elections for local officials in 1867. In contrast to their role in the elections of 1866, radicals were taking an active part in the campaign. By endorsing black suffrage in the Reconstruction Act, Republicans had already opened themselves to the Democratic charges of radicalism they had so successfully blunted in the previous year. Moreover, in three states—Kansas, Minnesota, and Ohio—Republicans had placed on the ballot proposals to eliminate white-only restrictions on voting from the state constitutions. Republican victories would be interpreted as a signal that northern voters were willing to endorse a more radical policy. They would strengthen the argument of the radicals and bring many hesitant Republican centrists into the radical camp.

As the struggle for control of the party intensified, the prac-

1. *Congressional Globe,* 39th Congress, 1st Session, 705 (February 7, 1866).

2. *Ibid.,* 673 (February 6, 1866). It is not possible within the framework of this essay to discuss fully the differences between radicalism and nonradicalism in the Republican party. I have dealt with the question in detail in my dissertation, "The Right Way," especially at pp. 34–54.

tical issues that divided Republicans became more and more directly involved in the campaign.[3]

One group of issues revolved about Reconstruction. Unsatisfied with the moderate Reconstruction program enacted by the 39th Congress and the first session of the 40th Congress, radicals continued to press for more thorough measures. Impeachment was only one of them. Despite opposition from conservatives like Trumbull, radicals increased pressure for Charles Sumner's proposal to enfranchise black citizens in all the states, northern as well as southern, by simple congressional enactment rather than through the cumbersome and time-consuming process of constitutional amendment. Radicals insisted that the southern states fulfill more requirements prior to restoration. Sumner still argued that Congress should insist on the establishment of a free public-school program in each state as a precondition for readmission. Some radicals still wanted southern states to undergo an indefinite period of probation before they returned to their old places in the Union. Stevens, Butler, and other radicals began for the first time since the war to agitate seriously for confiscation and land redistribution in the South.

Conservatives perceived in these efforts a program to establish a radical hegemony in the Republican party. "The ultraists . . . are determined to build up a party in the Southern States fully in accord with themselves," the conservative New York *Times* charged. "They scout and reject the moderation and tolerance of Senator WILSON, and hold such Senators as SHERMAN, FESSENDEN, and others of kindred temper in quite as much disfavor as Democrats themselves. Their plan is to consolidate the negro vote with that of the 'original Union men' of the South." [4]

This program ran counter to the policy more conservative Republican politicians advocated. Spurred by optimistic reports

3. For a fuller discussion of the intra-party divisions during the spring, summer, and fall of 1867 and a complete citation of sources, see Benedict, "The Rout of Radicalism: Republicans and the Elections of 1867," *Civil War History*, XVIII (December 1972), 334–44. See also Benedict, "The Right Way," 378–417, for a yet more complete analysis.

4. New York *Times*, May 2, 1867, p. 4.

of southern disillusion with northern Democrats and new flex-
ibility on the issue of Reconstruction, emanating especially
from the barnstorming Senator Henry Wilson of Massachusetts,
leading nonradicals hoped to build a southern Republican party
appealing to both races. Talk of confiscation or delay in restoration could only drive southern whites back to the Democrats.

The conciliatory policy now urged by Wilson; the New York
Tribune's editor, Horace Greeley; the Republican Congressional
Campaign Committee; and others infuriated the radicals.
Stevens publicly denounced the leading conciliationists, "a few
Republican meteors, always erratic in their course, . . . flit-
ting and exploding in the Republican atmosphere." Wendell
Phillips, the great radical agitator, accused Sherman and Fessen-
den of "bartering principle for patronage," while the *Anti-Slavery
Standard* predicted the disruption of the party.[5]

After the nonradicals successfully prevented the radicals
from taking up impeachment in the July session of Congress,
Sumner and Chandler joined the public criticism. In a well-
publicized interview with the radical Boston journalist James
Redpath, Sumner launched a broadside against his Senate
opponents. Criticizing the conservatism of recently elected senators like Roscoe Conkling and George F. Edmunds, whom he
called "a prodigy of obstructiveness and technicality," he saved
his most telling blows for Fessenden, "the head of the obstruc-
tives." [6] Chandler openly informed his audiences of the behind-
the-scenes maneuvering in Congress. Bitterly, he recalled how
nonradicals had defeated radical attempts to prevent adjournment after passage of the Reconstruction Act. Despite the "compromise" that provided the possibility of reconvening in July,
"these Conservatives had fixed it so they supposed we could

5. Stevens in the Gettysburg *Star and Herald,* quoted in the New
York *Times,* May 29, 1867, p. 5; Phillips's speech before the American
Anti-Slavery Society, quoted in the New York *Tribune,* May 8, 1867,
p. 1; New York *National Anti-Slavery Standard,* March 30, 1867, p. 2;
April 6, 1867, p. 2; October 26, 1867, p. 2. The influential abolitionist,
Parker Pillsbury, called upon the antislavery vanguard to leave the
party in a letter published by the *Standard,* November 2, 1867, p. 1.
6. Boston *Daily Advertiser,* September 4, 1867, p. 1.

not get together, and Mr. Johnson so understood it," Chandler charged. "But at the very last moment, when the session was given up as hopeless, and there was no intention of coming together, out came that opinion of Stanbery's, and the people rose up in their might and said Congress must get together, and watch this bad man. . . . [A]nd the very men who had been most opposed to the meeting of Congress, were there on the 3rd of July, at 12 o'clock. They did not dare to be a quarter of a second behind." [7]

The issue of impeachment also became involved with other questions, not directly related to Reconstruction. Most important of these was the controversy over the currency.[8] President Johnson's secretary of the treasury, Hugh McCulloch, favored a policy of contracting the currency as quickly as possible by offering long-term government bonds in exchange for the legal-tender notes the government had been forced to issue during the war. Congress had not endorsed this policy completely, but it had provided for cautious, limited contraction in 1866. By the fall of that year, however, even the slower contraction McCulloch enforced under Congress's legislation began to affect the economy. Business slowed and prices fell in the winter of 1866–67 and throughout 1867. The depression continued until 1868. Businessmen, especially manufacturers, reacted by demanding an end to contraction. Congressional Democrats, especially Westerners, seized the issue and began to call for currency expansion and the redemption of government bonds issued during the war in "greenbacks" rather than gold. Partly in response to the Democratic thrust, partly out of conviction, many Republicans took up the call, and by 1867 Congress voted to suspend further contraction.

This shift toward inflationary monetary policies thoroughly

7. Speech at Ashtabula, Ohio, October 1, 1867, quoted in the McPherson scrapbook: Campaign of 1867, II, 135–36, McPherson Mss.

8. For full discussions of the currency question during Reconstruction, see Robert P. Sharkey, *Money, Class, and Party: An Economic Study of Civil War and Reconstruction* (Baltimore, 1959) and Walter T. K. Nugent, *The Money Question During Reconstruction* (New York, 1967). See also Benedict, "The Right Way," 387–94.

alarmed those who held orthodox financial views. Many influential men, especially Easterners with established businesses, financiers, and intellectuals, began to organize in opposition to the trend toward "repudiation." Working to educate the public to what they conceived to be the facts of finance, the hard-money lobby offered cordial public support to McCulloch.

Closely related to the currency controversy was the tariff question. During the war, Congress had raised the tariff on imports to new heights, both to increase the income of the national government and to protect American industry from foreign competition. Although the tariff was accepted as a fiscal necessity during the war, many Republicans advocated the adoption of free-trade policies with the arrival of peace. Especially strong among former Democrats, free trade also appealed to Republican intellectuals influenced by English classical liberalism, including the editors of several important Republican newspapers and journals, such as Horace White of the Chicago *Tribune* and Edwin L. Godkin of the New York *Nation*, as well as intellectual politicians, of whom the most outstanding were Sumner, former Governor John A. Andrew of Massachusetts, Carl Schurz, and James A. Garfield, whose strongly pro-tariff constituency prevented him from going to the free-trade extreme, however. Of course, many Americans opposed the tariff for their own purely economic reasons—for example, importers and many farmers.

To a large extent, free tradism and hard-money views ran together, especially among those who favored the doctrines out of intellectual commitment rather than economic self-interest, and those who advocated both vigorously lobbied the government for what they called "fiscal reform."

Enthusiastic supporters of Secretary of the Treasury McCulloch, the hard-money, free-trade lobby naturally hesitated at supporting a movement aimed at removing the president who appointed and sustained him, even though nearly all of them supported congressional Reconstruction and many of them had been thorough radicals. But to make matters even worse for proponents of impeachment, the president pro tempore of the

Senate, the man who would replace Johnson if he were removed, was Benjamin F. Wade, a radical Republican with close connections with the soft-money, high-tariff Iron and Steel Association. In fact, rumors held that Wade would appoint the association's president, E. B. Ward, to replace McCulloch in the event of Johnson's removal. The fact that the two most vociferous leaders of the impeachment movement in the House, Stevens and Butler, also shared leadership of the soft-money forces in that body could only add to the fiscal reformers' disquiet. So to fiscal conservatives and free traders, a radical victory within the Republican party had implications for more than the course of Reconstruction. End the influence of conservative Republicans, fumed Grimes, a free trader as well as non-radical, "& [let] Thad Stevens & Butler be in control [*sic*] as they then would be with their revolutionary and repudiating ideas in the ascendancy & the government would not last 12 mos." [9]

Ultimately, the struggle for control of the party revolved about the battle for the 1868 Republican presidential nomination. In a party rife with factionalism, access to national patronage could mean the difference between power and oblivion for local rivals. Although many important Republicans were occasionally mentioned in 1867 as possible candidates, there were only three leading contenders. One was Wade. Another was Chief Justice Salmon P. Chase. Within Ohio politics Chase was clearly the more conservative, but most observers lumped both Wade and Chase together as radicals. When conservative Republicans desperately looked for a viable candidate to oppose the front-runners, they could find only one with the national following that would make victory possible—Ulysses S. Grant.

Although most historians assume Grant's nomination to have been a foregone conclusion, radicals were by no means reconciled to it in the spring, summer, and fall of 1867. The General had not even declared himself a Republican by the summer of 1867, and his past politics made him suspect in radical eyes. In

9. Grimes to Edward Atkinson, October 14, 1867, Atkinson Mss., Massachusetts Historical Society.

1864, Republicans had feared that the Democrats might nominate him for president. In 1865, Grant had sent President Johnson an optimistic report of conditions in the South, and Johnson had used it as the primary support for his contention that Southerners were ready for immediate restoration. During the 1866 elections, Grant had accompanied the President on the "swing around the circle," Johnson's political junket designed to help elect an anti-Republican Congress. Although he never made his position clear, his biographer believes that Grant generally supported Johnson's policies at least through 1866; his close friends and aides, Adam Badeau and John A. Rawlins, both endorsed Johnson.[10]

Radical distrust of Grant grew in 1867, as the President renewed his attack on Congress's Reconstruction policy after the July session adjourned without considering impeachment. Grant's agreement to replace the suspended Stanton as secretary of war shocked Republicans. Fearing that Johnson was driving for total control of the Army in order to check Reconstruction, radicals watched in dismay as the appointment of the popular Grant deflected criticism. "General Grant . . . ," mourned the editor of the radical New York *Independent*, Theodore Tilton, "appears to have become a cat's paw for the President." [11] The assurances emanating from Grant's friend and informal campaign manager, Elihu B. Washburne, that the General accepted Stanton's position only to prevent the appointment of a worse man, may have satisfied conservative Republicans, but many others still feared that, as Tilton charged, "GEN. GRANT has surrendered to the President." [12]

As the summer and fall of 1867 wore on and Republican tempers frayed, impeachment became as entwined with the presidential question as it had already become with the finan-

10. William B. Hesseltine, *Ulysses S. Grant, Politician* (New York, 1935), 61. Badeau to E. B. Washburne, October 20, 1865, Washburne Mss., Library of Congress; Rawlins to Mrs. Rawlins, August 30, September 1, 1866, quoted in James Harrison Wilson, *The Life of John A. Rawlins* . . . (New York, 1916), 334–36; Browning, *Diary*, II, 103–4.

11. New York *Independent*, August 29, 1867, p. 4.

12. *Ibid.*, September 5, 1867, p. 4.

cial reform issue. "[T]he impeachment movement," the Chicago *Tribune*'s Horace White warned Washburne, ". . . is an anti-Grant movement, the object being to get Wade into the Presidency long enough to give him prestige & patronage to control the next National Convention." [13]

The turning point in the radical-nonradical fight for dominance in the Republican party—and in the radicals' impeachment drive—came with the results of the 1867 elections. As has been already noted, conservative Republicans had long argued that Americans would not sustain a truly radical Republican party. The Republican performance in 1867 would test the theory. As James G. Blaine wrote afterward, "I felt . . . that if we should carry everything with a whirl in '67 such knaves as Ben Butler would control our National Convention and give us a nomination with which defeat would be inevitable *if not desirable*. . . ." [14]

But the elections bore out the conservatives' warnings. Only in Michigan and Kentucky did Republicans improve upon their showings of a year earlier. In the eighteen other states electing officials, Republicans lost significant ground. In Massachusetts, the Republican share of the vote dropped from 77 percent in 1866 to 58 percent in 1867. The Democrats swept California, charging that Republican policy would inevitably mean the enfranchisement of the state's Chinese population. The Republican vote in New Jersey fell 16,000 short of that polled in 1865. In Maryland, the Republican vote was reduced from 40 percent of the total to 25 percent. Wade lost his Senate seat as Democrats won control of Ohio's state legislature (state legislatures elected senators in the nineteenth century), and the Republican gubernatorial candidate squeezed out a victory margin of only 3,000 votes of 184,000 cast. The Republicans lost 13,000 votes from their 1866 total, while the Democrats gained 27,000. The poor showing eliminated Wade

13. White to Washburne, August 13, 1867, Washburne Mss.
14. Blaine to Israel Washburn, September 12, 1867, quoted in Gaillard Hunt, *Israel, Elihu and Cadwallader Washburn: A Chapter in American Biography* (New York, 1925), 122–23, at 122.

as a presidential contender and all but did the same for Chase. Republicans recorded parallel losses in all-important New York and Pennsylvania.

Fortunately for the Republicans, few important positions had been at stake. They had lost only a few major offices—the governorships of Connecticut and California and Wade's Senate seat. Conservative Republicans were not despondent. As Blaine wrote, "[The losses] will be good discipline in many ways and will I am sure be 'blessed to us in the edification and building up of the true faith' . . . ." [15]

But for the radicals and the impeachment movement, the defeat was a disaster—"a crusher for the wild men," the conservative Banks wrote happily.[16] The practical effects were felt immediately. The radical New York *Independent*'s correspondent found the change among congressmen arriving for the November meeting of Congress "startling." "Our friends have an overwhelming majority," he wrote, "but with the people apparently against the Radical members, it will be impossible to secure Radical legislation." As the session opened, he gloomily assessed the prospects: Congress would not enact any of the radical proposals to carry Reconstruction further, no law to enfranchise blacks throughout the country could pass. And "the impeachment movement is dead." [17]

Despite the defeats of 1867, radicals determined to continue their campaign for impeachment. But they knew it would be more difficult now to win the majority needed to bring the impeachment before the Senate. For although the election reverses did not induce individual Republicans to break ranks —that is, most Republicans who had been radicals during the first session of the 40th Congress remained so in the second, and the same was true of centrists and conservatives—they

15. *Ibid*.
16. Banks to Mrs. Banks, November 13, 1867, Banks Mss., Library of Congress.
17. New York *Independent,* October 24, 1867, p. 1; November 7, 1867, p. 1; November 14, 1867, p. 1.

did force each group to the right. The centrists, who might have favored impeachment had the elections demonstrated radical strength, now divided, most of them opposing impeachment. Confiscation, black enfranchisement by national law, and continued exclusion of southern states from the Union, all of which many radicals might have supported, now were out of the question.

Impeachment received a further blow when President Johnson refused to fulfill dire predictions that the Republican defeats would embolden him in obstructing Reconstruction. On the contrary, the President acted with remarkable—for him—circumspection. He removed no more military commanders in the South. He did not, as Republicans feared he might, recognize a rival Congress of Southerners and northern Democrats. He had not even replaced his Republican cabinet with a Democratic one, despite strong Democratic pressure to do so. In fact, he had been on his best behavior.

But the radicals did not believe that Johnson had turned over a new leaf. They surmised (accurately, it proved) that he had determined to add no more fuel to the impeachment controversy, but that he would act with vigor once that threat were removed. They had every reason to fear that in that case the congressional Reconstruction program would be defeated. The voters of the North were clearly growing tired of the controversy. If by use of the patronage and the Army under docile commanders Johnson and southern conservatives prevented ratification of the constitutions radical conventions were framing, Republicans would have to face the 1868 elections with a still unrestored Union. Exasperated northern voters might overwhelm them at the polls. Impeachment and removal would end that threat forever.

Presidential politics also played a role in the radicals' determination. The Grant movement was gaining strength rapidly. The elections of 1867 had demonstrated the weakness of the party organization and the tenuous hold Republicans had on the northern electorate. Party leaders decided that only the nomination of the popular, conservative general could guarantee victory in 1868. From New York, where only the discredited, pro-Johnson, conservative Thurlow Weed–William H. Seward wing of the Republican party had endorsed Grant before the elections (the radical faction favored Chase), one of Washburne's key organizers wrote, "I don't think Chase has a corporal's guard. Former Chase men have whipped off their livery, and the general cry is for Grant." In Pennsylvania, where conservative former Governor Andrew G. Curtin had earlier had little success in promoting Grant, he now found, "Everybody is for Grant and on the first opportunity our party will declare for him." The reason was patent: "Grant is the only man living who can carry this State next year on present issues." [18]

But despite looming political dangers, many radicals regarded the likelihood of Grant's nomination with despair. The men in the forefront of the Grant movement seemed to share little of the radicals' zeal for equal rights and thorough Reconstruction. "Out of every three Republicans whom one now meets," Tilton observed, "two are chiefly anxious for the success of Negro suffrage, and the third for the success of Gen. Grant." Disheartened, Wade, his ambition for the presidency dashed, lamented, "[I]t is very strange that when men talk of availability they always mean something squinting towards Copperheadism. They never think of consulting the Radicals, who are the only working men in the party. Oh, no; we must take what we get . . . ." [19]

The impeachment and removal of Andrew Johnson was the only hope radicals still had of averting the danger that they saw ahead. Wade, who would replace Johnson if he were removed, had publicly declared his preference for Chase rather than Grant. Many of Chase's partisans still remained in the Treasury Department, protected by McCulloch's reluctance to turn old Republicans out of office. Chase remained stronger

18. John Cochrane to E. B. Washburne, November 9, 1867; Curtin to Washburne, October 17, 1867, Washburne Mss.

19. New York *Independent,* November 14, 1867, p. 4; Wade in the New York *Times,* November 8, 1867, p. 8.

than Grant with southern Republicans, who feared the General's conservatism. With Wade as president, Grant might be denied the nomination. At least, the National Convention would be certain to frame a radical platform, which would commit Grant to radicalism or force him to withdrew his candidacy. As Chase's intimate friend and biographer, Jacob W. Schuckers, wrote six years later, "The impeachment programme had . . . two motives; the first and most important was, of course, to get Andrew Johnson out of the presidency, and the second and hardly less important was, to keep General Grant from getting in." [20]

When Congress met, the impeachers appeared to be in a hopeless minority. The Judiciary Committee had kept its proceedings strictly confidential, and most congressmen believed the majority report would be against impeachment, as the June vote in the committee had indicated. Since the whole House customarily concurred in majority reports from committees, many Republicans planned to vote against impeachment but to aver that they had simply endorsed a committee report, thus side-stepping the issue. The *Times* correspondent estimated that under these circumstances the impeachers could muster but fifty to fifty-five votes, with sixty Republicans and all forty-nine Democrats opposed, and fifteen undecided. But when the committee published its report on November 25, Republicans learned that John C. Churchill had changed his mind as a result of Johnson's interference with the military. The majority report would favor impeachment. Churchill's reversal caused wild excitement, and radicals believed they could muster a fifteen- to thirty-vote majority. In the confusion, both sides predicted victory.[21]

Conservatives were dismayed. "I have never been more than at this moment impressed with the peril of the Republican

20. Jacob William Schuckers, *The Life and Public Services of Salmon P. Chase, U.S. Senator and Governor of Ohio* (New York, 1874), 548.

21. New York *Times*, November 23, 1867, p. 1; Boston *Daily Advertiser*, November 25, 1867, p. 1; November 26, 1867, p. 1; New York *Independent*, November 30, 1867, p. 1.

party," George G. Fogg, the recently retired senator from New Hampshire, wrote Washburne. "I had hoped that the late elections had taught us something. I had hoped we would be allowed to breathe before being rushed forward into new disasters under the lead of men who are now little better than paroled prisoners of war." Washburne grimly agreed. Other conservative and moderate Republicans—and some radicals —echoed Fogg's forebodings and urged their representatives to abandon the impeachment issue and wrestle with finances instead. But the impeachers remained adamant. Fessenden gloomily anticipated a radical victory. He confessed, "This I shall regard as ruin to our party—and it will be a just punishment for our cowardice and folly." [22]

Conservative and anti-Wade men determined to fight impeachment with all their resources. Garfield and Spalding, Chase's chief conservative supporters in the House; Washburne and Bingham, leading Grant men; Blaine, Dawes, James F. Wilson, and others worked hard to defeat the impeachment resolution proposed by the Judiciary Committee majority. By December 5, they believed they had succeeded. [23]

Their work was made easier by the nature of the majority report. Written by Thomas Williams, it was an inflammatory indictment of the President, injudicious in language, even violent in spirit. Conservatives pointed to it as evidence that the impeachers were motivated more out of hatred for Andrew Johnson than concern for the country's well-being. The Re-

22. Fogg to Washburne, November 22, 1867, Washburne Mss.; Washburne to Fogg, November 25, 1867, Fogg Mss., New Hampshire Historical Society, Concord, N. H.; Fessenden to W. H. Fessenden, November 23, 1867, Fessenden Mss., Bowdoin College Library, Brunswick, Maine; William Henry Smith to C. S. Hamilton, December 2, 1867, Smith Mss., Ohio Historical Society Library, Columbus; Emory Washburne to Dawes, December 5, 1867, Dawes Mss.; Toledo *Blade*, November 30, 1867, p. 2; Boston *Daily Advertiser*, November 26, 1867, p. 2; Boston *Evening Journal*, November 27, 1867, p. 4.

23. Garfield to Hinsdale, December 5, 1867, quoted in Hinsdale, ed., *Garfield-Hinsdale Letters,* 117–18; Fessenden to Francis Fessenden, December 1, 1867, Fessenden Mss., Bowdoin College Library; New York *National Anti-Slavery Standard,* December 14, 1867, p. 2.

publican minority report, written by James F. Wilson, assumed an air of moderation. Yet it too was more of a brief for the defense than a dispassionate analysis of the case. The Democratic minority report, agreeing on the legal points with Wilson's, was of little importance. Both of the Republican reports emphasized the law of the case, radicals relying on their broad interpretation of the impeachment power and conservatives trying to narrow it.[24]

As the Republicans prepared to vote on the impeachment question, they were shocked by the President's annual message. Ending his passivity, Johnson once again became defiant. Beginning with a rather conciliatory reaffirmation of his interpretation of the constitutional basis for Reconstruction, Johnson went on to denounce the constitutionality of the Reconstruction Acts in less moderate terms. But he went further. Abandoning constitutional arguments, he proclaimed black suffrage "worse than the military despotism under which [the southern states] . . . are now suffering." Black men were inherently unable to govern themselves under republican institutions. They were "corrupt in principle and enemies of free institutions." "If the inferior [race] obtains the ascendency over the other, it will govern with reference only to its own interests—for it will recognize no common interest—and create such a tyranny as this continent has never yet witnessed." But most ominous was the President's unsubtle threat:

How far the duty of the President "to preserve, protect, and defend the Constitution" requires him to go in opposing an unconstitutional act of Congress is a very serious and important question, on which I have deliberated much, and felt extremely anxious to reach a proper conclusion. Where an act has been passed according to the forms of the Constitution by the supreme legislative authority, and is regularly enrolled among the public statutes of the country, executive resistance to it . . . would be likely to produce violent collision between the respective adherents of the two branches of the

24. Report on the Impeachment of the President, *House Report No. 7*, 40th Congress, 1st Session (November 25, 1867). The law of impeachment and the Judiciary Committee reports are discussed in Chapter 2, *supra*.

Government. This would be simply civil war; and civil war must be resorted to only as the last remedy for the worst of evils. . . . The so-called reconstruction acts, though plainly unconstitutional as any that can be imagined, were not believed to be within the class last mentioned.[25]

For the first time, the President had clearly indicated that he had considered forcible resistance to Congress. He had decided against it not because his action would have been illegal or unconstitutional but because in the President's opinion the Reconstruction Acts did not justify it.[26]

The presidential message reinforced the radicals' opinion that his removal was a necessity. "The propositions which the President has laid down . . . will lead to certain difficulty if they are acted upon," Boutwell warned. The Constitution authorizes Congress to pass bills, subject to the president's veto. "If the House and Senate by a two-thirds vote pass a bill [over the veto] it becomes a law, and until it is repealed by the same authority or annulled by the Supreme Court the President has but one duty, and that is to obey it; and no consideration or opinion of his as to its constitutionality will defend or protect him in any degree." Moreover, the President's vehement denunciation of black suffrage boded only evil. "Are we to leave this officer, if we judge him to be guilty of high crimes and misdemeanors, in control of the Army and the Navy, with his declaration upon the record that under certain circumstances he will not execute the laws?" Boutwell asked. "He has the control of the Army. Do you not suppose that

25. Richardson, ed., *Messages and Papers of the Presidents,* VI, 558–81.

26. The President in reality was warning Congress against any attempt to suspend him from office pending a trial on impeachment. He gave as an example of an act to which resistance would be justified one "to abolish a coordinate department of the Government." *Ibid.,* 569. On November 30, Johnson asked his cabinet's advice on his course in case Congress should attempt to suspend him during an impeachment trial. The members agree he should not submit. The critical voice was that of Grant, who would control the Army. He told the President he would support the President with military force, even at the risk of civil war. Browning, *Diary,* II, 167–68 (November 30, 1867).

next November a single soldier at each polling place in the southern country, aided by the whites, could prevent the entire negro population from voting? And if it is for the interest of the President to do so have we any reason to anticipate a different course of conduct?" [27] The tone of the President's message, Ben Perley Poore reported, had influenced eight to ten Republicans to vote for impeachment. But he believed the impeachers still lacked the necessary votes.[28]

As the senior signer of the majority report, George S. Boutwell opened debate on impeachment on December 5. He devoted his long address primarily to the legal question. The House, he knew, was well aware of the President's activities. The question would turn on whether they were impeachable, for, he acknowledged, "If the theory of the law submitted by the minority be in the judgment of this House a true theory, then the majority have no case whatever." He altered his address before it was published in the appendix of the *Congressional Globe,* but observers wrote that the House listened in rapt attention. As published, Boutwell's speech embodied the clearest, most eloquent, and most convincing argument for the liberal view of the impeachment power. Boutwell began by expressing his sympathy for those who feared the effects of an impeachment. He acknowledged that the House could decide that impeachment was inexpedient even if members believed the President liable to the process. He affirmed that he himself would be inclined to allow the President to finish his term if he did not believe evil consequences were sure to follow. Then, in a concise and convincing manner, he discussed the impeachers' view of the law of the case (see pp. 33–36, *supra.*)

Completing the legal argument, Boutwell turned to the facts, which he believed were self-evident. The President had taken upon himself the responsibility of reconstructing the southern states. The minority might argue that Congress had ratified that

27. *Congressional Globe,* 40th Congress, 2nd Session, appendix, 62 (December 6, 1867).
28. Boston *Evening Journal,* December 4, 1867, p. 2.

usurpation by acquiescing in the continued existence of his restored state governments. But, Boutwell reminded his listeners, the President had concealed his purposes. Congress had believed the President's plan a temporary one, to be annulled or approved when Congress met. "The public mind did not comprehend the character and extent of the usurpation." The President had vetoed all Congress's Reconstruction bills, he had urged the Southerners to reject the Fourteenth Amendment, he had appointed to office men who could not take the test oath, he had surrendered the abandoned lands and confiscated railroad property, he had appointed and paid provisional governors in the southern states although Congress had neither created the office nor appropriated money to reimburse its holders. The ultimate purpose of all this, Boutwell concluded, was manifestly to return the former Rebels to power in the state and national governments despite Congress's judgment that this must not be done. "[W]hen you consider all these things, can there be any doubt as to his purpose, or doubt as to the criminality of his purpose and his responsibility under the Constitution?" Boutwell asked. He continued:

It may not be possible, by specific charge, to arraign him for this great crime, but is he therefore to escape? These offenses which I have enumerated . . . are the acts, the individual acts, the subordinate crimes, the tributary offenses to the accomplishment of the great object which he had in view. But if, upon the body of the testimony, you are satisfied of his purpose, and if you are satisfied that these tributary offenses were committed as the means of enabling him to accomplish this great crime, will you hesitate to try and convict him upon those charges of which he is manifestly guilty, even if they appear to be of inferior importance, knowing . . . that in this way, and this way only, can you protect the State against the final consummation of his crime? [29]

Wilson followed Boutwell's effort on December 6. Boutwell's attack on the minority's legal argument was so powerful that Wilson immediately retreated from it. No member of the minority believed their legal doctrine "of the slightest im-

29. Boutwell's speech in the *Congressional Globe,* 40th Congress, 2nd Session, appendix, 54–62 (December 5, 6, 1867).

portance so far as a correct determination of this case is concerned. . . . It is immaterial what opinion members may have of it," he began. Nonetheless, he devoted half of his speech to defending his position that impeachment was only for indictable crimes and attacking its opponents. In essence, Wilson turned the very superiority of Boutwell's argument against him. He pointed out the palpable fact that it was inconsistent with the committee report. In his speech, Boutwell had eschewed the value of English precedents as irrelevant to impeachment in American constitutional law; the report cited English cases. In his speech, Boutwell had asserted that under the minority's view of the law an officer could commit murder in such a way as to be outside the jurisdiction of United States courts and yet be immune to impeachment; the report had stated that murder would not be an impeachable offense, since it did not relate directly to officeholding. Wilson's blunt analysis of the inconsistencies between Boutwell's brilliant speech and Williams's mediocre majority report did tremendous damage to the impeachers' case.

Wilson went on to emphasize the full implications of the majority position. Boutwell had insisted that the impeachment power "is subject to no revision or control, and that its exercise is to be guided solely by the conscience of the House. Correctly interpreted," said Wilson, "this doctrine, as it seems to me, comes to this: that whatever this House may declare on its conscience to be an impeachable offense, reduce to the form of articles, and carry to the Senate for trial, that body is only to be allowed to declare whether the officer impeached is guilty of the facts presented against him, but is not to be permitted to say that such facts do or do not constitute a crime or a misdemeanor. Does he desire us to intrust the character, extent, and uses of this power to the shifting fortunes of political parties? What could be more dangerous to the peace and safety of the Government than this?"

Finally, Wilson discussed the individual charges. He pointed out that the report of the Joint Committee on Reconstruction, of which Boutwell was a member, assigned patriotic motives

to the President when discussing his Reconstruction policy in
June of 1866, long after Boutwell claimed to have discerned the
President's master design to return power to the Rebels. He reit-
erated his conviction that the return of property to the Rebels
was by advice of the cabinet and showed no evidence of criminal intent. But Wilson abruptly left this discussion and closed
his address by returning to the legal issue. "Sir, we must be
guided by some rule in the grave proceeding . . . . If we
cannot arraign the President for a specific crime for what are
we to proceed against him? For a bundle of generalities such
as we have in the volume of testimony reported by the committee to the House in this case? If we cannot state upon paper
a specific crime how are we to carry this case to the Senate for
trial?" So despite his disclaimer, Wilson relied after all on his
legal objections, and with that he moved that the impeachment resolution be laid on the table.[30]

The radicals were outraged. By moving to lay the resolution on the table, Wilson had cut off debate. Over forty radicals had prepared speeches on the question, many of them
filled with vituperation toward the conservatives and their
arguments, which the radicals sincerely believed to be specious.
Moreover, Wilson's maneuver again opened the possibility of
dodging the issue, enabling members to say they favored tabling to avoid bitterly divisive argument that might disrupt the
party.[31] Furious, the radicals began the difficult job of fili-
bustering the House. Logan and Schenck led the radical forces.
With seven roll-call votes on adjournment, the radicals delayed
the vote into the dinner hour, mustering from fifty to sixty votes
against the anti-impeachers' one hundred plus. But at five
o'clock the anti-impeachers broke ranks, over twenty of them
voting with the radicals to adjourn, giving them an 80 to 77
victory.

The next day the radicals began where they had left off, but

30. Wilson's speech, *ibid.,* 62–65 (December 6, 1867).
31. Boston *Evening Journal,* December 5, 1867, p. 2; Boston
Daily Advertiser, December 9, 1867, p. 1; New York *Independent,*
December 12, 1867, p. 4.

they could not continue forever. Logan implored his opponents to allow the minority ten minutes to explain the reason for its filibuster. If the majority granted their request, Logan promised, the impeachers would agree to vote. But this would require unanimous consent, and although many of the anti-impeachers were willing, Rufus P. Spalding objected. "I will not give them a single minute now," he announced bitterly. Again the radicals moved an adjournment. Again the clerk read the name of each representative in turn. Again the effort failed.

Logan now asked Wilson to withdraw his tabling motion, promising to end the delay if the majority would agree to vote on the direct issue. Wilson agreed, and the House defeated the majority resolution 57 to 108. Three absent Republicans were announced in favor of impeachment and two against. All those who favored impeachment were Republicans; sixty-six Republicans voted against it; two more were so declared. The radicals had not been able to muster a majority even of their own party.[32] "You will see how Congress backed down on impeachment, & can guess the effect of it on the whole of the South, followed by such a message as the last," radical Representative George W. Julian wrote his wife. "It is pitiful!" [33]

The pattern of the Republican vote on impeachment indicated the importance of the money question in determining representatives' positions. Voting records on the currency-expansion issue during the 40th Congress correlated with the vote on impeachment almost as well as did voting records on Reconstruction issues during the second session of the 39th Congress, when Republicans had passed the Reconstruction Act.[34] Chart 1 compares the impeachment vote with Re-

32. *Congressional Globe,* 40th Congress, 2nd Session, 64–67 (December 6, 1867), 67–69 (December 7, 1867).

33. Julian to Mrs. Grace Giddings Julian, December 8, 1867, Julian Mss., Indiana State Historical Library, Indiana Division.

34. The correlation between voting records on Reconstruction issues in the 40th Congress, second session, and the vote on impeachment was much higher than the impeachment roll call's correlation with voting records on currency questions or on Reconstruction votes of the 39th Congress, second session. *(Note continues on page 84)*

CHART 1

Comparison of Radicalism During the Second Session of the 39th Congress (December 1866–March 1867) to the Impeachment Vote (December 7, 1867)

REPUBLICAN RADICALISM	AGAINST IMPEACHMENT		FOR IMPEACHMENT	
GROUP 5 *Ultra Radicals*			I. Donnelly *(1)*	
GROUP 4 *Radicals*	F. C. Beaman J. H. Driggs T. D. Eliot F. A. Pike P. Sawyer H. Van Aernam H. D. Washburn *(7)*		S. M. Arnell J. M. Ashley G. S. Boutwell H. P. T. Bromwell S. Clarke A. Cobb E. R. Eckley A. C. Harding G. W. Julian W. D. Kelley	J. W. McClurg L. Myers C. O'Neill H. E. Paine T. Stevens R. E. Trowbridge R. T. Van Horn H. Ward T. Williams S. F. Wilson *(20)*
GROUP 3 *Radical Centrists*	W. B. Allison B. C. Cook N. F. Dixon B. Eggleston C. T. Hulburd W. H. Koontz G. F. Miller	J. K. Moorhead S. Perham R. P. Spalding C. Upson M. Welker J. F. Wilson *(13)*	G. W. Anderson J. M. Broomall R. W. Clarke S. M. Cullom W. Higby W. Lawrence	B. F. Loan J. Lynch U. Mercur G. S. Orth G. W. Scofield W. B. Stokes *(12)*
GROUP 2 *Conservative Centrists*	O. Ames J. Baker J. D. Baldwin N. P. Banks T. W. Ferry	J. A. Garfield E. C. Ingersoll W. B. Washburn E. B. Washburne *(9)*	H. Maynard H. Price *(2)*	
GROUP 1 *Conservatives*	D. R. Ashley J. F. Benjamin J. A. Bingham H. L. Dawes G. M. Dodge C. D. Hubbard	J. H. Ketcham A. H. Laflin G. V. Lawrence J. M. Marvin T. A. Plants *(11)*	J. F. Farnsworth R. C. Schenck F. Thomas *(3)*	
GROUP 0 *Extreme Conservatives*	I. R. Hawkins *(1)*			

γ (gamma) $= +.6433$

CHART 2

Republican Positions on the Currency Question During the 40th Congress (1867–69) Compared to the Vote on the Impeachment

REPUBLICAN POSITIONS ON THE CURRENCY QUESTION	AGAINST IMPEACHMENT		FOR IMPEACHMENT	
GROUP 2 *Expansionists*	J. Baker R. P. Buckland B. C. Cook B. Eggleston I. R. Hawkins E. C. Ingersoll H. D. Washburn		H. P. T. Bromwell B. F. Butler A. Cobb J. Coburn I. Donnelly J. F. Farnsworth J. H. Gravely B. F. Hopkins	M. C. Hunter W. Lawrence W. Loughridge G. S. Orth J. P. C. Shanks A. F. Stevens W. B. Stokes
		(7)		*(15)*
GROUP 1 *Suspensionists*	W. B. Allison F. C. Beaman J. F. Benjamin J. A. Bingham G. M. Dodge J. H. Driggs T. W. Ferry B. M. Kitchen T. A. Plants D. Polsley	P. Sawyer M. Welker	G. W. Anderson R. W. Clarke S. Clarke S. M. Cullom E. R. Eckley W. Higby N. B. Judd G. W. Julian B. F. Loan J. A. Logan	J. Mullins C. A. Newcomb D. A. Nunn H. E. Paine W. A. Pile R. C. Schenck R. E. Trowbridge R. T. Van Horn W. Williams
		(12)		*(19)*
GROUP 0 *Contractionists*	O. Ames D. R. Ashley J. D. Baldwin N. P. Banks H. L. Dawes N. F. Dixon T. D. Eliot W. L. Fields J. A. Garfield J. A. Griswold G. A. Halsey J. Hill C. D. Hubbard C. T. Hulburd J. H. Ketcham A. H. Laflin G. V. Lawrence	J. M. Marvin D. McCarthy J. K. Moorhead S. Perham L. P. Poland R. P. Spalding H. H. Starkweather T. E. Stewart N. Taylor G. Twichell H. Van Aernam C. Van Wyck C. C. Washburn W. B. Washburn J. F. Wilson F. E. Woodbridge	G. S. Boutwell J. M. Broomall J. C. Churchill J. Covode U. Mercur H. Price G. W. Scofield H. Ward	
		(33)		*(8)*

γ (gamma) $= +.6345$

publicans' positions on Reconstruction, while Chart 2 compares the vote with positions on the money question. The γ (gamma) correlation value of each is high and almost equal— + .6433 for the comparison of votes in impeachment and on Reconstruction issues (Chart 1) and + .6345 for the comparison between the impeachment vote and votes on the financial issue (Chart 2).[35]

The influence of the money question is apparent if one isolates Republicans identified as radical-centrists during the second session of the 39th Congress. This was the group that divided most evenly on impeachment in December 1867 (see Chart 3). The contractionists in that group opposed impeachment by a two-to-one margin, while expansionists and those who favored at least a temporary suspension of contraction favored impeachment by a similar margin.

A close look discloses that it was especially the contractionists whose votes on impeachment seem to have correlated to their fiscal positions. They divided 33 to 8 against impeaching the President, while Republicans favoring currency expansion or a suspension of contraction favored impeachment by much more modest margins. Even contractionists who had voted with the radicals or radical-centrists during the controversy over the Reconstruction Act opposed impeachment by an eight-to-five margin (Chart 4). Among expansionists, on the

---

But by this time radicalism on Reconstruction issues was so bound up with impeachment that the high correlation doesn't prove much. These charts are based upon scale analysis of House voting patterns. For an explanation of scale analysis, see Charles M. Dollar and Richard J. Jensen, *Historian's Guide to Statistics: Quantitative Analysis and Historical Research* (New York and other cities, 1971), 116–21. Qmin (minimum value of the Q correlation) between individual roll calls was set at ±.6. The roll calls upon which the scales are based are given in the Appendix.

35. γ (gamma) is a measure of correlation for ranked ordinal variables developed by Leo A. Goodman and William H. Kruskal. I have used the computation method described in Theodore K. Anderson and Morris Zelditch, Jr., *A Basic Course in Statistics with Sociological Applications,* 2nd ed. (New York and other cities, 1968), 152–55. +1.000 would be a perfect positive correlation.

CHART 3

*Position of Republican Radical Centrists
(Group 3 of Chart 1) on the Currency Question
Compared to Their Votes on Impeachment*

REPUBLICAN POSITIONS ON THE CURRENCY QUESTION	AGAINST IMPEACHMENT		FOR IMPEACHMENT	
GROUP 2 *Expansionists*	Cook Eggleston	(2)	W. Lawrence Orth Stokes	(3)
GROUP 1 *Suspensionists*	Allison Welker	(2)	Anderson R. W. Clarke Cullom	Higby Loan (5)
GROUP 0 *Contractionists*	Dixon Hulburd Moorhead	Perham Spalding J. F. Wilson (6)	Broomall Mercur Scofield	(3)

γ (gamma) $= + .4211$

other hand, there seems to have been no countervailing force of similar strength. Three of the four expansionists who had voted with conservatives or conservative-centrists earlier voted as one would expect them to as conservatives—against impeachment (Chart 5).

So the radical drive for impeachment had failed. But although intra-party rivalry and tangential issues like the money question had played a role in its defeat, ultimately those Republicans who opposed impeachment endorsed the position of the Republican minority of the Judiciary Committee—impeachment lay only for positive violations of law that would be indictable in ordinary courts, despite the weight of precedent and authority that held the other way.

The conservatives had betrayed the nation with their pettifogging lawyers' arguments, radicals believed. They would sacrifice southern loyalists and the security of the Union out of

CHART 4

*Position of Republican Contractionists
(Group 0 of Chart 2) on Reconstruction Issues
Compared to Their Votes on Impeachment*

REPUBLICAN POSITIONS ON RECONSTRUCTION ISSUES	AGAINST IMPEACHMENT		FOR IMPEACHMENT	
GROUP 5 *Ultra Radicals*				
GROUP 4 *Radicals*	Eliot Van Aernam	*(2)*	Boutwell Ward	*(2)*
GROUP 3 *Radical Centrists*	Dixon Hulburd Moorhead	Perham Spalding J. F. Wilson *(6)*	Broomall Mercur Scofield	*(3)*
GROUP 2 *Conservative Centrists*	Ames Baldwin Banks	Garfield W. B. Washburn *(5)*	Price	*(1)*
GROUP 1 *Conservatives*	D. R. Ashley Dawes Hubbard	Laflin G. V. Lawrence Marvin *(6)*		

γ (gamma) $= +.6782$

pretended devotion to spurious legal doctrines. "If the great culprit had robbed a till; if he fired a barn; if he had forged a check; he would have been indicted, prosecuted, condemned, sentenced, and punished," Tilton moaned. "But the evidence shows that he only oppressed the Negro; that he only conspired with the rebel; that he only betrayed the Union party; that he only attempted to overthrow the Republic—of course, he goes unwhipped of justice. . . . So a President of the United States begins by insulting, continues by bullying, and ends by conquering Congress. . . . At the last moment the

CHART 5

Position of Republican Expansionists
(Group 2 of Chart 2) on Reconstruction Issues
Compared to Their Votes on Impeachment

REPUBLICAN POSITION ON RECONSTRUCTION ISSUES	AGAINST IMPEACHMENT	FOR IMPEACHMENT
GROUP 5 *Ultra* *Radicals*		Donnelly *(1)*
GROUP 4 *Radicals*	H. D. Washburn *(1)*	Bromwell Cobb *(2)*
GROUP 3 *Radical* *Centrists*	Cook Eggleston *(2)*	W. Lawrence Orth Stokes *(3)*
GROUP 2 *Conservative* *Centrists*	Baker Ingersoll *(2)*	
GROUP 1 *Conservatives*	Hawkins *(1)*	Farnsworth *(1)*

γ (gamma) $= + .5152$

brave men among them were denied even the right of opening their lips on the question. . . . [A] Republican majority of cowards gagged a Republican minority of statesmen. Thaddeus Stevens, George Boutwell, John Logan, and others of like heroic mold, stood by their country, and were throttled by their friends . . . ." [36]

The bitterness left by the struggle over impeachment strained the Republican party almost to the breaking point. Radicals began to prepare for an open rupture in the party. In conference they discussed the possibility of perfecting a new party organization in the House, made up of radicals alone. Radical

36. New York *Independent,* December 12, 1867, p. 4.

splinter groups considered calling a meeting in Washington for February 1868 to adopt a platform of principles to which they would demand that the Republican party adhere. If the regular party refused to endorse those principles, these radicals would bolt.[37]

If the radicals were furious, conservatives were elated. Republicans could now turn to financial questions in peace, Fessenden happily wrote. "It extinguishes the aspirations of the Radical-Radicals. . . . For once, Mr. Sumner cannot boast of the fulfillment of his prophecy, and his bitterness beats 'wormwood and gall,' " he exulted. "It is of no use, however. They are in a minority of their own party—and must stay there." [38]

The Democrats happily recognized that they now faced a party divided. Some Democrats determined to emphasize Grant's early statements against Negro suffrage and his friendliness to Johnson, rather than attacking him. "I shd be sorry to have assisted in overcoming Radical hostility to his nomination in the Republican convention by persuading them that he *is* in sympathy with them," the editor of the New York *World,* Manton Marble, wrote one of Johnson's supporters in the Senate.[39] But Andrew Johnson did not share such political wisdom. Freed, he thought, from the threat of impeachment, Johnson was led by his boundless conviction of the correctness of his principles and his passionate hostility toward his critics to pursue a course that reunited the fragmenting Republican party and nearly brought about his removal.

37. New York *National Anti-Slavery Standard,* December 14, 1867, p. 2; New York *Times,* December 21, 1867, p. 4.
38. Fessenden to Elizabeth Fessenden Warriner, December 15, 1867; Fessenden to William H. Fessenden, December 7, 1867; Fessenden to Samuel Fessenden, December 7, 1867, Fessenden Mss., Bowdoin College Library; John Binney to Fessenden, December 9, 1867, Fessenden Mss., Library of Congress.
39. Marble to James R. Doolittle, December 29, 1867, quoted in "Doolittle Correspondence," *Publications of the Southern Historical Association,* XI (January 1907), 6–7.

4

Johnson Forces
the Issue

THE DEFEAT of impeachment following upon the Republicans' mediocre showing in the 1867 elections had the effect radicals feared. Johnson and his supporters, convinced that the tide of Reconstruction was at last beginning to turn, pressed their opposition to Republican Reconstruction measures with renewed vigor. In Louisiana, the archconservative General Winfield S. Hancock, whom Johnson had designated to replace Sheridan, reversed his precedessor's policies, restoring to power the Johnsonian government officials whom Sheridan had removed. In Virginia, the conservative commander John M. Schofield continued his opposition to radical Republicans. He stolidly resisted radical efforts to persuade him to remove officials of the provisional government whose terms had expired, preferring to hold over the conservative and Democratic officers of the Johnson government rather than name radical Republicans. He was determined, he later wrote, to execute the Reconstruction Acts in Virginia in such a way as to "save that State from the great evils suffered by sister States." [1]

Hoping that Johnson would now act upon their complaints, Southerners renewed their attacks on the remaining military commanders in the South and increased their obstruction of the Reconstruction process. In Georgia, the provisional govern-

1. See the correspondence in *House Executive Documents Nos. 172 and 209,* 40th Congress, 2nd Session, relative to Louisiana; Schofield, *Forty-Six Years in the Army* (New York, 1897), 397.

ment signaled its reawakened recalcitrance by refusing to pay
the expenses of the constitutional convention meeting pursuant
to the Reconstruction Act, forcing General Pope, the district
commander, to remove the governor and state treasurer. With
this, Georgians opened a new wave of attacks upon Pope's
"despotism." Disheartened at Johnson's failure to support him,
Pope wrote Grant, "The indications are now that the managers
of the disloyal faction in the South will succeed in breaking
down every General who performs his duty." Pope suggested
that Johnson replace him with "some officer . . . whom the
President will trust . . . ." [2] On December 28, Johnson acted,
removing Pope, his subordinate, Wager Swayne, commander in
Alabama, and General Edward O. C. Ord, commander in Arkansas and Mississippi. General George Meade replaced Pope and
promptly instituted a more conservative policy, ordering the
military to consider itself subordinate to the civil authority, forbidding interference with the Johnson government officials
without his direct order, and allowing these officials to remain
in office despite the expiration of their terms. He also allowed
the state courts to exclude blacks from jury duty.[3] In Ord's
place Johnson appointed conservative General Alvan C. Gillem.

Despairing, Freedmen's Bureau Commissioner Oliver Otis
Howard lamented, "The President . . . musters out all my
officers. . . . Measures are on foot . . . which are doubt-
less intended to utterly defeat reconstruction." The angry radical Washington correspondent of the Boston *Commonwealth*
wrote, "Thus Johnson defeats Congress at every point. . . .
While Congress is passing acts to reconstruct the South, the
President is driving a carriage and six through them." [4]

2. *House Executive Document No. 30,* 40th Congress, 2nd Session,
12–18, *passim;* Elizabeth Studley Nathans, *Losing the Peace: Georgia
Republicans and Reconstruction, 1865–1871* (Baton Rouge, 1968), 70–
72; Pope to Grant, December 27, 1867, HQA, Letters Received, R.G.
108, N.A.
3. Walter L. Fleming, *Civil War and Reconstruction in Alabama*
(New York, 1949), 492–500.
4. Howard to Edgar Ketchum, December 30, 1867, Howard Mss.,
Library of Congress; Boston *Commonwealth,* January 4, 1867, p. 2.

Southern Republicans were desperate. Foster Blodgett, the chairman of the Central State Committee of the Georgia Republican party, pleaded with congressional Republicans for help. "The fact is that Reconstruction is now on a pivot . . . ," he warned. "The action of Congress for the next 10 or 15 days will decide whether the whole South will be Republican or Democratic." He concluded, "Our Northern friends seem to know nothing of the intense bitter hatred that is manifested towards us." Judge John C. Underwood, one of Virginia's leading radicals, appealed to Washburne to persuade Schofield to remove the Virginia provisional government. "Every State, city & county office with very few exceptions [is] in the hands of the rebels holding over," he complained.[5]

The chairman of the Alabama party joined the frantic appeal, as Republicans there blamed their failure to win a majority for the new constitution on Swayne's removal. "Unfriendly military management has killed us," one of them wrote. "The rebels have had all their own ways in many counties. What next can we do?" From Texas, Mississippi, and Louisiana, Republicans urged their allies finally to erase the Johnson state governments. They echoed Underwood's plea: "Can Congress save us from annihilation?"[6]

Even the Chicago *Tribune,* which had vigorously opposed impeachment, implored, "Cannot Congress devise some means of checkmating the villainous conspiracy of Johnson and Co. to defeat the restoration . . . of the Southern States to the Union?"[7] Privately, the *Tribune*'s editor, Horace White,

5. Blodgett to John Sherman, December 30, 1867, Sherman Mss. (this was a circular letter sent to many congressmen); Underwood to E. B. Washburne, December 9, 1868, Washburne Mss.

6. B. W. Morris to [the Republican Congressional Campaign Committee], January 4, 1868; E. I. Costello to T. L. Tullock, January 17, 1868, in the files of the Select Committee on Reconstruction, 40th and 41st Congresses, R.G. 233, N.A. (file 40A–F29.8 and 40A–F29.23, respectively); Charles Buckley to E. B. Washburne, January 9, 1868; George Ely to Washburne, February 9, 1868; W. H. Gibbs to Washburne, January 18, 1868; Underwood to Washburne, December 16, 1867, Washburne Mss.; *House Miscellaneous Documents Nos. 43, 54, 57,* 40th Congress, 2nd Session.

7. Chicago *Tribune,* December 30, 1867, p. 2.

wrote Washburne that he shared the "rather gloomy feeling
you express concerning the present phase of reconstruction."
And he urged "that inasmuch as Johnson carries all his points,
by sheer audacity and doggedness, it is necessary for Congress
to meet him on the same ground, and to be as audacious and
obstinate as he is." [8]

The temporizing policies of the conservative and center
Republicans had allowed the President to take the offensive.
To radicals this was patent. "Our legislation on reconstruction was a monstrous blunder . . . ," Senator Timothy Otis
Howe of Wisconsin fumed. "We declared those State organizations illegal. . . . We asserted our complete authority over
them & then instead of abolishing them as we ought, we
declared them provisional & subordinated them to a military
system at the head of which is Andrew Johnson." [9] The entire
congressional Reconstruction policy had been predicated on the
hope that the President would honestly enforce the law. He
had not. But rather than remove him, the conservatives and
centrists had forced Congress to amend its Reconstruction laws
continually. "Congress enacts measure after measure and
adjourns in the pleasing delusion it has everything its own
way," the Boston *Commonwealth* lamented. "While Congress
acts as if he were an obstinate and stupid blockhead, [John-
son] . . . works quietly and steadily in the White House,
saying nothing, devoting himself with an energy almost sub-
lime to the accomplishments of his wicked ends . . . ." [10]

In response to the President's new offensive, confused Republicans prepared to pass yet another supplementary Reconstruction bill. Once again, some radicals pressed their allies
to replace completely the Johnsonian provisional governments,
but that proposal was defeated in the House Reconstruction

8. White to Washburne, January 16, 1868, Washburne Mss.
9. Howe to Horace Rublee, January 15, 1868, Howe Mss.; New
York National *Anti-Slavery Standard,* January 11, 1868, p. 1; Boston
Commonwealth, January 4, 1867, p. 2.
10. *Ibid.*

Committee, only Stevens holding out for it.[11] Instead, the committee made a final effort to strip away Johnson's influence over the enforcement of the Reconstruction Acts. Under the leadership of the conservative Bingham, it reported a bill prohibiting the President from appointing or removing military commanders in the South, placing the duty instead upon the General of the Army, Grant. Furthermore, it authorized Grant personally to replace any official of the Johnsonian governments. Finally (and pointedly), the bill declared any interference with its provisions a "high misdemeanor"—an impeachable offense.[12] The nonradicals had gone as far as they could go without impeaching the President or turning control of the South over to the radicals.

The bill passed the House with complaints from only a few radicals and the Democrats, but in the more conservative Senate it occasioned three weeks of debate between Democrats and Republicans trying to make a record for the upcoming presidential election. The endless debate wore on Republicans' nerves. Popular reaction to the "Military Dictator Bill," as Democrats labeled it, was not good. "We cannot be blind to the fact that a reaction has set in," Friedrich Hassaurek, the influential German Republican, warned Sherman. Hassaurek himself shared the feeling. "I [am] . . . not in favor of changing the American system of Government, merely because a certain individual happens to be in the Presidential chair," he informed Sherman bluntly. The Republicans must change their course. "We are losing ground daily. Men who have voted

11. James M. Ashley proposed a bill that authorized the constitutional conventions in the South to elect provisional governors and executive committees to govern each state. They would have the power to remove all Johnsonian state officials who opposed Reconstruction or could not take the test oath. The bill also revoked the paramount authority of the military authorities over these governments. *Congressional Globe*, 40th Congress, 2nd Session, 53 (December 5, 1867). The bill is described at *ibid.*, 264–65 (December 18, 1867). In the Senate, radicals tried and failed to force the conservative Judiciary committee to frame a bill similar to Ashley's. *Ibid.*, 384 (January 8, 1868), 405–6 (January 9, 1868).

12. *Ibid.*, 476 (January 13, 1868).

with us for many years, are going over to the opposition. The train-bands and camp-followers who scent the coming storm, are leaving us by hundreds, and, if the brakes are not put on in time, not even Gen. Grant's great popularity will be able to save us next October and November." The Chicago *Tribune,* impatient with delay and everlasting agitation, warned, "The people demand that the reconstruction imbroglio be brought to an end, and they will not go back to fight the battle ever again, *no matter how it is ended."* [13] Grant too opposed the bill, and Republicans decided to abandon it. [14] The conservative policy was no longer viable. Rather than take the politically radical step of removing Johnson, the conservatives and more conservative centrists had hedged him about with more and more restrictive laws, until these laws threatened a constitutionally radical alteration in the relations between Congress and the executive, from which many Americans recoiled.

The political situation was unraveling. Gloomily, Boutwell predicted again that Johnson and his southern allies would succeed in preventing southern blacks from voting in the next presidential election. "In February, 1869, we shall receive certificates of the election of electors who have given their votes to the candidates of the Opposition; and this country will be brought again to the extremity of civil war, or we shall be compelled to surrender . . . to the rebels, . . . who are yet struggling through their alliance with the Executive to destroy the Government." [15] Republicans feared they stood at the edge of disaster not only for themselves but for the nation.

13. Hassaurek to Sherman, January 27, 1868, Sherman Mss.; Chicago *Tribune,* January 30, 1868, p. 2; John Binney to Fessenden, February 5, 1868, Fessenden Mss., Library of Congress; Hinsdale to Garfield, January 20, 1868, quoted in Hinsdale, ed., *Garfield-Hinsdale Letters,* 127–30; Boston *Commonwealth,* January 11, 1868, p. 2; New York *Nation,* January 16, 1868, p. 41.

14. William T. Sherman to Ellen Ewing Sherman, January 23, 1868, W. T. Sherman Mss., University of Notre Dame Archives, South Bend, Ind. Also quoted in Mark A. DeWolfe Howe, ed., *Home Letters of General Sherman* (New York, 1909), 367–68.

15. *Congressional Globe,* 40th Congress, 2nd Session, 595 (January 17, 1868).

And it was all unnecessary. The nation would have been spared this "agony of strife," as Sumner called it, if only the President had remained true to his first Reconstruction policy. Even as they discussed their new legislation, Republicans knew the truth of Boutwell's conviction: "I know Andrew Johnson will thwart these measures as he has thwarted others." [16] And yet, from all their sources of information, they knew the people would not support a new attempt at impeachment. There was no escape.

As Republicans struggled to cope with the President's offensive in the South, Johnson continued the battle in Washington, D.C. On December 12, in compliance with the Tenure of Office Act, the President sent the Senate his reasons for suspending Secretary of War Stanton. Not questioning the Senate's right to restore Stanton to his office, Johnson argued that Stanton should have resigned when his opposition to the President's policy became irreconcilable and that his failure to do so and subsequent actions demonstrated Stanton's intent to embarrass the administration. He argued the necessity for confidence between a President and his immediate subordinates. He pointed out the injustice of holding an executive responsible for acts of officers beyond his control. In all, it was a strong performance.

But of great importance for the future was the President's failure to insist that Stanton was not covered by the act. At the time he discussed the bill with the cabinet, Johnson informed the Senate, all his advisers seemed to agree that Lincoln's appointees were not covered by the Tenure of Office Act. But he added that he did not recall whether the point was distinctly decided and, by conceding the Senate's jurisdiction over the removal, abandoned that line of defense.[17] The Senate

16. *Ibid.*
17. U.S. Senate, *Message of the President of the United States, and the Report of the Committee on Military Affairs, Etc., in Regard to the Suspension of Hon. E. M. Stanton from the Office of Secretary of War* (Washington, 1868), 3–11. The President's message is also printed in the *Senate Executive Journal*, XVI, 95–105 (December 12, 1868).

referred the message to the Committee on Military Affairs, which spent nearly a month considering it and preparing a report.

But Johnson did not intend to acquiesce if the Senate decided adversely to his wishes. Shortly after his appointment as secretary of war ad interim, Grant had agreed not to consent to his removal. Grant would either remain or turn the office back to the President. Johnson later claimed that he believed this would force Stanton to go into the courts to press his claim to the office, thereby offering a test of the constitutionality of the Tenure of Office Act. But Stanton's most recent biographers suggest that Johnson was far more interested in gaining control of the office of secretary of war than in testing Congress's law.[18] Even if Johnson did desire a court test, this does not mean that he was merely an honest statesman trying to win a legal decision against a law he considered unconstitutional. The Tenure of Office Act was part of a profound and bitter struggle over fundamental *political* questions. To ask the courts to decide this struggle, in which millions of Americans passionately adhered to one side or the other, was to risk the disaster that followed the Supreme Court's *Dred Scott* decision under similar circumstances. Johnson and his supporters were well aware of the true nature of the question. Widespread rumors held that five of the eight justices of the Supreme Court believed congressional Reconstruction unconstitutional. By appealing to these justices, Johnson hoped to win a victory against a policy he had been unable to defeat by appealing to the popular voice. If the Court ruled the Tenure of Office Act unconstitutional, Johnson would perfect his control of the Army. By retaining the office, Grant would have signified his decision to support the President. If he returned the office to the President but did not retain it, Johnson could fill it with whomever he pleased and refill it with other friends if the Senate refused to confirm his first choice. When the Senate adjourned, he could appoint a supporter secretary of war ad

18. Thomas and Hyman, *Stanton,* 589.

interim, who would remain undisturbed until the Senate met again. With a loyal supporter as secretary of war, with Grant cooperating, with more conservative military officers in the South, Johnson might prevent the ratification of the new constitutions framed under the Reconstruction law and frustrate Congress's program. In light of the aggressive southern policy Johnson inaugurated after the failure of the first attempt at impeachment, there is every reason to believe this was his intention. The Supreme Court was not to be a neutral arbiter; it would be the President's weapon.[19]

Grant could not help but understand the stakes involved. Even if he retained the secretaryship with every intention of seeing the Reconstruction Acts faithfully executed, there would be nothing to prevent the President from removing him too if the Court ruled the Tenure of Office Act unconstitutional. Moreover, such a course would certainly jeopardize his prospects for the Republican presidential nomination. Even if he were nominated, the radicals would be more inclined than ever to bolt. Finally, Grant learned that if the Court ruled that the Tenure of Office Act *was* constitutional after all, he would be liable to a $10,000 fine and a five-year prison term. So when, on January 10, 1868, the Military Affairs Committee finally reported a resolution denying the Senate's advice and consent to Stanton's removal, Grant determined not to risk the consequences of resistance.

On January 11, Grant informed the President that he had decided that the law left him no alternative but to relinquish his office to Stanton if the Senate passed the committee's resolution. Johnson now offered Grant the argument he had not offered the Senate. He had suspended Stanton not under the provisions of the Tenure of Office Act, he insisted, but under

19. For the best and most insightful analyses of the Supreme Court's role during Reconstruction, see Stanley I. Kutler, *Judicial Power and Reconstruction Politics* (Chicago and London, 1968), and Charles Fairman, *History of the Supreme Court of the United States: Volume VI, Reconstruction and Reunion, 1864–1868, Part One* (New York, 1971).

his presidential powers under the Constitution. He had appointed Grant by virtue of the same powers and not pursuant to the congressional law. In the heat of Johnson's personal plea that Grant honor his earlier commitment, the General must have tried to hedge. Johnson thought Grant had agreed. Grant later denied it, but there is no question as to the sincerity of Johnson's conviction that the General had agreed to fulfill the role he had assigned him.[20] But upon further consideration Grant became more and more dissatisfied with his position.

Hoping to ease the situation, Grant and General William T. Sherman, in Washington to help recodify the Army's war regulations, decided to suggest that the President name the conservative Republican former Governor of Ohio, Jacob D. Cox, to replace Stanton. This, Sherman believed, was "a mode practicable & easy to get rid of Stanton forever." Cox, though one of the most conservative of Republicans, had not deserted the party. Radicals might be disgruntled, but conservative and moderate Republicans would be likely to accede to the compromise, confident that Cox would enforce the law.[21] But when Sherman proposed his idea to Johnson, he found the President uninterested. Sherman and Grant now realized that Johnson was intent on something more than ridding himself of an odious subordinate, that, as Sherman wrote, "there must be something behind the scenes." [22]

The Senate considered the resolution to refuse its consent to Stanton's removal on January 11 and 13. As a whole, the Re-

20. See the correspondence between Grant and Johnson debating what actually occurred at this meeting in McPherson, ed., *Political History of Reconstruction,* 283–88, and the written testimony of Johnson's cabinet in support of the President's contentions, *ibid.,* 289–92.

21. Sherman was quite confident of this. It is probable that he discussed his plan with his brother, the senator. He certainly knew the reluctance of such men as his brother, Fessenden, Grimes, Trumbull, and others to force a confrontation with the President. Before the Senate voted on accepting Stanton's removal, Thomas Ewing, Jr. told Johnson he had been assured that Cox's nomination would settle the matter. Ewing to Johnson [January 12(?), 1868], Johnson Mss.

22. W. T. Sherman to Ellen Ewing Sherman, January 13, 1868, W. T. Sherman Mss., University of Notre Dame Archives. The letter is excerpted in Howe, ed., *Home Letters of General Sherman,* 364–65.

publicans were determined to sustain the Secretary of War. But not all were zealous. Edmund G. Ross, the senator from Kansas, voted with the Democrats and Johnson Conservatives to amend the resolution to agree to Stanton's removal. Frederick T. Frelinghuysen, James Harlan, John B. Henderson, and Peter G. Van Winkle, all of whom seem to have been present, did not vote. Henderson, Van Winkle, and Frelinghuysen had opposed making the Tenure of Office Act applicable to members of the cabinet. Ross had been absent. But the President himself seemed to concede that the bill applied to Stanton, so any nascent opposition was blunted. Nonetheless, Senator Sherman, who had insisted when the bill passed that department heads were exempt from its operation, Grimes, Henderson, Ross, William Sprague, and Van Winkle all abstained on the final vote. In this group were four of the seven Republicans who would vote to acquit Andrew Johnson of high crimes and misdemeanors after he removed Stanton in violation of the law. But two other Republicans who would vote for acquittal, Fessenden and Trumbull, were among Stanton's most vigorous defenders.[23]

The next day Grant turned the keys to the secretary of war's office over to Stanton. Furious, Johnson accused the General of double-dealing. A bitter wrangle ensued, which wedded Grant firmly and finally to the Republicans and reassured them of his position.[24] Johnson now turned to General Sherman. The President was determined to remove Stanton in violation of the Tenure of Office Act. He intended either to force him out of the War Office building and order other government officials to ignore him or to remove him and send Sherman's

23. *Senate Executive Journal,* XVI, 129 (January 11, 1868), 129–30 (January 13, 1868). The senators I have identified as abstaining had voted on roll calls taken shortly before the votes in question. *Ibid.,* 129 (January 11, 1868); *Congressional Globe,* 40th Congress, 2nd Session, 473 (January 13, 1868); Francis Fessenden, *Life and Public Services of William Pitt Fessenden,* 2 vols. (Boston and New York, 1907), II, 149–52; Thomas and Hyman, *Stanton,* 572.
24. *Ibid.,* 570–71. The correspondence involved in the controversy in McPherson, ed., *Political History of Reconstruction,* 282–93.

name to the Senate for confirmation. At the same time, Johnson determined to take the ominous step of creating a new Army department, the Army of the Atlantic, with headquarters in Washington. Sherman would be placed in command. This, he told Secretary of the Navy Welles, was in preparation for the crisis when it came. He agreed with Welles that if an order went out for his arrest, as part of a radical "plot" to seize the government, Grant would take Congress's part. With Sherman the head of an Army department centered in Washington, Johnson believed he too would have access to military power. Sherman resisted the appointment, but on February 6 Johnson ordered Grant to issue an order creating the department and giving command to Sherman. At the same time, he acted to promote Sherman to General of the Army—Grant's rank— sending the nomination to the Senate on February 13. "This would set some of them thinking," his private secretary quoted the President as saying.

Sherman was thunderstruck. He wrote the President that he did not want the command and hinted at his resignation. He telegraphed his brother, John Sherman, to oppose confirmation of his new rank in the Senate. "The President would make use of me to beget violence . . . ," he wrote. "He has no right to use us for such purposes, though he is Commander-in-Chief." On February 19, Johnson acceded to Sherman's pleas and rescinded his transfer to the new command. Despite the apparent collapse of his plans, however, on February 21 Johnson finally ordered Stanton's removal. He had been "very determined to pursue an aggressive course," his secretary had written. He would follow it to the bitter end.[25]

25. W. T. Sherman to Johnson, January 31, February 14, 1868, quoted in Rachel Sherman Thorndike, ed., *The Sherman Letters: Correspondence Between General and Senator Sherman from 1837 to 1891* (New York, 1894), 300–4; Welles, *Diary,* III, 271–72 (February 5, 1868); W. T. Sherman to Ellen Ewing Sherman, January 28, 30, 1868, W. T. Sherman Mss., University of Notre Dame Archives (excerpts quoted in Howe, ed., *Home Letters of General Sherman,* 369–70); Sherman to Thomas Ewing, Sr., February 13, 14, 1868, quoted in *ibid.,* 370–74; Johnson to Grant, February 6, 1868; Johnson to Sherman, February 19, 1868, HQA, Letters Received, R.G. 108, N.A.; W. T. Sherman to John Sherman, February 14, 1868; W. T. Sherman to Grant, February

The message appointing a new secretary of war ad interim in place of Stanton (the appointee was General Lorenzo Thomas, the nondescript Adjutant General of the Army) arrived at the Senate while it was debating the bill to repeal the absolute-majority requirement for ratifying new constitutions in the southern states. Chandler had casually gone to President pro tem Wade's table to read the incoming message. When he realized what it meant, he dropped the papers and rushed to Alexander Ramsey, Jacob M. Howard, and Sumner. Senators ran up to Wade's place to see what had happened. As word spread through the chamber, representatives who had been on the floor rushed to their side of the Capitol to inform their colleagues, who had just received a message from Stanton telling them of the situation. Several senators hurried to Stanton's offices to urge him to hold on. Representatives broke into agitated groups—Wilson, Bingham, Williams, Halburt E. Paine, and Frederick A. Pike at one end of the House and Blaine, Butler, Dawes, and Lawrence at the other. John Covode rummaged through papers on his desk and found an old impeachment resolution. He jumped up to move its adoption, but other representatives shouted him down. On February 10, the House had transferred the impeachment question from the Judiciary to the Reconstruction Committee, where Bingham, with the support of the majority of Republicans and General Grant, had smothered the question. Now Washburne moved the reference of Stanton's message to the committee, and Pike shouted, "Now all in favor of impeachment stand up." All the Republicans rose. Bingham was fuming. The President had not left well enough alone. He had revived "a contest which can exert no other than evil influence upon the welfare of the country," he said bitterly.[26]

14, 1868; W. T. Sherman to John Sherman (telegram), February 14, 1868, quoted in Thorndike, ed., *Sherman Letters*, 305–6; Moore Notes, February 17, 1868, Johnson Mss.

26. New York *Herald*, June 22, 1868, p. 5; *Congressional Globe*, 40th Congress, 2nd Session, 1326–27 (February 21, 1868). For impeachment in the Reconstruction Committee, see *ibid.*, 1087–88 (February 10, 1868); Bingham to Mrs. Bingham, February 16, 1868, Bingham Mss., Ohio Historical Society Library.

At the War Office, Stanton did not know what to do. Radicals like Chandler, Sumner, and Boutwell were urging him to stay. Sumner sent a one-word telegram: "Stick." But if he were to risk defiance, Stanton wanted the support of the united party. He sent his son, Edwin L. Stanton, to get the advice of the conservatives. Nonradical Republican Senator George F. Edmunds told him that "Fessenden, Frelinghuysen, and all to whom he has spoken say you ought to hold on to the point of expulsion until the Senate acts." So Stanton determined to stay.[27]

As Stanton waited in the War Office, the Senate went into executive session. For seven hours senators argued over what to do. Edmunds proposed a resolution simply disapproving the President's action, but other senators moved amendments. Chandler tried to amend Edmunds's proposition by adding a provision that Johnson's act was disapproved "as a violation of the rights of the Senate and unauthorized by law." Radical Richard Yates suggested a resolution that Stanton's removal and the appointment of a replacement "is simple resistance to law and revolutionary in character . . . ." Both suggestions were defeated. Instead, the Republicans turned to a substitute offered by Henry Wilson. Not as violent as Yates's proposal, Wilson's still averred: "That we do not concur in the action of the President . . . ; that we deny the right of the President so to act, under the existing laws, without the consent of the Senate." Its effect if passed was clear. The House had refused to impeach Andrew Johnson in December at least in part because many representatives did not believe he had committed a specific violation of law; the Senate—the body before which an impeachment would be tried—would now declare its solemn judgment that he had. Fessenden, Edmunds, and probably others fought the resolution with all their resources. But noth-

27. E. L. Stanton to E. M. Stanton, February 21, 1868, Stanton Mss.; Sumner to Stanton, February 21, 1868, quoted in E. D. Townshend, *Anecdotes of the Civil War* (New York, 1884), 133*n*. In the Stanton papers at the Library of Congress are messages of February 21 from Boutwell, Howard, Wilson, Yates, and Thayer.

ing could alter the outcome. The case seemed too clear, the emergency too great. Wilson's resolution passed 28 to 6. Edmunds was the only Republican to vote against it. But a significant number of Republicans did not vote. These were mainly conservatives—John Conness, Henry W. Corbett, Fessenden, Joseph S. Fowler, Frelinghuysen, Grimes, Henderson, Edwin D. Morgan, and Sherman.[28] But other conservatives *had* voted. Van Winkle and Trumbull voted with the majority. So did Edmund G. Ross. All three would change their minds. But that night, when Illinois Representatives Shelby Moore Cullom and Burton C. Cook spoke to Trumbull, he was earnest for impeachment.[29]

In Fessenden's opinion, the worst had happened. The Senate had passed a resolution "upon the strength of which Mr. Johnson will probably be impeached—and that will end us," he prophesied gloomily. "I am utterly discouraged and out of spirits," he confessed. "Either I am very stupid, or my friends are acting like fools, and hurrying us to destruction." [30] But the radicals' anxiety was mixed with anticipation. The President had revived the radicals' sagging hopes for securing Reconstruction through his removal. "Even the weak kneed Republicans may find it impossible not to stand up to the work," Schenck wrote hopefully.[31] Except for a few self-characterized "grumblers" (as Fessenden described himself and Grimes), Johnson had succeeded in uniting a party that had been on the verge of disruption. Welles knew it. "A little skillful management would have made a permanent break in that party," he wrote shortly afterward. "But the President

28. *Senate Executive Journal*, XVI, 170–72 (February 21, 1868). Of those not voting, Howard, Corbett, Chandler, and Fessenden were almost certainly present. Conness, Frelinghuysen, Henderson, and Howe had voted on an earlier question. Sherman and Howe had both committed themselves in debate on the Tenure of Office Act to the position that cabinet members were not covered by it.

29. Cullom, *Fifty Years of Public Service* (New York, 1911), 154.

30. Fessenden to Elizabeth Fessenden Warriner, February 22, 1868, Fessenden Mss., Bowdoin College Library.

31. Schenck to Sally Schenk, February 21, 1868, Schenck Mss., Rutherford B. Hayes Library, Fremont, Ohio.

had no tact himself to affect it, he consulted with no others, the opportunity passed away, and by a final hasty move, without preparation, without advising with anybody, he took a step which consolidated the Radicals of every stripe . . . ." [32]

The next day, February 22, the Reconstruction Committee reported an impeachment resolution to the House of Representatives. Every Republican member endorsed it, including both Bingham and Stevens. Citing as evidence only Johnson's order removing Stanton and his order to Thomas to take his place, the committee proposed: "That Andrew Johnson, President of the United States, be impeached of high crimes and misdemeanors in office." To the Democrats, impeachment was the culmination of radical efforts. It had been defeated before, but now "a minority of the party on the other side, forcing its influence and power upon a majority of a committee of this House, has at last succeeded in compelling its party to approach the House itself in a united . . . form to demand . . . impeachment . . . ." [33] But they completely misconstrued the situation. The radicals could not impeach the President alone. The President himself made it possible, and the conservatives were leading the movement. By his decision to disregard the laws Congress had passed to circumscribe his power to obstruct Reconstruction, Johnson left them no choice. Conservative Republicans could bear no more. "I have been among those who have hesitated long before resorting to this measure," the archconservative Austin Blair conceded. "I thought it better, as I know many other persons did, that we should bear much and suffer very much rather than resort to this extreme measure. I had constantly hoped that we had got to the end of the usurpations and the defiances which have been hurled at Congress from time to time by the President of the United States; but at last I am convinced, as I believe all at least upon this side are, that there is to be no end of this course of conduct." The President must be removed. [34]

32. Welles, *Diary,* III, 315 (March 17, 1868).
33. *Congressional Globe,* 40th Congress, 2nd Session, 1336 (February 22, 1868).
34. *Ibid.,* 1367 (February 22, 1868).

James F. Wilson, who had led the battle against the first impeachment, reluctantly agreed. "Guided by a sincere desire to pass this cup from our lips, determined not to drink it if escape were not cut off by the presence of a palpable duty, we at last find ourselves compelled to take its very dregs." [35]

Republicans looked to the result with confidence. "I am glad . . . that we have delayed thus long," Blair averred. "I was not willing, and should not be now, that this measure should be undertaken upon any doubtful case. I desired that we should have a complete and perfectly clear case upon which to present the President . . . for trial, so that there would be no honest man in the United States that could look upon this case and not say that there was abundant reason for what the House of Representatives was doing." [36] For the President had acted in total defiance of Congress. He had not argued that the Tenure of Office Act did not apply to Stanton. He had not denied Congress's right to advise and consent to Stanton's removal when he submitted his reasons for his action. He had suspended Stanton according to the letter of the Tenure of Office Act; now he defied the Senate's decision. It was a challenge pure and simple. "[T]here is no question of law involved at all," Blair insisted. "The President has openly and clearly violated the law. He has thrown down the gauntlet to Congress, and says to us as plainly as words can speak it: 'Try this issue now betwixt me and you; either you go to the wall or I do.' And there is nothing left to Congress but to take it up." [37]

Yet the case was not so clear-cut as Republicans may have believed. Lawyers know that an argument can be made for both sides of almost any question. The Democrats proceeded to make one. The president had as much authority as Congress to decide whether a law is constitutional, they insisted. "[T]he President of the United States has a primary right to judge of the Constitution of the United States and the laws passed under the Constitution, subject to all the penalties to

35. *Ibid.,* 1386 (February 24, 1868).
36. *Ibid.,* 1367–68 (February 22, 1868).
37. *Ibid.,* 1368 (February 22, 1868).

which he may be liable if he violates any law when that law is adjudged to be constitutional by the Supreme Court of the United States." [38] If the President can be impeached for violating the Tenure of Office Act, the Democrats argued, then Congress could pass any unconstitutional law, "and you then impeach the President because he wishes to test the constitutionality of your rule." [39]

Democrats argued that the Tenure of Office Act did not apply to Stanton. The Senate had refused to concur in the House's amendment subjecting cabinet officers to the bill. The result had been a compromise, which had provided that cabinet members would be subject to the act for the term of the president who appointed them and one month thereafter. Democrats insisted that this meant Johnson's cabinet was not covered. Johnson could have removed his department heads any time since one month after President Lincoln died. Since Stanton had never been reappointed by President Johnson, he had merely been holding over at the will of the President. The only historian to have delved into the impeachment intensively has concluded that the Democrats were correct in their analysis. James G. Blaine, who voted for impeachment, reached the same conclusion twenty years later.[40]

But the situation was not so simple. When senators had met representatives in conference committee to reconcile their differences on the bill, they had found their counterparts, in Sherman's words, "very tenacious." In order to save the bill, the Senate members agreed to the amendment requiring that the Senate advise and consent to the removal of cabinet officers during the term of the president who appointed them and one month thereafter. The senior House member of the conference committee informed his colleagues that the amendment "is in fact an acceptance by the Senate of the position taken by the House." [41] In the Senate, the chairman of the conference

38. *Ibid.,* 1337 (February 22, 1868).
39. *Ibid.*
40. DeWitt, *Impeachment and Trial,* 195–99; Blaine, *Twenty Years of Congress . . .* 2 vols. (Norwich, Conn., 1884–86), II, 352–54.
41. *Congressional Globe,* 39th Congress, 2nd Session, 1340 (February 19, 1867).

committee, George H. Williams, explained that the amendment was designed to vitiate the objection that by refusing to consent to the removal of cabinet members, a Senate controlled by one party could force an incoming president of the opposing party to retain his predecessor's cabinet against his will. He and Sherman, the other Republican senator on the conference committee, had agreed that the protected term of cabinet members would end under the bill one month after the president who appointed them left office. "If the President dies the Cabinet goes out; if the President is removed for cause by impeachment the Cabinet goes out; at the expiration of the term of the President's office the Cabinet goes out." [42]

The compromise section of the Tenure of Office Act in effect gave cabinet officers a fixed term for the only time in American history. And for that reason the House conferees were generally justified in claiming the Senate had acceded to the House's demands. But it was not so certain that the Senate had agreed that the law covered Johnson's cabinet. Like all other executive officers in the government, the terms of department heads would expire and the office would become vacant. The president would then have to name a replacement or reappoint the former occupant. Upon Senate confirmation the new appointee's term would run, as his predecessor's had, until one month after the president left office, unless the Senate agreed to his removal. But since the terms of department heads were indeterminate when Johnson became president, there had been no necessity to officially reappoint members of Lincoln's cabinet to office. What was their status now? Were they merely holding over, subject to removal at the president's will, two years after the end of his predecessor's term?

After Sherman and Williams had made their explanations, leaving this point untouched, Doolittle had insisted that by the terms of the compromise Johnson's cabinet was not covered. Sherman had agreed, and Howe had followed by expressing sorrow that the Senate had not concurred in the House's amendment. He too believed Johnson's cabinet was

42. *Ibid.,* 1515 (February 18, 1867).

not covered. No other senator discussed the matter before the Senate concurred in the conference committee report.[43] So when the Tenure of Office bill passed, the meaning of the provision in question was hazy. The House believed the Senate had acceded to its demands completely and that Johnson's cabinet was protected. Two Republican senators had insisted on a different interpretation, and the Senate, unaware of the House's interpretation, seemed to acquiesce in those senators' opinions. But the President himself had not insisted that his cabinet was excluded and, by proceeding under the act to suspend Stanton, had inclined the Senate to accept the House position. The debate over the resolution denying Johnson's right to remove Stanton without the Senate's advise and consent was not made public, but senators must have discussed the differing interpretations of the act's applicability, and the final vote clearly shows that by this time they concluded that the act protected Stanton after all. By the terms of the amendment, Stanton's term as secretary of war had ceased one month after President Lincoln's assassination. If he continued to act as secretary of war after that time, it was because of a virtual reappointment by the new president.[44]

The Republicans gave the Democratic argument short shrift. The President had acted in conformity with the Tenure of Office Act. He had waited for the Senate to express an opinion. It had. He could not now insist that he never believed Stanton to be protected by the act; he could not now insist that he had not intended to violate the law.

Furthermore, the President had not only violated the Tenure of Office Act. He had appointed Lorenzo Thomas Secretary of War ad interim to replace Stanton before he was confirmed by the Senate. This action of itself violated the Constitution, even in the absence of the Tenure of Office Act. The president could replace an officer ad interim while the Senate was not in session, but while the Senate sat, all appointees

43. *Ibid.*, 1514–18 (February 18, 1867).
44. *Ibid.*, 40th Congress, 2nd Session, 1352 (February 22, 1868).

must be confirmed before taking office, Republicans argued.

Even if the Democrats were right and the President could disobey a law to challenge its constitutionality in the courts, he could not claim that as a defense. "Suppose the courts should hold the act to be constitutional, would the fact that his intent was to have that question decided be a good plea to an indictment for a violation of its provisions? . . . Whoever acts in the way and for the purpose suggested does so at his peril," Representative Wilson insisted. If the court decided the law unconstitutional, the offender would be acquitted. If not, he would be liable to punishment. "[W]e will gratify his desire by carrying his case to the highest court known to the Constitution of the Republic," Wilson affirmed, "the high court of impeachment." It would decide the constitutionality of the law. And since the Senate had passed the law over the President's veto in the first place, it was not hard to foresee its decision as to the law's constitutionality.[45]

Moreover, Republicans denied the President's right to disobey a law merely because he believed it unconstitutional, or even to get the question into the courts. This was the prerogative of the citizen; he can challenge a law and risk the consequences. But this is not the prerogative of the officeholder. When the president accepts office, "he merges his individuality into that official creature which binds itself by an oath as an executive officer to do that which, as a mere individual, he may not believe to be just, right or constitutional. Such an acceptance removes him from the sphere of the right of private judgment to the plane of the public officer, and binds him to observe the law, his judgment as an individual to the contrary notwithstanding," James F. Wilson argued. If an officeholder believes he cannot in good faith execute the law as his duty requires, he must resign.[46] To hold otherwise would be to give the president absolute power to decide which laws to execute and which to ignore. The implications for the

45. *Ibid.*, 1387 (February 24, 1868).
46. *Ibid.*

Reconstruction laws were clear. Bingham, the House's leading conservative, admitted:

> I would be willing to delay indefinitely . . . the final action of the House upon this question, if I were fully assured that the President from this time forth would have respect to the obligations of law, and not undertake to usurp the authority of this Government in defiance of the people's Constitution and the people's laws. But . . . I have had evidence enough in the transaction . . . to satisfy me that the President of the United States is so bent upon his own destruction, or upon the destruction of the peace of this great country, that he is capable of rushing to any extreme of madness whatever.
>
> . . . I am precluded from the conclusion that he meant anything else than to defy your power and say to you . . . "Whatever laws you have passed or whatever laws you may pass I will disregard them on my own judgment whenever I see fit as being not in pursuance of the Constitution of the United States, and let you do your worst." [47]

The legal question melted into the political one. If the President's legal position were upheld, Republicans feared, he would use it to overthrow Congress's laws on the political question of Reconstruction. As a result, no matter how grossly the President had violated the laws, his trial on impeachment could not help but acquire a political cast. This was one of the two great weaknesses of the Republican position. The other lay in the nature of the law the President had violated.

House Republicans were not aware of how committed some of their Senate counterparts were to the opinion that the Tenure of Office Act did not cover Johnson's cabinet. The House members of the conference committee that had fashioned the compromise amendment had assured them the Senate had given in. They knew the President had not challenged the House interpretation, that he had acted upon it by submitting Stanton's removal to the Senate for its consent, and that the Senate had acted upon it by refusing its consent. House Republicans did not know upon what fragile ground they stood.

Republicans would have recognized another problem arising out of the nature of the Tenure of Office Act had they been

47. *Ibid.,* 1342 (February 22, 1868).

privy to the conclusion at which John Norton Pomeroy, the great constitutional analyst, arrived at almost the same time that impeachment proceedings commenced. Pomeroy agreed totally with the radical position on impeachment. In a brilliant discussion, he would demonstrate that impeachment was a political process and that no other conclusion was tenable. The case became all the more certain when the president actually violated a law or refused to carry it out. But, he added:

> To the general rule stated in the foregoing paragraphs, there are, I think, two important exceptions. A statute may be passed of such a form and character as to be addressed directly to the President; it presumes to regulate his official action; no private person and no subordinate officer is affected by its provissions. If the Chief Magistrate enforces this law, no question as to its validity can be raised. . . . It is only by refusal to execute such a statute that the President can possibly create an issue between himself and Congress. In such a case the President, unless he chooses to acquiesce, may plainly exercise an independent judgment, and act upon his own separate convictions.

And he illustrated his proposition by citing the Tenure of Office Act.[48]

Despite their unanimous belief that the Senate would convict the President for his violation of the Tenure of Office Act, many Republicans were loath to present such a narrow impeachment.[49] The Republicans who had voted for impeachment in December believed subsequent events had vindicated their course, and they again argued their interpretation of the law. Radicals like William D. Kelley, Ashley, Stevens, and Sidney Clarke brought up Johnson's offenses before Stanton's removal and included them in their charges. Other radicals,

48. Pomeroy, *Constitutional Law,* 444–45, 482–92. Pomeroy's work was published in 1870, but his language clearly indicates that he wrote his section on impeachment before the proceedings against Johnson.

49. DeWitt suggests that Republicans arraigned the President's conduct before Stanton's removal because they doubted the sufficiency of that action alone for impeachment. A reading of the debate on impeachment in the House uncovers no such doubts. DeWitt's conclusion reflects his misunderstanding of the division among Republicans on the law of impeachment.

like Logan and Butler, brought in Johnson's earlier activities indirectly, arguing that these proved the President's criminal intent in removing the Secretary of War. A few of the anti-impeachers of December conceded that they had voted against impeachment out of expediency and that the President was liable for his obstructionism before 1868. But nearly all of the early opponents of impeachment adhered to the positions they had then assumed. Bingham, Blair, Wilson, Luke P. Poland, Spalding, and others all based their charges on Johnson's violation of law alone. That offense had been necessary for impeachment; it would be sufficient for conviction.

The House voted on the impeachment resolution on February 24. It passed overwhelmingly, every Republican present voting for it. Of the fifteen absentees, ten were declared in favor.[50] Speaker Colfax, carefully balancing his committee between conservatives and radicals, appointed Stevens and Bingham to inform the Senate of the House's action. This would demonstrate to the senators the House Republicans' complete unanimity. To the committee to frame the specific articles of impeachment, the Speaker named Boutwell, Stevens, Bingham, Wilson, Logan, George W. Julian, and Hamilton Ward. This committee was weighted in favor of the radicals but still included the two most important opponents of impeachment in December, Wilson and Bingham.

Radical-conservative differences on impeachment came into the open once more as the committee reported its impeachment articles. Despite the radical preponderance on the committee, the members had refused to follow Stevens's lead in framing the articles, accusing the President only of crimes connected with Stanton's removal. Disappointed, the ailing Stevens wrote Butler, "[T]he Committee are likely to present no articles having any real vigor in them." Too weak to do the job himself, he suggested that Butler write several more, em-

50. The House debate on impeachment is in the *Congressional Globe*, 40th Congress, 2nd Session, 1336–69 (February 22, 1868), 1382–1402 (February 24), appendix, 155–258, 263–66 (February 22, 24, 1868).

bracing broader grounds than the committee's, which would be "worth convicting on." [51] The committee reported its articles on February 29, and after two days of speeches pro and con, Butler gained an opportunity to offer another. The proposed article declared the President, "designing and intending to set aside the rightful authority and powers of Congress, did attempt to bring into disgrace, ridicule, hatred, contempt, and reproach the Congress of the United States . . . , to impair and destroy the regard and respect of all the good people of the United States for the Congress and legislative power thereof . . . and to excite the odium and resentment of all the good people of the United States against Congress and the laws by it duly and constitutionally enacted . . . ." As specific instances, Butler cited the President's speeches made during the 1866 congressional elections. Butler's article was clearly based on the radical conception of impeachable "high crimes and misdemeanors." It asserted no violation of law, but rather a political offense. By a vote of 48 to 74, the House rejected it.[52] Without Republican dissent, the House then approved the committee's articles.[53]

As the House proceeded to select the men who would manage the impeachment, a new crisis erupted. The names had been decided upon in caucus, and when the ticket was printed Stevens and Butler preceded Bingham in order of preference. The implication was that Stevens would chair the committee, with Butler often replacing him owing to his illness. Bingham was outraged. "I'll be damned if I serve under Butler," he shouted. "It is no use to argue, gentlemen, I won't do it." Boutwell tried to calm him but to no avail, and the radicals gave in, agreeing that the committee itself would name a chairman. Of the seven men nominated by the caucus, Bing-

51. Stevens to Butler, February 28, 1868, Butler Mss., Library of Congress.

52. The original article is in the *Congressional Globe*, 40th Congress, 2nd Session, 1542–43 (February 29, 1868), a slightly amended version in *ibid.*, 1613–14 (March 2). Butler's proposed article is quoted in *ibid.*, 1615 (March 2).

53. *Ibid.*, 1616–18 (March 2, 1868).

ham received the most votes. Serving with him would be Boutwell, Wilson, Butler, Thomas Williams, Logan, and Stevens.[54]

In committee, Stevens, Logan, and Butler voted to name Boutwell chairman, with Bingham receiving the votes of Wilson and Williams. The angry Bingham again threatened to quit the committee, and, to the dismay of his radical colleagues, Boutwell acquiesced, resigning the chair and nominating Bingham in his place. He knew impeachment could not succeed if the leading conservative in the House left the committee.[55] With this decided, Butler renewed his efforts to broaden the grounds of the impeachment. With Wilson alone registering opposition, Butler persuaded the managers to incorporate his proposed article into the impeachment.[56]

Butler reported the new article to the House next day, where it met the opposition of representatives who argued that it charged no indictable crime. Butler retorted that he had supposed the doctrine that impeachment lay only for indictable crime "was dead and buried—I knew it stunk." [57] The House agreed with Butler by an 87 to 43 vote, with eleven Republicans voting with the opposition and seven apparently present abstaining.[58] The House then adopted another article, without Republican opposition, which incorporated the position several radicals had taken in the debate a week earlier.[59] This article described the earlier acts of the President as demonstrating his criminal intent when he removed Stanton. Johnson had conspired to remove Stanton to prevent the execution of the law requiring all military orders to be issued through the

54. New York *Herald,* March 3, 1868, p. 3; *Congressional Globe,* 40th Congress, 2nd Session, 1618–19 (March 2, 1868).

55. George S. Boutwell, "The Impeachment of Andrew Johnson: From the Standpoint of One of the Managers of the Impeachment Trial," *McClure's Magazine,* XIV (December 1899), 181.

56. Journal of the House Managers of Impeachment, R.G. 233, N.A.; Hans Trefousse, *Ben Butler: The South Called Him Beast!* (New York, 1957), 195–96.

57. *Congressional Globe,* 40th Congress 2nd Session, 1640 (March 3, 1868).

58. *Ibid.,* 1642 (March 3, 1868).

59. *Ibid.*

office of the General of the Army and to obstruct execution of the Reconstruction Acts. This was a compromise resolution. It alleged an indictable crime, but also listed nonindictable offenses that, taken together with the crime, constituted a long-term criminal conspiracy. The two charges became the tenth and eleventh articles.

As the House framed its articles of impeachment, the Senate fashioned rules of procedure for the trial. Wade appointed Jacob M. Howard, Trumbull, Conkling, Edmunds, Oliver P. Morton, Samuel C. Pomeroy, and Reverdy Johnson a committee to consider the question and report rules to the Senate. Just as in the House, Wade had carefully balanced radical and conservative sentiment on the committee.

The committee reported on February 29, proposing twenty-four rules to govern the trial.[60] When the Senate considered them, some important problems came to the fore. The first was a disagreement as to the nature of the Senate when trying an impeachment. The original rules described the Senate during the trial as a "high court of impeachment." It would "resolve itself into a high court of impeachment" to hear evidence and arguments. Before the Senate could resume legislative duties, it would have to adjourn the "high court" and resolve itself once more into the Senate. Many senators, led by Conkling and Morton, who obviously had objected to this in committee, took exception to such procedure. They feared its implications. Surprisingly, no senator argued that the Senate should try the impeachment in a political capacity. All agreed that impeachment was a judicial proceeding. Despite his opinions, Sumner remained silent. What senators feared was that Chief Justice Chase, who would preside over the trial, might claim a vote as a member of the "high court." If the Senate retained its normal character while sitting in judgment, the Chief Justice could make no such claim, as he was not a member of the Senate. After two days of confusing debate, the

---

60. They may be found in the *Congressional Globe,* 40th Congress, 2nd Session, 1515–16 (February 29, 1868).

Senate on a key vote agreed to Conkling's objections.[61] Chase's position was unknown at the time, although some Republicans suspected he opposed conviction.[62] The division, therefore, did not run along conservative-radical lines. After the vote, the Senate agreed to eliminate the term "high court of impeachment" wherever it occurred in the rules.[63]

Closely related to the nature of the proceeding was the question of the Chief Justice's role. The original rules authorized Chase to rule on all questions of law and evidence, his rulings to stand as the judgment of the "court" unless overruled by a majority vote. Senator Charles D. Drake opposed this provision and moved to strike it. Drake feared the prestige of a ruling by the Chief Justice of the United States on a matter of law or procedure. "It is not proper that the judgment of the Senate upon questions of law, which it must ultimately decide, . . . should be warped, in any degree affected by the previous announcement of an opinion upon that question by so high a judicial officer as the Chief Justice." [64] Howard proposed instead to substitute a more ambiguous rule: "The Presiding Officer may in the first instance submit to the Senate, without a division, all questions of evidence and incidental questions; but the same on demand of one fifth of the members present, shall be decided by yeas and nays." Drake accepted this modification, indicating his conviction that this proposition meant that all questions of law would have to be put to the senators for decision, but on the face of it Howard's amendment was unclear on that point.[65] The Senate accepted the modified proposition on a nonpartisan division.[66]

A final source of controversy among the senators was the

61. *Ibid.*, 1592 (March 2, 1868).

62. Daniel Sickles to E. B. Washburne, March 1, 1868, Washburne Mss.

63. For the discussion of this question, see the *Congressional Globe*, 40th Congress, 2nd Session, 1521–26 (February 29, 1868), 1591–92, 1593–94, 1602–1603 (March 2, 1868).

64. *Ibid.*, 1598 (March 2, 1868).

65. *Ibid.*, 1596 (March 2, 1868).

66. *Ibid.*, 1601 (March 2, 1868).

proper limitation of time allotted to managers and counsel. The original rule from the special committee allowed each side one hour to argue preliminary and interlocutory questions. Frelinghuysen proposed to allow two hours. Howard objected strenuously. Republicans were in a difficult situation. For political reasons, speed was of the utmost importance. A long period of uncertainty would allow time for reflection and reaction among conservative Republicans, especially businessmen interested in stability.[67] On the other hand, Republicans dared not move so quickly as to compromise the appearance of a fair trial. To a certain degree the two considerations were contradictory, and therefore more radical senators were inclined to favor speed at the expense of impartiality. "[I]f I can prevail," Sumner informed Francis Lieber, the respected student of systems of government, the trial "shall proceed . . . without intermission, to the end." Many believed the proceedings would take three weeks, but Sumner hoped to arrive at a verdict within ten days of its commencement.[68]

Howard was not in such haste, but he objected to allowing two hours for each point. He pointed to the issue of the jurisdiction of the Senate sitting without southern members. "Why, sir, an ingenious counselor could spend several days, not to say several weeks, in discussing that question." [69] On this issue, the Senate did display its attitude toward the imperatives of impeachment, and the result should have been sobering to those who believed in the certainty of conviction. Frelinghuysen's proposal lost by only four votes, 20 to 24, with eleven Republicans joining the Democrats.[70]

67. See, for instance, Daniel Sickles to E. B. Washburne, March 17, 25, 1868, Washburne Mss.; B. Gratz Brown to Wade, March 26, 1868, Wade Mss., Library of Congress; E. D. Morgan to William Wheeler, March 25, 1868, Morgan Mss.; Charles Moorfield Storey to Henry L. Dawes, March 6, 1868, Dawes Mss.; Francis W. Bird to Sumner, February 24, 1868; Edward L. Pierce to Sumner, March 4, 1868, Sumner Mss.
68. Sumner to Lieber, March 27, 1868, Sumner Mss.
69. *Congressional Globe,* 40th Congress, 2nd Session, 1571 (March 2, 1868).
70. *Ibid.,* 1578 (March 2, 1868).

On March 2 the Senate passed the amended version of the rules proposed by the special committee. That did not finally settle the issues, however. To the dismay of the radicals, they came up again during the trial, and several of the most important decisions were overturned. Chase undermined the first decision—the status of the Senate during the trial—by clever maneuvering. The Senate had decided that it did not become a distinct body while sitting in judgment. It did not become a "high court of impeachment." But on March 5, as Chase was administering an oath of affirmation to the senators to do impartial justice, the Democrats objected to Wade's sitting as part of the "court," since he would become president were Johnson convicted. He could not do impartial justice. The more conservative Republicans suggested that such an objection must come from the President's counsel rather than from the Senate itself, but more radical members suggested a different justification for swearing Wade. The Senate when sitting on trial, Morton insisted, is still the Senate and Wade was a senator. He might be disqualified if the Senate became a court, but it did not. The Democrats proceeded to argue the question at length.

Finally, Grimes moved an adjournment of the "court." Howard objected that the Senate had decided that it did not resolve into a court when discussing impeachment. Henry B. Anthony suggested that "the proper motion would be that the Senate proceed to the consideration of legislative business." But the Chief Justice retorted, "The court must first adjourn," and he put the question on adjournment, to which the Senate agreed.[71] From that day, the "court" always adjourned before resolving once more into the Senate.

The next day, Howard, realizing that the Democrats were using the issue of Wade's eligibility to stall the proceedings, raised a point of order to cut off debate. He pointed out that the rules of procedure adopted by the Senate required the

71. The whole discussion may be found in *Trial of Andrew Johnson,* III, 360–88 (March 5, 1868).

presiding officer to administer the oath and did not provide for challenge. He objected that the motions to disqualify or delay Wade's swearing in were therefore out of order. But after some discussion, Chase ruled that the rules adopted by the Senate would apply only after the Senate had organized for impeachment and that it had not yet done so. In other words, the Senate was indeed a distinct body when considering impeachment. Drake immediately appealed the ruling, but the Senate sustained the Chief Justice, 24 to 20. Fifteen Republicans had joined the Democrats to support Chase's interpretation.[72] The Chief Justice administered his *coup de grâce* after the Democrats withdrew their objection to Wade's participation. He announced to the Senate that, in his judgment, "the Senate is now organized as a distinct body from the Senate sitting in its legislative capacity. . . . Under these circumstances, the Chair conceives that rules adopted by the Senate in its legislative capacity are not rules for the government of the Senate sitting for the trial of an impeachment, unless they be also adopted by that body." Chase announced that he wanted the opinion of the Senate on this issue, but he framed the question in an ambiguous way. "Senators," he said, "you who think that the rules of proceeding adopted on the 2d of March . . . shall be considered the rules of proceeding in this body will say 'ay'; contrary opinion, 'no.'" There was no way to vote "no." If a senator believed the Senate sitting on impeachment was not distinguished from the Senate discussing legislation, then the rules adopted on March 2 were, of course, binding on the Senate now. Therefore he would have to vote "ay." If another senator agreed with the Chief Justice, then the rules had to be readopted. To readopt them, he too would have to vote "ay." Chase could not lose.[73] He interpreted the Senate vote as endorsing his position, effectively destroying the contrary opinion that the Senate was the same body in all its capacities. This opened the way for Chase to cast the deciding

72. *Ibid.,* 388–94 (March 6, 1868).
73. *Ibid.,* I, 12 (March 6, 1868).

vote in case of a tie on points of law, and perhaps would allow him to vote on the articles themselves if his vote would decide conviction or acquittal, although that would be a much more dubious proposition, as traditionally the presiding officer votes only in the case of an actual tie. In the case of conviction on impeachment, two-thirds of the senators must vote for removal in order to render the presiding officer's the deciding vote.

The next step in undermining the Senate's original rules regarding the position of the Chief Justice came as the trial began. The rule in regard to the Chief Justice's right to decide points of law and procedure preliminary to a Senate vote had been equivocal. The Senate had stricken a provision granting undoubted authority to Chase to make those decisions but had replaced it with the unclear provision discussed earlier (see p. 116). Now Chase stated his decision (which he may or may not have been authorized to state in the first place, depending on the interpretation given the rule) that the rule did allow him to make preliminary determinations on points of law, particularly upon objections to evidence. Senator Drake appealed the decision, but Chase ruled him out of order. Only the managers for the House or the counsel for the President could appeal, he insisted. The managers promptly did so. "We have been too long in parliamentary and other bodies not to know how much disadvantage it is to be put in that position—the position . . . of appealing from the ruling of the presiding officer of the Senate," Butler observed.[74] The ruling would endanger the House's case for another reason: according to Chase's ruling, only the managers could raise a point of law, but once the Chief Justice decided it, another rule stated that his decision could be appealed only by a senator. The managers could not appeal it themselves. So unless a senator did appeal, the House managers could not debate the point at issue in an effort to change the ruling. As there was no court of appeal to correct an error, this enforced silence might be critical

74. *Ibid.,* 176 (March 31, 1868).

and a mistake irreparable. Bingham and Boutwell endorsed Butler's protest in an effort to demonstrate to conservative senators that this was not the opinion of the most radical manager alone. Senator Wilson then moved that the Senate retire for consultation, but this immediately raised a new question, for on this motion the Senate divided 25 to 25, and Chase took immediate advantage of this to vote in the affirmative, breaking the tie and asserting his right to a casting vote.

In the critical conference that followed, Sherman proposed a rule declaring that all questions other than those of order must be submitted to the Senate, but a motion by Henderson to postpone Sherman's proposition passed 32 to 18. Henderson wrote years later that he felt the impeachment proceedings were "a monstrosity." That conviction, he wrote, was shared by "several of the lawyers in that body . . . , for the Senate was to act both as judge and jury." Henderson determined to "separate the jurisdiction of the jury from that of the judge . . . . I wanted a judge, preferably the Chief Justice, to decide the judicial points, as the Senate was like a mob, deciding everything for themselves." [75]

To reach his objective, Henderson proposed a resolution declaring the presiding officer's decision the judgment of the Senate unless a senator asked for a formal vote. Sumner moved to substitute a declaration that the Chief Justice "is not a member of the Senate, and has no authority, under the Constitution, to vote on any question during the trial, and he can pronounce decision only as the organ of the Senate, with its assent." But the Senate defeated Sumner's amendment, 26 to 22, and a similar one by Drake, 20 to 30. The senators then adopted Henderson's proposal, 31 to 19, nineteen Republicans joining the Democrats and Johnson Conservatives. The next day, the Senate refused to declare that Chase had cast his tie-

75. John B. Henderson, "Emancipation and Impeachment," *Century Magazine,* LXXXV (December 1912), 202. Henderson wrote that his efforts were "in vain." That did not mean he failed to win approval for his motions. In fact, they passed. He must have meant that despite their passage the Senate did not act in accordance with proper judicial procedure. Others, of course, disagreed.

breaking vote the previous day without authority. The conservative position on the duties and nature of the Senate during an impeachment had been accepted. The Senate was a court; the Chief Justice was a member of it. Implicitly, the impeachment was of a judicial nature, to be tried according to the forms of law and not by an essentially political tribunal.[76]

The impeachment trial would also progress more slowly than many Republicans had hoped. The Senate summoned the President to answer the House's charges on March 13. According to the rules adopted by the Senate, the President or his counsel were to be prepared with their answer. If they did not appear or failed to file an answer, an automatic plea of not guilty was to be recorded and the trial would begin.[77] But instead of meeting the Senate requirement, the defense lawyers asked forty days to prepare the President's answer, pointing out that more time had been granted in earlier impeachments.

"The managers appeared at the bar of the Senate impressed with the belief that the rule meant precisely what it says," Bingham argued impatiently. The defense argued that a requirement to appear and answer never meant the defendant had to answer the bill the same day. But manager Wilson called attention to the difference in the rule's wording—that it went so far as to provide for a constructive plea if the defense were not ready. But the President's lawyers hit the managers and the Senate in their weakest spot. "A case like this, Mr. Chief Justice, in which the President of the United States is arraigned upon an impeachment presented by the House of Representatives, a case of the greatest magnitude we have ever had, is, as to time, to be treated as if it were a case before a police court, to be put through with railroad speed on the first day the criminal appears," Henry Stanbery declaimed. He made explicit the dichotomy for the senators: speed or the appearance of a fair trial.

76. The discussions and votes on these issues are in *Trial of Andrew Johnson*, I, 175–87 (March 31, 1868), 187–88 (April 1, 1868).
77. Rule VIII, quoted *ibid.*, 14.

Bingham pleaded with the senators to adhere to their own rule, but they were not disposed to do so. After a consultation, the Senate agreed to require the respondents to file an answer to the charges on March 23, a delay of ten days. The managers then asked the Senate to authorize the trial to proceed immediately after the managers replied to the defense's answer, but the Senate refused by a vote of 25 to 26, sixteen Republicans joining the Democrats and Johnson Conservatives. But the Senate then reversed itself, authorizing the trial to begin immediately after the managers' reply "unless otherwise ordered by the Senate for cause shown." [78] When the President's counsel, after answering the House charges on March 23, asked for a thirty-day delay of the actual trial, the Senate refused to agree; the Republicans were unanimous in denying the request.[79]

Trying to speed the trial, the House adopted a short reply to the President's answer and presented it the next day. But now Senator Reverdy Johnson moved a ten-day delay in the trial. Sumner demanded that the Senate adhere to its own rule, but again the radicals were overruled, and in consultation the Senate agreed to a one-week delay, the trial to begin on March 30. When the trial began, over one month had elapsed since the President had challenged Congress with Stanton's removal.[80]

Throughout the trial, radical attempts to speed the proceedings failed. Until April 17, the Senate heard the impeachment proceedings from noon until about five o'clock in the afternoon. The pattern was established early, on a roll-call vote on April 2. The radicals had resisted Doolittle's motion to adjourn, but the Chief Justice broke the tie vote.[81] The radicals did not challenge the five-o'clock adjournment again until April 16, when Sumner tried but failed to get even enough support to require a record vote.[82] The same day, Sumner pro-

78. *Ibid.,* 17–34, 35 (March 13, 1868).
79. *Ibid.,* 82 (March 23, 1868).
80. *Ibid.,* 84–86 (March 24, 1868).
81. *Ibid.,* 276 (April 3, 1868).
82. *Ibid.,* 632 (April 17, 1868).

posed a new order that the Senate sit in trial from 10 A.M. to 6 P.M. The next day, the Senate refused to adopt Sumner's order, only thirteen Republicans favoring it. Instead, the senators agreed to meet at 11 A.M., leaving the adjournment time undetermined. Implicitly, this meant that the Senate would continue to adjourn at five o'clock.[83] One week later, the Senate moved its meeting time back to noon, on the motion of Grimes, who all knew now opposed conviction. Only thirteen Republicans refused to accede.[84] Radicals made one more abortive attempt to step up the pace of the trial. On April 30, they tried to persuade the senators to sit through night sessions. Again they failed.[85]

Sumner had hoped for a trial of ten days; instead, it had lasted five weeks before actual testimony even began. Two and a half months would pass before the Senate even approached a vote on the final questions. This was the result not only of Democratic delaying tactics. As Garfield wrote on April 28:

This trial has developed, in the most remarkable manner, the insane love of speaking among public men. . . . [W]e have been wading knee deep in words, words, words . . . and are but little more than half across the turbid stream. I verily believe there are fierce impeachers here, who, if the alternative of conviction of the President, coupled with their silence; and an unlimited opportunity to talk, coupled with his certain acquittal, were before them would instantly decide to speak.[86]

The effects of this were to become clear. It would give time for a reaction to set in. Hard-money and low-tariff men would grow more and more fearful of a Wade administration. The President would have time to allay fears of his intentions and reach some sort of accommodation with Republican conservatives. But despite these votes on procedural matters, few doubted that the President would be convicted in the end. As Ben Perley

83. *Ibid.*, 631 (April 16, 1868), 632–33 (April 17, 1868).
84. *Ibid.*, II, 141 (April 24, 1868).
85. *Ibid.*, 307–8 (April 30, 1868).
86. Garfield to J. H. Rhodes, April 28, 1868, Garfield Mss.

Poore wrote, "A Senator may have desired to elevate the trial above the proceedings in a Magistrate's Court, and yet have no desire to shield the great criminal." [87]

87. Boston *Evening Journal*, April 18, 1868, p. 4; Thomas Ewing, Sr., to Hugh Ewing, February 28, 1868, Hugh Ewing Mss., Ohio Historical Society Library; Julian to Mrs. Laura Giddings Julian, February 29, April 21, 1868, Julian Mss.; Patrick Riddleberger, *George Washington Julian, Radical Republican: A Study in Nineteenth Century Politics and Reform* (Indianapolis, 1966), 234–35; J. M. Ashley to William H. Smith, March 21, 1868; Joseph H. Barrett to Smith, April 1, 1868, Smith Mss., Ohio Historical Society Library; Henry S. Lane to John Hanna, March 27, 1868, Hanna Mss., Lilly Library, Indiana University, Bloomington; Godlove S. Orth to Conrad Baker, April 28, 1868, Baker Mss., Indiana State Historical Library, Indiana Division.

5

Trial

MOST HISTORIANS have interpreted the attempt to remove President Johnson as blatantly political, insupportable in law, a blunder from which the nation was saved by seven noble Republican senators who would not succumb to the political pressure around them. This is true even of those historians who have begun to recognize the circumstances in which impeachment took place and have debunked the idea that the President was an innocent victim unable any longer to disrupt the "radical" program. But such a view is naive in the extreme.[1]

Extralegal considerations did play a large part in the impeachment proceedings. But these considerations weighed not only upon the Republicans who voted for conviction. It goes almost without saying that the Democrats and the few "Johnsonized" Republicans who had been cooperating with them would under no circumstances have voted to remove the President and turn the office over to the Republicans. In fact, they were more consistently antipathetic to the entire proceeding than even the most hostile of the Republicans (see Chart 6). If one argues that Johnson's conviction would have resulted from votes motivated by political considerations, one must concede that the same considerations secured his acquittal.

1. See the Bibliographical Review for a brief historiography of impeachment.

CHART 6

Senators and Impeachment
40th Congress, Second Session

MAIN SCALE—GENERAL IMPEACHMENT ISSUES

GROUP 0 Democrats and Johnson Conservatives

James A. Bayard, Del.

Garrett Davis, Ky.

James Dixon, Conn.
    (Johnson Conservative)

James R. Doolittle, Wis.
    (Johnson Conservative)

Thomas C. McCreery, Ky.

David T. Patterson, Tenn.

Willard Saulsbury, Del.

George Vickers, Md.

Charles R. Buckalew, Pa.

Thomas A. Hendricks, Ind.

Reverdy Johnson, Md.

Daniel S. Norton, Minn.
    (Johnson Conservative)

—*Motion declaring impeachment illegal without participation of senators from southern states, motion to adjourn* sine die *May 16, admissibility of hearsay evidence showing Johnson hoped only to test the constitutionality of the Tenure of Office Act, motion to deny a defense request for delay, admissibility of report of Johnson speeches of 1866, motion to delay vote on articles, motion to adjourn* sine die *May 26.*

GROUP 1 Republicans Voting Against Conviction and/or to Sustain the Defense Position on Most Questions

Joseph S. Fowler, Tenn.

Edmund G. Ross, Kans.

William P. Fessenden, Maine

James W. Grimes, Iowa

John B. Henderson, Mo.

Lyman Trumbull, Ill.

Peter G. Van Winkle, W.Va.

Henry B. Anthony, R.I.

—*Motion to postpone vote on conviction, admissibility of evidence that Johnson hoped only to test the constitutionality of the Tenure of Office Act, votes on the articles, motion to vote first on Article XI, motion to extend the hours of trial, motion to adjourn over weekend, admissibility of testimony regarding cabinet discussions of the Tenure of Office Act, admissibility of testimony that Johnson attempted to bring the Tenure of Office Act before the courts, votes on defense requests for delays, admissibility of evidence of Johnson's intentions as expressed after he attempted to remove Stanton.*

GROUP 2   Republicans Apparently Uncommitted to Conviction, Favoring Delay, and Not Strongly Committed to Conviction by End of Trial

    George F. Edmunds, Vt.   James W. Patterson, N.H.
    Waitman T. Willey, W.Va.   John Sherman, Ohio
    Frederick T. Frelinghuysen, N.J.   William Sprague, R.I.
    Justin S. Morrill, Vt.   *Cornelius Cole, Calif.*
    Oliver P. Morton, Ind.

  —*Motion to proceed with Article XI first, motion to adjourn after failure to convict on Article XI, admissibility of evidence of Johnson's intentions as expressed after his attempt to remove Stanton, motion to require defense to respond to impeachment articles without delay, admissibility of General Sherman's evidence.*

GROUP 3   Republicans Apparently Uncommitted to Conviction as the Trial Began but Opposing Delay and Committed to Conviction by Its End

    Alexander G. Cattell, N.J.   Timothy O. Howe, Wis.
    Henry W. Corbett, Ore.   Lot M. Morrill, Maine
    Aaron H. Cragin, N.H.   *George H. Williams, Ore.*
    Orris S. Ferry, Conn.   *Richard Yates, Ill.*

  —*Motion to take up a resolution to investigate charges of intimidation of senators, motion to extend hours of trial, admissibility of evidence that Johnson sought to get a court test of the Tenure of Office Act, motion to strip the Chief Justice of power to decide legal questions and to declare him not a member of the court of impeachment, motions to speed voting on articles.*

GROUP 4   Republicans Strongly Committed to Conviction

    Zachariah Chandler, Mich.   Thomas W. Tipton, Nebr.
    Edwin D. Morgan, N.Y.   Henry Wilson, Mass.
    Samuel C. Pomeroy, Kans.

  —*Censure of defense counsel for impugning the Senate, admissibility of evidence of Johnson's intentions as expressed after he attempted to remove Stanton, motions to eliminate impeachment rules authorizing senators to file written opinions.*

GROUP 5   Republicans Strongly Committed to Conviction

    Simon Cameron, Pa.   James W. Nye, Nev.
    Roscoe Conkling, N.Y.   Alexander Ramsey, Minn.
    John Conness, Calif.   William A. Stewart, Nev.
    Charles D. Drake, Mo.   Charles Sumner, Mass.
    James Harlan, Iowa   John M. Thayer, Nebr.
    Jacob M. Howard, Mass.

         Not Voting: Benjamin F. Wade, Ohio (Rep.)

For a list of the roll calls upon which this chart (page 128) is based, see the Appendix. Italicized senators voted less consistently than others in their groups, leaning toward the groups nearest their names.

SUBSCALE—DIVISIVE VOTES, PRIMARILY EARLY IN THE TRIAL

GROUP 0 Democrats, Johnson Conservatives, and Republicans Not Strongly Committed to Conviction

Anthony, R.I. (Rep.)
Bayard, Del. (Dem.)
Buckalew, Pa. (Dem.)
Davis, Ky. (Dem.)
Dixon, Conn.
  (Johnson Conservative)
Doolittle, Wis.
  (Johnson Conservative)
Edmunds, Vt. (Rep.)
Fessenden, Maine (Rep.)
Fowler, Tenn. (Rep.)
Frelinghuysen, N.J. (Rep.)
Grimes, Iowa (Rep.)
Henderson, Mo. (Rep.)
Hendricks, Ind. (Dem.)

Johnson, Md. (Dem.)
McCreery, Ky. (Dem.)
Norton, Minn.
  (Johnson Conservative)
Patterson, Tenn. (Dem.)
Ross, Kans. (Rep.)
Saulsbury, Del. (Dem.)
Sherman, Ohio (Rep.)
Sprague, R.I. (Rep.)
Trumbull, Ill. (Rep.)
Van Winkle, W.Va. (Rep.)
Vickers, Md. (Dem.)
Willey, W.Va. (Rep.)
Williams, Ore. (Rep.)

—*Admissibility of General Sherman's testimony that Johnson intended only to test the Tenure of Office Act's constitutionality, adjournment over weekend, admissibility of testimony that Johnson illegally planned to gain control of the Treasury, motion to deny the Chief Justice's right to cast deciding votes in case of ties, motion to vote on Article XI by clause.*

GROUP 1 Republicans Relatively Committed to Conviction

Cattell, N.J.
Conness, Calif.
Corbett, Ore.
Cragin, N.H.
Drake, Mo.
Ferry, Conn.
Howard, Mich.

Howe, Wis.
Morrill, Vt.
Morton, Ind.
Nye, Nev.
Patterson, N.H.
Wilson, Mass.

—*Motion to lengthen hours of trial.*

GROUP 2 Republicans Committed to Speedy Trial and Conviction

Harlan, Iowa
Morgan, N.Y.
Morrill, Maine

Ramsey, Minn.
Tipton, Nebr.
Yates, Ill.

—*Adjournment to allow defense to prepare for trial.*

GROUP 3   Republicans Committed to Speedy Trial and Conviction

Cameron, Pa.	Pomeroy, Kans.
Chandler, Mich.	Stewart, Nev.
Cole, Calif.	Sumner, Mass.
Conkling, N.Y.	Thayer, Nebr.

Not Voting: Wade, Ohio (Rep.)

For a list of the roll calls upon which this chart is based, see the Appendix.

Moreover, not all of the seven Republican holdouts were moved solely by legal requirements. Most Republicans believed that impeachment was necessary for the future success of the Republican party and therefore for the security of southern black and white loyalists. The President had embarked on a bold offensive to defeat Reconstruction in the South. Before the House impeached him, he had removed every military commander in the South who was committed to carrying out the spirit of the Reconstruction Acts; he had twice replaced Stanton, quarreled with Grant, and begun to create a new military headquarters in Washington to be commanded by a more friendly general equal in rank to the General of the Army. If impeachment failed, Republicans believed, "the President will have schemes enough to endanger the peace of the country. It would open a Pandora's box." [2]

Smarting under the blows of the President's "winter offensive" and apparently unable to cope with it, watching as the anti-Republican reaction gained strength among the voters, Republicans seized the opportunity Johnson had given them to

2. John Meredith Read to E. B. Washburne, April 30, 1868; W. H. Gibbs to Washburne, April 11, 1868, Washburne Mss.; Edward L. Pierce to Sumner, May 7, 1868, Sumner Mss.; C. H. Allen to Conrad Baker, February 28, 1868; Godlove S. Orth to Baker, April 16, 1868, Baker Mss.; Colfax to Kline G. Shyrock, March 7, 1868, Colfax Mss., Chicago Historical Society; Colfax to Jonathan Russell Young, April 8, 1868, Young Mss., Library of Congress; Oliver Pillsbury to William Eaton Chandler, April 25, 1868, Chandler Mss., New Hampshire Historical Society, Concord, N.H.; Francis Lieber to Martin Russell Thayer, March 2, 1868, Lieber Mss., Huntington Libary, San Marino Calif.

escape from their predicament. "What we never could get of the virtue of the Republican party we seem likely to get from its fears," Phillips commented acidly.[3] But other Republicans held different views. When Richard Henry Dana visited Washington, he found some Republicans who thought "it would be the ruin of the Rep. party to fail. Others say that it will lose us the election if we succeed. If the Pr. is convicted, we are responsible for Ben Wade, and all that happens & shall have distributed our offices before election. Wrongs to be redressed & offices to be given are the stock of party."[4]

Thomas Ewing, Jr., recognized the importance of the political prospects. From New Hampshire, where he was campaigning for the Democrats, he wrote, " [T]he general cry and belief, is the party will be damned if they don't convict, and therefore the newspapers and leaders generally of the radical wing threaten to shoot doubters But if it begin to appear from the spring elections that the radicals from some cause are losing 4 or 5 per cent of their votes, then the more conservative men and papers will cry out that the party will be damned if they *do* convict, and Fessenden, Trumbull, Sherman, Grimes, and others will rally courage enough to refuse to perjure themselves for Ben Wade & Co."[5]

In fact, the Republicans did lose votes in the spring elections. They garnered 51.7 percent of the vote in New Hampshire as compared to 52.3 percent the year before and 53.5 percent in 1866. This represented a 1.1 percent loss in the Republican percentage between 1868 and 1867 and a 3.5 percent loss between 1868 and 1866.[6] This was not the 4 or 5 percent loss Ewing had hoped for, but it demonstrated that impeachment had not reversed the downward trend that began

3. New York *National Anti-Slavery Standard,* April 4, 1868, p. 2.
4. Dana to Mrs. Sara Dana, March 22, 1868, Dana Mss., Massachusetts Historical Society.
5. Ewing to Hugh Ewing, March 8, 1868, Hugh Ewing Mss., Ohio Historical Society Library.
6. That is, the .6 percent decline in the Republican share of the total vote amounted to 1.1 percent of the 52.3 percent of the vote Republicans received the year before.

in 1867. The Republican decline continued in Connecticut's election held on April 6. Republicans lost the gubernatorial race for the second successive year, winning but 47.9 percent of the vote compared to 49.6 percent in 1867 and 50.1 percent in 1866. The Republican percentage here had been reduced by 3.6 percent over the previous year and 4 percent since 1866.[7] By May 3, Fessenden wrote, "I am satisfied that with present light the thing never would have begun. People now see, as I always told them . . . , that the result is to be disastrous any way."[8]

Furthermore, men like Fessenden, Trumbull, and Grimes disliked the radicals nearly as much as or more than they disliked Andrew Johnson, and it was the radicals who stood to gain most by Johnson's removal. Fessenden, in fact, preferred the President to the radicals in personal terms. He had not suffered so much as they from Johnson's use of the patronage. Secretary of the Treasury McCulloch had been reluctant to use the Treasury service as a political weapon and had retained Republicans in office wherever he could, paying special attention to the personal appointments of his predecessor, Fessenden. The Senator from Maine could not generally get his friends appointed, but many of his allies already in office remained there. "It is quite evident that there had been a disposition to avoid treading on my toes," he wrote. Johnson's "wish to oblige me," as Fessenden put it, could not help but favorably impress him, especially when he compared the President's attitude towards him to the radicals'. "Say what they will, Andy is a good hearted fellow, and with all his faults stands, or ought to, a much better chance for 'Kingdom-come' than some men I could name who count themselves as saints."[9]

7. Because of Connecticut's well-gerrymandered legislative districts, however, Republicans actually increased their narrow control of the state legislature slightly.

8. Fessenden to William H. Fessenden, May 3, 1868; Fessenden to James D. Fessenden, April 22, 1868. Fessenden Mss., Bowdoin College Library.

9. Fessenden to Elizabeth Fessenden Warriner, December 8, 1866, May 13, 1866, March 4, 1867, Fessenden Mss., Bowdoin College Li-

In a way, the impeachment was a personal victory for Sumner over Fessenden, or at least Fessenden might have so considered it. Sumner had predicted that reluctant Republicans would be forced to impeach Johnson eventually. When concervatives had defeated impeachment in December 1867, Fessenden had crowed, "For once, Mr. Sumner cannot boast of the fulfillment of his prophecy . . . ." [10] Sumner's obvious triumph may well have added to Fessenden's chagrin when impeachment finally came. At any rate, he had, as he wrote his son, "opposed it from the beginning." [11]

But far more than personal hostilities influenced several of the "recusant" senators—as they came to be called—against removing Johnson. As Hans Trefousse has pointed out, the character and politics of Johnson's would-be successor played a large role in the President's acquittal. He had delivered a speech in Lawrence, Kansas, a year before, which the Boston *Daily Advertiser* described as "simply and wholly . . . an avowal of agrarian sympathies." [12] He had expanded on it to question the fundamental value of freedom so long as working-men were at the mercy of capitalists. But these opinions were merely vagaries. What really aroused powerful interests against him (and *for* him, it should be remembered) were his high-tariff, soft-money opinions. The tariff and financial questions were living issues, over which men fought passionately, and

---

brary; Jellison, *Fessenden,* 213. Fessenden was the only Republican to write McCulloch regularly on patronage matters, and McCulloch regularly obliged him. Fessenden to McCulloch, August 15, 17, 29, September 7, 11, 15, November 11, 1866, January 9, 27, June 4, 15, July 27, September 2, 1867, McCulloch Mss., Library of Congress; Fessenden to Elizabeth Fessenden Warriner, February 6, 1867, Fessenden Mss., Bowdoin College Library; McCulloch to Fessenden, September 11, 1866, Fessenden Mss., Library of Congress. Postmaster General Alexander W. Randall also willingly helped Fessenden at least once in 1867. Randall to Fessenden, September 16, 1867, Frederick M. Dearborn collection, Houghton Library, Harvard University.

10. Fessenden to Elizabeth Fessenden Warriner, December 15, 1867, Fessenden Mss., Bowdoin College Library.

11. Fessenden to William H. Fessenden, May 3, 1868, Fessenden Mss., Bowdoin College Library.

12. Boston *Daily Advertiser,* June 17, 1867, p. 2.

much more controversial than scattered musings over the rights of labor. These issues had already played a large part in the impeachment controversy and had helped to defeat the impeachment resolution of December 1867. The immediate threat apparent in Johnson's activities in February 1868 had persuaded Republican contractionists in the House to risk impeachment, but as time wore on many fiscal reformers, especially those outside the House, began once more to worry about the effect of Wade's elevation to the presidency. When *Iron Age*, the organ of the protectionist iron industry, called for a meeting of high-tariff men to take advantage of Wade's prospective administration to pass a new tariff bill, the free-trade-oriented Chicago *Tribune* warned, "[T]hey are doing more to defeat the impeachment of Johnson than any other equal number of men in the country, and far more than the President's counsel." [13] The rumor (well founded, judging from Wade's correspondence) that he intended to name E. B. Ward, a leading opponent of contraction, secretary of the treasury worried the hard-money lobby.

Another rumor held that Wade intended to name Butler secretary of state. The controversial radical's intense hostility toward England was well known, and Republicans feared the damage he might do the delicate *Alabama* claims negotiations and the designs he might hold on Canada. By May 2, former Representative John B. Alley warned Butler that leading senators had determined to prevent anyone involved with impeachment, whether manager or senator, from going into Wade's cabinet.[14]

"I have a few words to whisper in your private ear, concerning what conservative Republicans think," Garfield wrote James Harrison Rhodes on May 7. "They say that 'Conviction means a transfer to the Presidency of Mr. Wade, a man of violent passions, extreme opinions, and narrow views; . . . a grossly profane coarse nature who is surrounded by the worst and most violent elements in the Republican party . . . that

13. Chicago *Tribune,* April 21, 1868, p. 2.
14. Alley to Butler, May 2, 1868, Butler Mss.

already the worst class of political cormorants from Ohio and elsewhere are thronging the lobbies and filling the hotels in high hopes of plunder when Wade is sworn in.' " [15] The President's counsel, insistent as they were that political considerations should not enter into the trial, were not averse to making subtle appeals to these fears—especially William M. Evarts, who, as the only defense counselor openly committed to Grant as the prospective Republican presidential nominee, could hint of such matters with a particular authority.[16] Johnson would be convicted for certain, the Chicago *Tribune* concluded, if Wade were not the man who would replace him. Before the vote, Fessenden called on the conservative Senator George F. Edmunds and virtually told him as much.[17]

These fears must be placed in perspective. When Republicans spoke fearfully of the calamity of a Wade administration, they referred to the effect his policies might have not only on the country but on the party. Naturally, free traders believed high tariffs hurt the nation, and hard-money men believed the financial strength of the United States required a commitment to the resumption of specie payments. But these men, and others not strongly committed to one view or the other, knew

15. Garfield to Rhodes, May 7, 1868, quoted in Theodore Clarke Smith, *The Life and Letters of James Abram Garfield,* 2 vols. (New Haven, 1925), I, 425.

16. *Trial of Andrew Johnson,* II, 270–71 (April 28, 1868).

17. Chicago *Tribune,* May 6, 1868, p. 2; George F. Edmunds, "Ex-Senator Edmunds on Reconstruction and Impeachment," *Century Magazine,* LXXXV (April 1913), 863–64. See also the New York *Nation,* May 14, 1868, pp. 382, 384–85; Atkinson to Charles Eliot Norton, February 26, 1868, Norton Mss., Houghton Library, Harvard University; Atkinson to Sumner, February 25, May 1, 1868; Sumner to Lieber, May [?], 1868. Sumner Mss.; Charles A. Trowbridge to Wade, March 30, 1868; Ward to Wade, March 30, 1868, Wade Mss.; Henderson, "Emancipation and Impeachment," 206–7; Horace White to E. B. Washburne, May 1, 1868, Washburne Mss.; Joseph H. Defrees to Richard Thompson, February 24, 1868, Thompson Mss., Indiana State Historical Library, Indiana Division; Timothy Otis Howe to Grace T. Howe, May 9, 1868, Howe Mss.; Garfield to Rhodes, May 20, 1868, quoted in Smith, *Garfield,* I, 425–26; Trefousse, "Ben Wade and the Failure of the Impeachment of Johnson," *Bulletin of the Historical and Philosophical Society of Ohio,* XVIII (October 1960), 241–52.

that one of the strengths of the Republican party was that men of all economic opinions were united on the issues that now divided Republican from Democrat—security for northern and loyal southern interests in Reconstruction. The Republican party could—and did—mute its position on the other issues. So long as Andrew Johnson was president, men of such opposite tariff and financial views as Horace Greeley and Edward Atkinson, William D. Kelley and James A. Garfield, Richard Henry Dana and Benjamin F. Butler could share the same platform and vote the same ticket. But let Ben Wade become president, let high-tariff and soft-money interests begin a campaign to put their views into law, and many believed with Atkinson that "the Republican party would cease to exist." [18] The major political issue would shift from one on which Republicans were united, although with differing degrees of commitment, to one on which they were hopelessly divided. This was the real apprehension of the conservatives. It was this to which Fessenden referred when he wrote that "the result is to be disastrous any way."

Chief Justice Chase too was deeply involved in politics. As soon as he showed his position on the "Senate as court" question, Democrats began to eye him as a possible presidential candidate, especially if impeachment succeeded. By April 19, he had informed Alexander Long, an extreme Peace Democrat from Ohio, that he would not refuse a Democratic nomination if that party accepted universal suffrage. They would make the issue against Republicans on amnesty for all former Rebels, an end to military protection for southern loyalists, and opposition to confiscation.[19] Despite his professed conviction that the impeachment proceedings should progress under rules similar to those pertaining to trials in court, he privately informed correspondents and wavering senators of his belief that the articles

18. Atkinson to Sumner, March 4, 1868, Sumner Mss.
19. Chase to Long, April 19, 1868, quoted in Robert B. Warden, *An Account of the Private Life and Public Services of Salmon P. Chase* (Cincinnati, 1874), 686–87.

did not warrant conviction, a grave violation of judicial ethics.[20]

Finally, neither the President nor his counsel were willing to rely solely on the strength of legal arguments for acquittal. In choosing his lawyers, Johnson carefully included conservative Republicans Benjamin R. Curtis and William M. Evarts, who in 1867 had become one of Grant's earliest supporters for the presidency, and War Democrats William S. Groesbeck and Thomas A. R. Nelson, as well as his former attorney general, Henry Stanbery. The President's advisers urged him to appeal to the moderate Republicans, to make the case as much as possible an "inter-Republican issue." [21]

But most important were the assurances the President gave of good behavior for the rest of his term.[22] House conservatives had been impelled to vote for Johnson's impeachment because they were convinced that the removal of Stanton in apparent violation of law was merely the first step in a program to overthrow the Reconstruction Acts. Despite their desire to decide Johnson's guilt or innocence on legal points alone, conservative Republicans (Welles later named Fessenden and Grimes) informed Evarts that they would feel freer to vote against conviction of the President if they were assured he did not intend to retaliate against Republicans or interfere in Reconstruction. They suggested that the President name the conservative military commander of Virginia, John M. Schofield, secretary of war. He had enforced the Reconstruction Acts, but in such a

20. Chase to Gerritt Smith, April 19, 1868; Chase to Henry B. Anthony, May 22, 1868, in *ibid.,* 686–87 and 699n, respectively; Jerome Mushkat, ed., "The Impeachment of Andrew Johnson: A Contemporary View," New York *History,* XLVIII (July 1967), 280.

21. Gaillard Hunt, "The President's Defense: His Side of the Case as Told by His Correspondence," *Century Magazine,* LXXXV (January 1913), 430–33; Thomas Ewing, Sr., to Johnson, March 1, 1868, Johnson Mss.

22. George P. Brockway has thoroughly discussed Johnson's extralegal efforts to persuade wavering Republican senators to vote against conviction in an unpublished study, "Political Deals That Saved Andrew Johnson." I am indebted to Mr. Brockway for much of the following information.

way as to aid conservative Republicans against radicals. His presence in the War Department would reassure the people and the party. Evarts approached Schofield on Johnson's behalf and asked him to accept the office. The general agreed, on the condition that the President would enforce the Reconstruction laws. On April 23, Johnson prepared the nomination, and on April 24 sent it in to the Senate, where, Johnson's secretary, who had delivered the message, wrote, "I could see it created considerable interest." [23]

On May 4, Senator Edmund G. Ross, another who would vote for acquittal, informed acting Attorney General Orville H. Browning that he hoped the President would demonstrate his good intentions by forwarding to the Senate the new constitutions Arkansas and South Carolina had adopted under the Reconstruction laws. Browning and Stanbery urged the President to send the constitutions in, over the objections of the uncompromising Welles, and Johnson did so on May 5.[24] In a final maneuver, Reverdy Johnson arranged a meeting between Grimes and the President. Grimes told the President that senators inclined to acquit him were wavering out of fear of what Johnson might do after impeachment failed. Johnson assured him he intended to do nothing in violation of the law or the Constitution, and Grimes, satisfied, relayed the message to other conservatives.[25]

Perhaps even more important than the President's assurances to conservative Republicans was the actual cessation of

23. James Lee McDonough and William T. Alderson, eds., "Republican Politics and the Impeachment of Andrew Johnson," *East Tennessee Historical Quarterly*, XXVI (Summer 1967), 177–83; Moore notes, April 23, 24, May 1, 1868, Johnson Mss.; Welles, *Diary*, III, 364–65 (May 20, 1868), 409–10 (July 21, 1868).

24. Browning, *Diary*, II, 195 (May 5, 1868); Richardson, ed., *Messages and Papers of the Presidents*, VI, 632.

25. Samuel Sullivan Cox, *Union—Disunion—Reunion: Three Decades of Federal Legislation, 1855 to 1885* (Providence, 1886), 592–94. By May 14, Henderson assured Republican representatives that Johnson intended to enforce the Reconstruction laws and even change his cabinet to give Republicans control. *House Report No. 75*, 40th Congress, 2nd Session, 18.

his interference while impeachment progressed. In explaining "What Has Happened During the Impeachment Trial," the Chicago *Tribune* wrote simply, "Andrew Johnson has been a changed man. The country has been at peace. The great obstruction to the law has been virtually suspended; the President . . . has been on his good behavior." [26] The President's new docility enabled Republicans to recoup some of their losses in the South. In six of the unreconstructed states, Republicans were able to win ratification of the new constitutions framed under the Reconstruction laws, although by narrow margins in several. In Alabama, where the removal of General Swayne proved critical, Republicans failed to win the absolute majority of registered voters required to ratify the new constitutions. The opposition had refused to vote at all. But Congress decided to repeal the absolute-majority requirement to enable it to restore Alabama nonetheless. By the time senators voted on impeachment, it was clear that only Virginia, Mississippi, and Texas would remain unrestored and liable to presidential interference. It is remarkable how quickly the sense of crisis that gripped the capital a few months earlier eased.

To a large extent, therefore, impeachment had succeeded in its primary goal: to safeguard Reconstruction from presidential obstruction. Only after the political exigencies that in part had motivated impeachment were removed did the seven "recusant" Republicans vote to acquit the President.

All this evidence of politicking during the impeachment proceedings did not mean that the seven "recreants" (the New York *Tribune*'s term) voted to acquit Johnson solely for political reasons or out of personal dislike for the radicals. Far from it. The recusants shared a real distaste for the political nature of the proceedings in which they were involved. Unlike a few radicals, they never suggested that impeachment might be primarily a political proceeding. They were revolted at every political interference in the impeachment. They voted consistently to expand the role of the Chief Justice—the one non-elected of-

26. Chicago *Tribune,* May 14, 1868, p. 2.

ficer sitting with the Senate. They voted in favor of considering the Senate a "court" during impeachment and continually referred to it as such. What the evidence does demonstrate was the futility of trying to separate politics from law in the impeachment proceedings. As the defense counsel had pointed out, this was not the trial of a petty thief but of the President of the United States, a man whose office was political, whose duties were political, who had the support of a political party and millions of its adherents. From no court in the country could political considerations have been eliminated, much less the Senate, a political body with political functions, elected through the political process. Yet, as the Boston *Daily Advertiser* pointed out, "[T]he Constitution commits the trial of the President to a political body of that description; . . . it requires the Senators to form their opinions upon questions of policy in order to act as legislators, . . . and . . . it requires them afterwards, upon an impeachment by the House, to sit in judgment upon the very matters . . . which they may have had occasion to consider as legislators." [27] The senators—and historians—who wanted the President judged purely on legal principles and by legal procedures wanted the impossible.

Moreover, there is a certain naïveté in the assumption, which many historians seem to make, that if all political influences had been removed from impeachment and only legal principles consulted, all the senators would have reached the same conclusion, presumably acquittal. A case is seldom that clear-cut, and the impeachment case was among the foggiest ever pleaded, for it turned largely on the construction of a law the language of which had been purposely obfuscated to satisfy the demands of both the Senate and the House without appearing to require a concession by either. Of the six opinions filed by the seven recusant senators, five of them turned on the disputed point—whether Secretary of War Stanton had been covered by the Tenure of Office Act. They concluded that the act did

27. Boston *Daily Advertiser,* January 22, 1867 p. 2. The *Advertiser* made these observations when the impeachment question first arose, in January 1867.

not protect him from removal without the Senate's consent. Nearly every senator who voted to convict concluded the opposite.

In almost every legal case there is enough leeway for the judge to decide it according to the dictates of his concept of justice, his beliefs, and his attitudes. In the impeachment there was more leeway than in most, and various considerations led the seven recusants in a different direction from their colleagues. But one should not assume that these were the only honest men, that the thirty-five Republicans who voted to convict the President had not wrestled with the legal principles involved in the case with as much diligence as those who acquitted him.

Such an interpretation overlooks the fact that more than half of the Republicans in the House who voted to impeach the President had refused to do so earlier, when he was charged with crimes of a manifestly political nature. Eminent conservative lawyers in the House, including Bingham, James F. Wilson, Luke Poland, Garfield, and Blaine, had resisted all attempts to make the impeachment a political question. They had voted to impeach Johnson only when satisfied that he was guilty of a criminal violation of a congressional statute.

Many senators who finally voted to convict the President were motivated by the same desire for impartial justice as historians and partisans ascribed only to the recusants. George F. Edmunds, the highly respected constitutional lawyer from Vermont, for example, had been the *only* Republican senator to vote against the resolution of February 21 that declared the sense of the Senate to be that the President had acted contrary to law in removing Stanton. Yet he decided Johnson was guilty, and later expressed his conviction that had Wade not been president pro tem of the Senate, Fessenden and others certainly would have reached the same conclusion.[28] Six senators who voted to convict Johnson voted with the acquitters on questions pertaining to the Senate's status as a court during

28. *Senate Executive Journal,* XVI, 171 (February 21, 1868); Edmunds, "Ex-Senator Edmunds on Reconstruction," 863–64.

impeachment and the related issues of the proper role of the Chief Justice (see Chart 6). The senators in Group 2 of the main scale of Chart 6 differed from those in Group 1—all of whom but Henry B. Anthony voted for acquittal—primarily on a *legal* issue: the relevance of testimony showing that Johnson intended only to force a test of the constitutionality of the Tenure of Office Act before the courts.[29] Those who believed it was relevant—that such an intent could exculpate the President— voted to acquit him, with the exception of Anthony. Those who did not, voted to convict.[30]

Furthermore, these six senators—and several others— quickly reversed themselves and voted to admit this evidence despite their first impression, deciding to allow the defense the widest range of freedom. Here they demonstrated their true commitment to full and fair trial. Despite their conviction that Johnson's intention to raise a court case, even if proven, could not vitiate his guilt, they allowed the President's counsel to present evidence on the subject, evidence that could only bolster the President's case and weaken the managers' before the nation.

Contemporaries recognized most senators' commitment to impartial justice. Those who confidently expected conviction did so because they were certain of the President's guilt. And the violent reaction against the Republicans who acquitted him must be understood as the reaction of men who believed the President so patently guilty that they could not conceive of any impartial judge coming to a contrary conclusion unless influenced by extraneous and corrupt considerations.

Those who were not convinced of the President's guilt— with the exception of men like the myopic Welles, who did not comprehend the differences among Republicans—also believed

29. The six were Anthony, Edmunds, Frelinghuysen, Sherman, Sprague, and Willey.
30. Senator Waitman T. Willey often voted with the acquitters on this question. Significantly, Henderson later informed the great historian, William A. Dunning, that Willey had pledged to vote for acquittal if his vote was needed. Dunning, *Reconstruction, Political and Economic, 1865–1877* (New York and London, 1907), 107.

most senators would judge fairly. The New York *Herald*'s
Washington correspondent counted eleven Republicans certain
to acquit the President and two more as doubtful. Grimes, the
first Republican to decide for acquittal, wrote before the trial
began, "About a dozen men are determined to convict, about
the same number are determined to acquit, and the balance
intend to hear the evidence and weigh the law before they
pronounce judgment." [31]

Historians should view the trial of impeachment for what
it was: not as an attempt by a violent majority to remove an innocent president for partisan purposes but as one of the great
legal cases of history, in which American politicians demonstrated the strength of the nation's democratic institutions by
attempting to do what no one could justifiably expect them to
do—to give a political officer a full and fair trial in a time of
political crisis.

Despite the political crisis that gave birth to the impeachment, despite the political rewards and penalties resting on its
success or failure, legal considerations determined the votes of
the critical middle group of senators whose decision would
either convict or acquit the President. There were numerous
minor elements in the House's case for impeachment, and a
complete analysis of them would require a longer monograph
than I have undertaken here. Nonetheless, that is a job that
needs doing. The only detailed study of the trial, DeWitt's
Impeachment and Trial of Andrew Johnson, is primarily a
narrative account that draws superficial conclusions about the
nature of the charges and defense and is not marked by a real
consideration of the questions involved. Here only the major
points may be discussed.

There were four main thrusts to the House's charges, only

---

31. New York *Herald,* March 2, 1868, p. 5; Grimes to H. W.
Starr, March 6, 1868, quoted in Salter, *Life of James W. Grimes,* 336;
Hiram Ketchum to William M. Evarts, March 24, 1868, Evarts Mss.,
Library of Congress; Thomas Ewing, Sr., to Hugh Ewing, April 15,
1868, Hugh Ewing Mss., Ohio Historical Society Library.

three of which played important roles in the trial. First, the President had violated the Tenure of Office Act by issuing orders to replace Stanton and appoint General Lorenzo Thomas secretary of war ad interim after the Senate had refused its consent to Stanton's removal. Second, even if the Tenure of Office Act were not applicable, the President had no authority to issue orders to remove an officer and name a replacement while the Senate was in session. The articles embraced several accusations subordinate to these two major charges—charges of conspiracy to violate the law by force, by threat, and by intimidation, made in different forms and involving slightly different points. The third major accusation, embodied in the eleventh article of impeachment, charged the President with devising means to prevent the execution of the Reconstruction laws and the law requiring the issuance of all military orders through the General of the Army, as well as the Tenure of Office Act. Although the article seemed on the surface to charge an indictable crime, as interpreted by the managers, particularly Boutwell, it became essentially a political article embodying not only the President's indictable violations of law but all the things he had done to prevent a final settlement of the war issues, to perpetuate chaos in the South, and to resist the will of Congress.[32] The fourth charge, embodied in the tenth article of impeachment (Butler's article)—that the President had attempted to bring Congress into ridicule and disrepute—was only slightly emphasized by the managers.

The President's counsel delivered their formal answer on March 23, as the Senate required, but it was not until they opened the case for the defense that it became clear in all its ramifications.

Once again opponents argued the nature of an impeachable offense. House managers Butler and Logan once more argued the political nature of impeachment. An impeachable offense, Butler insisted, was "one in its nature or consequences subversive of some fundamental or essential principle of govern-

32. See Boutwell's argument in *Trial of Andrew Johnson,* II, 109–17 (April 23, 1868).

ment, or highly prejudicial to the public interest, and this may consist of a violation of the Constitution, of law, of an official oath, or of duty, by an act committed or omitted, or, without violating a positive law, by the abuse of discretionary powers from improper motives, or for any improper purpose." [33] If the Senate accepted this definition, the House's case would be strengthened immeasurably. Not only would it buttress the eleventh article, which charged both indictable and nonindictable offenses, but it meant that the managers need not prove an actual violation of the Tenure of Office Act. Even if he had the legal right to remove Stanton, the President was liable to impeachment if he did so for improper purposes. [34]

The President's counsel, of course, denied the managers' contention and in their turn went as far as they could in the opposite direction. Nelson argued that a "high crime or misdemeanor" meant more than merely an infraction of law. The words referred to serious crimes punishable by both fine and imprisonment. Furthermore, he suggested that the terms referred only to acts that were crimes and misdemeanors when the Constitution was adopted, not to those enacted by statute later. This was the most extreme position taken by any of the President's counsel. [35] Evarts and Stanbery insisted that impeachment lay not for any indictable violation of law but only for a criminal act directly subversive of fundamental principles of government or the public interest. Under this restricted interpretation, counsel could argue that the removal of Stanton, even if it violated the law, did not warrant the President's removal. [36] Only Groesbeck limited himself to the position taken by the anti-impeachers in December 1867—that impeachment

33. *Ibid.,* I, 88 (March 30, 1868), italics omitted.
34. *Ibid.,* 94–95 (March 30, 1868). The managers' arguments on the definition of an impeachable crime in *ibid.,* 88–89, 94–95, 123–47 (March 30, 1868, Butler); *ibid.,* II, 19–23 (April 22, 1868, Logan).
35. *Ibid.,* 139–40 (April 23, 1868).
36. *Ibid.,* 286–89 (April 29, 1868). Stanbery argued that the alleged violation was merely one of form, of a law designed merely to regulate the mode of executive administration, not an act that of itself was a crime. *Ibid.,* 364 (May 2, 1868).

must be based on an indictable crime—without trying to restrict it further.[37]

If more than one-third of the Senate accepted Nelson's
view or that propounded by Evarts and Stanbery on the nature
of impeachable offenses, Johnson must have been acquitted.
If over two-thirds accepted the interpretation of Butler and
Logan, then there could be no doubt of his conviction. But if
enough senators to determine the case beleved an official became
liable to impeachment only for violation of law, then the case
would turn on the main issues—the removal of Stanton and the
appointment of Thomas ad interim.

The first task facing Johnson's defense counsel was to show
that the President could not be convicted for issuing his order
to remove Stanton after the Senate had refused its consent
under the Tenure of Office Act. This would be no easy job.
The facts were clear: the President had issued the order. The
counsel would have to vitiate his guilt somehow, despite his
act.

Johnson's counsel's first line of defense was that the Tenure
of Office Act itself was unconstitutional and therefore null.
Johnson had then violated no law in trying to remove Stanton.
But the Senate had already registered its conviction that the
law was constitutional by passing it over the President's veto.
The defense could have had slight confidence in this tack. They
next insisted that Johnson had not in fact removed Stanton.
"There is not a judge or a lawyer in this Senate who does not
know that in every law-book which has been written in 200
years a distinction is taken between a crime and an attempt to
commit a crime," Nelson argued. "That there was an attempt
to remove there is no sort of question; . . . [but] how is it that
[Johnson] can be found guilty of removing Mr. Stanton from
his office . . . when there was no removal at all?" [38]

This technical objection underlined the importance of the

37. *Ibid.*, 190 (April 25, 1868).
38. *Ibid.*, 153 (April 24, 1868); Curtis, *ibid.,* I, 383 (April 9,
1868); Stanbery, *ibid.,* II, 363–64, 370–71 (May 2, 1868).

question of the nature of impeachment and the Senate's status while trying it. For, as Butler acknowledged, if the Senate sitting in judgment on trial of impeachment was a court, then all the rules and procedures and technicalities of the common law applied to its proceedings. The managers urged a more relaxed rule. They agreed, in Logan's words, "that in determining this general issue senators must consider the sufficiency or insufficiency in law or in fact of every article of accusation. But the insufficiency which they are to consider is not the technical insufficiency by which indictments are measured. No mere insufficiency of statement—no mere want of precision— no mere lack of relative averments—no mere absence of legal verbiage, can inure to the benefit of the accused. The insufficiency which will avail him must be such an entire want of substance as takes all soul and body from the charge and leaves it nothing but a shadow." [39]

The President's counsel naturally argued in the opposite vein, pointing to precedents for their position and warning of the consequences of accepting the managers' position. If the Senate swerved from a purely judicial proceeding, Evarts insisted, then its conviction would be no more than a bill of attainder—"a proceeding by the legislature, as a legislature, to enact crime, sentence, punishment, all in one." [40]

This controversy helps to put the opposing interpretations of impeachment in perspective and illustrates the inherent problems involved. What Evarts objected to was the implication he found in the managers' arguments that the Senate was not bound to observe the rules of law. In fact, the managers did more than merely imply this doctrine—they stated it openly. "You are a law unto yourselves, bound only by the natural principles of equity and justice . . . ," Butler insisted.[41] In Evarts's opinion, this meant that the House and Senate, when-

39. Butler, *ibid.,* I, 89–90 (March 30, 1868); Logan, *ibid.,* II, 18 (April 22, 1868); Bingham, *ibid.,* I, 24 (March 13, 1868).
40. *Ibid.,* II, 276–80 (April 28, 1868); quoted material on 278.
41. *Ibid.,* I, 90 (March 30, 1868).

ever the support of two-thirds of their members could be mustered, might impeach and remove any government officer without averring any legal grounds at all. This would destroy the checks and balances that maintained the stability of the three branches of the national government. Certainly the fears had merit.

But the managers also felt impelled by weighty considerations. The traditional safeguards of the common law were intended to afford every possible protection to the innocent. In the abstract, society decided that its interests were best served by risking the escape of the guilty in order more certainly to protect the rights and liberty of the innocent. It is not at all certain that the same decision should obtain in cases of impeachment, where the person accused of wrongdoing may hold tremendous power over society itself, and where conviction means no more than removal from office. The managers took this view of the case. "[I]t is a question only of official delinquency, involving, however, the life of a great state, and with it the liberties of a great people," Williams maintained. "[I]n cases such as this, the safety of the people, which is the supreme law, is the true rule and the only rule that ought to govern." [42]

The question of the President's liability for the mere attempt to commit a crime demonstrates the strength of the managers' argument. Should the President of the United States be allowed to retain his office after attempting to commit a crime, merely because he did not succeed? Is not the fact that a man in such a responsible and powerful position attempted to violate the law reason to fear for the safety of the nation and reason enough to take steps to avert the danger? Should wrongdoers in high office retain the capability for evil because of the technical insufficiency of charges against them? The House managers and President's counsel arrived at opposing conclusions. There were strengths and weaknesses in each.

The third line of defense was that Stanton was not covered by the Tenure of Office Act at all. The President's counsel

42. *Ibid.,* II, 259, 260 (April 28, 1868).

pointed, of course, to the disputed proviso that department heads should hold office during the term of the president who appointed them and one month thereafter unless removed with the advice and consent of the Senate. They argued that Stanton's protected term ran only through Lincoln's first term and one month thereafter, ending under the law on April 4, 1865. To this the managers answered simply that the law protected department heads not during the presidential term when appointed but "during the term of the President by whom they may have been appointed." The language had been framed in that way to cover any term that the appointing president might hold. The President's counsel then argued that if this were true, then Stanton's protected term ended one month after the death of the president who had appointed him, Lincoln, and that since then he had been holding office at the pleasure of President Johnson under the 1789 law that created the War Department. The managers answered that Johnson had no term. The Constitution sets the president's term at four years; if the president does not complete that term, "the powers and duties of the said office . . . shall devolve on the Vice-President" (the Constitution's words), not the term. President Johnson was completing President Lincoln's term, and Stanton was protected until one month after it ended: April 4, 1869.

The President's lawyers denied this interpretation. The president's term was not absolute, but conditional, they insisted. It lasted, in effect, only if he lasted. If he resigned, died, or was removed, his term ended and his replacement entered upon a term of his own. If this were not the case, they asked, then when did the protected term of department heads appointed by Johnson cease? When was one month after the term of the president who appointed them if that president had no term? There seems to have been no right or wrong answer to this dispute. The United States Constitution defines the president's term at four years and does not indicate that the president's term devolves upon his successor with the powers and duties of the office. On the other hand, the provisions of the Tenure of Office Act cited by the President's counsel certainly did not make much sense if Johnson had no term. Once again, there was leeway for each senator to decide this question as he saw fit.[43]

The managers presented two further arguments on the point. The managers and the President's counsel had agreed that the Tenure of Office Act forbade the removal of any government official until his replacement was confirmed by the Senate. If nothing had been added, Stanton clearly would have been covered. All agreed to that. But the law had provided for an exception to the rule: department heads would have a fixed term—the term of the president who had appointed them and one month thereafter. But for that exception, the House managers insisted, every United States officer would be protected by the Tenure of Office Act. If Stanton's term had ended, as the defense argued, one month after the close of Lincoln's first term or one month after his death, then Stanton no longer fitted into the exception. In that case, said the impeachers, he must come under the operation of the general provisions of the bill. Like all officeholders not covered by the exception, Stanton could not be removed until the Senate confirmed a successor. He was not serving at the pleasure of the President, under the law of 1789, but until the Senate confirmed a successor, under the law of 1867. Johnson's counsel answered that the *office* of secretary of war, not Stanton himself, had been excepted by the provision from the operation of the bill. The proviso gave that *office* a fixed term and nowhere else was it mentioned. Bingham pointed out, however, that the general provisions of the law covered "every person holding any civil office" who had been confirmed by the Senate "except as herein otherwise provided." If Stanton were no longer among those excepted, then he certainly fitted into the category of "every person holding any civil office."

On the face of it, the managers had the better of the argu-

43. Boutwell, *ibid.*, 93–94 (April 22, 1868); Logan, *ibid.*, 48–49 (April 22, 1868); Stevens, *ibid.*, 221–22 (April 27, 1868); Bingham *ibid.*, 452 (May 5, 1868); Curtis, *ibid.*, I, 379–82 (April 9, 1868); Groesbeck, *ibid.*, II, 194–95 (April 25, 1868); Stanbery, *ibid.*, 366–70 (May 2, 1868).

ment, but Evarts weakened their position by pointing out that if their interpretation was correct, then Stanton could never in the future be removed without the Senate's consent, even when a new president took office. Yet the Senate had insisted upon excepting department heads from the general operation of the bill, precisely to allow incoming presidents freedom of action.[44] Nonetheless, the law was certainly unclear; again senators would have to decide the proper construction for themselves.

Finally, the managers argued that Johnson himself had acknowledged that the law protected Stanton when he suspended him according to its provisions in August 1867, and then sent in reasons for that suspension as the law required when Congress met. The President, the managers argued, was estopped from now contending that the act did not cover Stanton after all.[45] Johnson's lawyers attacked this argument vigorously. Estoppel related to facts, they insisted, not matters of law. A party's deeds could not prevent the judge from construing the law in a civil court, and it could not prevent senators from construing the law in deciding the impeachment. Moreover, the rule applied not to criminal cases but to civil actions, where the opposing party put reliance on the estopped party's words or behavior. "That the President of the United States should be impeached and removed from office, not by reason of the truth of his case, but because he is estopped from telling it, would be a spectacle for gods and men," Curtis declaimed. "Undoubtedly it would have a place in history which it is not necessary for me to attempt to foreshadow." [46] But Stevens retorted with a different interpretation. "The gentleman treats lightly the question of *estoppel;* and yet really nothing is more powerful, for it is an argument by the party against himself . . . ." [47]

44. Stevens, *ibid.,* 223–24 (April 27, 1868); Williams, *ibid.,* 237 (April 27, 1868); Bingham, *ibid.,* 450 (May 5, 1868); Evarts, *ibid.,* 350–51 (May 1, 1868).
45. "Estoppel" is a legal term. It arises when a party to an action by word or deed accepts the truth of a certain set of facts and then later denies that truth. The law "estops" him from so doing.
46. Curtis, *ibid.,* I, 394 (April 9, 1868).
47. *Ibid.,* II, 22 (April 27, 1868). Also Butler, *ibid.,* I, 103–4 (March 30, 1868).

Still another point to be weighed and decided by the senators individually.

Concluding arguments on the construction of the law, the President's counsel posed an argument that showed how they had won their reputations as among the most astute legal practitioners in the United States. They argued that even if the President's interpretation were wrong, even if Stanton was in fact protected by the law's terms, Johnson's only crime was to have made a mistake. It was a brilliant maneuver. All their arguments as to whether Stanton was covered had been aimed not so much at convincing the Senate that he was not, as at convincing them that a reasonable man might believe he was not.

Once again the question of the nature of impeachment loomed in importance. If the process could be based only on a criminal violation of statute, then two elements were necessary: a guilty act and a guilty intent. Defense counsel had already argued that the President had not succeeded in committing the act. Now they argued that he had no criminal intent.[48] There was no question that the charges relating to the removal of Stanton in violation of the Tenure of Office Act and the appointment of Thomas contrary to its provisions would fall if Johnson's lawyers could prove that the President had not believed Stanton was covered. But that was the rub. This was a matter of fact, an assertion to be proved.

Johnson's defenders pointed to the brief phrase in the President's message to the Senate giving the reasons for Stanton's suspension, in which Johnson mentioned that at least one cabinet member had suggested that Lincoln's appointees were not covered under the bill. This evidence was weakened, however, by the immediately following sentence: "I do not remember that the point was distinctly decided . . . ."[49]

Counsel for the President also proposed to submit the message Johnson had sent to the Senate in response to the resolu-

48. Curtis, *ibid.,* 378 (April 9, 1868); Groesbeck, *ibid.,* II, 192–93, 197 (April 25, 1868); Stanbery, *ibid.,* 372–73 (May 2, 1868).
49. Richardson, ed., *Messages and Papers of the Presidents,* VI, 587–88.

tion it had passed condemning the attempted removal of Stanton and the appointment of Thomas as a violation of law. In that message, prepared on February 22, Johnson had insisted that he had always believed that Stanton was not covered by the Tenure of Office Act, and had justified his removal under that construction.[50] The managers objected immediately. The President had not sent that message until after the House Reconstruction Committee had reported the articles of impeachment. It was no more, Bingham insisted, "than a volunteer declaration of the criminal, after the fact, in his own behalf[.]" [51] Chief Justice Chase ruled the evidence inadmissible.[52]

Finally, the defense offered to prove that the subject had come up when the cabinet discussed the bill after its passage. They asked Welles to testify to that effect, but again the managers objected. Other questions confused the issue, and the senators refused to admit the testimony, 22 to 26. But eleven Republicans, including the seven recusants, Sherman, Anthony, Sprague, and Waitman T. Willey, voted to overrule the managers' objections.[53]

In a second argument that Johnson lacked criminal intent, his counsel suggested that he could, without intending to commit a crime, violate or refuse to enforce a law he believed unconstitutional. In their broadest assertions, Johnson's counsel argued that the president has a right independent of Congress or the Supreme Court to decide the constitutionality of the laws.

50. *Ibid.,* VI, 622–27, at 622–25.
51. *Trial of Andrew Johnson,* I, 540 (April 15, 1868). At this time accused criminals were not allowed to testify on their own behalf in the courts of most jurisdictions, including those of the United States. The movement to change this, begun in Maine, was only then gaining momentum.
52. The entire discussion is in *ibid.,* 437–45 (April 15, 1868).
53. *Ibid.,* 693–97 (April 18, 1868). The issue was not clear because at the time Welles offered to testify the defense counsel were pursuing the argument that Stanton had indicated in the cabinet that he did not believe himself covered by the bill. They wanted to show this in order to argue that Johnson had not intended to use force in removing him, believing he would step down without resistance. The senators considered this an invalid defense and therefore voted to sustain the managers' objections.

If he believes an enactment to violate the Constitution, his oath binds him not to enforce it. "A private individual, if he violates the laws of the land, is amenable for their violation . . . ," Nelson argued, "but the President of the United States, having the executive power invested in him by the Constitution, has the right to exercise his best judgment in the situation in which he is placed, and if he exercises that judgment honestly and faithfully, not from corrupt motives, then his action cannot be reviewed by Congress or by any other tribunal than the tribunal of the people in the presidential election . . . ."

"How can it be said that he had any wrongful or unlawful intent when the Constitution gave him the power to judge for himself in reference to the particular act?" he concluded.[54]

The managers quickly pointed out the implications of this argument. "If [the President] . . . has the power to sit in judgment judicially—and I use the word of his advocate—upon the tenure-of-office act of 1867, he has like power to sit in judgment judicially upon every other act of Congress," Bingham argued. Under this interpretation of presidential power, Boutwell warned, "for the purpose of government, his will or opinion is substituted for the action of the law-making power, and the government is no longer a government of laws, but the government of one man." And he added, "This is also true if, when arraigned, he may justify by showing that he has acted upon advice that the law was unconstitutional." Moreover, the requirement of criminal intent did not mean that the President's motives had to be inherently evil. "His offence is that he intentionally violated a law. Knowing its terms and requirements, he disregarded them." [55]

The Senate received an opportunity to vote upon the issue on April 18, when the defense tried to introduce evidence that the entire cabinet advised the President that the Tenure of Of-

54. *Ibid.*, II, 167, 169 (April 24, 1868). Also Stanbery, *ibid.*, 382–83 (May 2, 1868).
55. Bingham, *ibid.*, 407–8 (May 4, 1868); Boutwell, *ibid.*, 72–75 (April 22, 1868), quoted material on 72. Also Stevens, *ibid.*, 229 (April 27, 1868); Williams, *ibid.*, 256 (April 27, 1868).

fice Act was unconstitutional when it first came before them in
February 1867. After a full discussion by both managers and
counsel, the Senate refused to admit the evidence, 20 to 29.
But over a third of the senators had indicated their conviction
that the evidence had been relevant. Among that number were
nine Republicans, including the seven who would vote not
guilty.[56]

Winning even more support were Curtis's and Groesbeck's
more limited arguments on the subject. Taking ground similar
to that of John Norton Pomeroy in his treatise on the Constitution, Curtis conceded that the President ordinarily could
not refuse to enforce a congressional enactment. The President
"asserts no such power," Curtis insisted. "He has no such idea of
his duty." But under certain circumstances the President may
disobey or refuse to enforce a law. In particular, he might do
so "when . . . a question arises whether a particular law has
cut off power confided into him by the people, through the
Constitution, and he alone can raise that question . . . ."
Even in this case, Curtis acknowledged, the President could not
determine for himself whether or not to execute the law. He
could only, by refusing once, bring the case before the Supreme
Court to enable it to decide who is right, he or Congress. In
raising such a case, the President manifested no criminal intent
and therefore could not be removed.[57]

But Curtis's argument had one great weakness. If senators
conceded that the President could protect his prerogatives in
the way Curtis indicated, they must still be convinced that the
offending law actually threatened those prerogatives. The Senate, by passing the Tenure of Office Act, had already decided
that an absolute right of removal was not a presidential prerogative, and this substantially diminished the power of Curtis's
argument. Groesbeck remedied the flaw by broadening
slightly the circumstances under which the president could
challenge a law to include those doubtful cases in which a congressional enactment contradicts long-standing constitutional

56. *Ibid.,* I, 676–79 (April 17, 1868), 680–93 (April 18, 1868).
57. *Ibid.,* 386–88 (April 9, 1868).

doctrine. This fitted the case at hand perfectly. Even if the removal power did not reside solely in the president, constitutional theorists had long held that it did. The Tenure of Office Act denied that well-established doctrine. The president could challenge it.[58]

The managers tried their best to ignore the difference between the broad and narrow interpretations of the president's right to resist the law, opposing the narrow view with the same arguments as they did the broad. Bingham argued that the president might interpret any law as somehow restricting the powers of his office and, with an effective flourish, quoted Curtis's own work, *Executive Power*, in which the President's defender had insisted that "the powers of the President are executive merely. He cannot make a law. He cannot repeal one. He can only execute the laws. He can neither make nor suspend nor alter them." [59] But despite Bingham's efforts, the defense lawyers had opened a wide hole in the prosecution's case. The Senate overruled the managers when they objected to defense testimony that Johnson desired a court test of the law—testimony primarily from General Sherman—on the ground that this was no defense and that, even if it were, Johnson's mere statement to Sherman that this was his intention did not prove that it really was. On the key votes, between twenty-three and fifteen Republicans voted to admit the evidence.[60]

The managers received an even worse setback when the Senate voted to accept testimony that Johnson desired a court test of the law *after* he had removed Stanton and impeachment was already under discussion. "If, after this subject was introduced into the House of Representatives, the President became alarmed at the state of affairs, and concluded that it was best to attempt by some means to secure a decision of the court upon the question of the . . . tenure-of-office act, it cannot avail him in this case," Wilson argued. "We are inquiring as to the intent which controlled and directed the action of the President at

58. *Ibid.*, II, 200–206 (April 25, 1868).
59. *Ibid.*, 411–12 (May 4, 1868).
60. *Ibid.*, I, 515–518, 521 (April 13, 1868).

the time the act was done; and if we succeed in establishing that intent . . . , no subsequent act can interfere with it or remove from him the responsibility which the law places upon him because of the act done." [61] Retreating under the power of this attack, the defense limited their argument as to what the testimony proved, now saying that they intended only to show that Johnson intended no use of force.[62] After this modification in the defense position, the Senate accepted the testimony, overruling repeated objections by the managers, with from fifteen to eighteen Republicans voting in the majority.[63]

But while more than enough senators to acquit Johnson seemed to agree that he should not be removed if he merely intended to challenge the constitutionality of the Tenure of Office Act before the courts, this did not mean that the defense had won its case. They had to prove that this was in fact Johnson's intention. And here was where the real case for estoppel lay. For Johnson had never indicated any intention to challenge the law before the courts until the Senate refused to accede in Stanton's removal. He had suspended Stanton in conformity with the law; he had denominated his successor secretary of war ad interim, clearly implying that he did not consider Stanton's removal final; he had sent his reasons for the suspension to the Senate as the law required. How could he now insist that he had always intended to challenge its constitutionality?

The same considerations constituted a forceful argument for estoppel regarding the President's contention that he did not believe that Stanton was covered by the law. The defense's arguments against estoppel—that it could not prevent the Senate from deciding a point of law—did not apply here. The President's actual intent was a matter of fact, to be determined from the evidence. And all his acts indicated that he had not questioned Stanton's protection under the law.

Second, the two averrals were patently inconsistent. If

61. *Ibid.*, 603 (April 16, 1868).
62. *Ibid.*, 603–4 (April 16, 1868).
63. *Ibid.*, 597–623 (April 16, 1868).

Johnson had wanted to bring the constitutionality of the Tenure of Office Act before the courts for adjudication, how could he have intended to do so by removing an officer to whom he believed the act did not apply? Why did he not instead remove a non-cabinet officer, one to whom the law clearly pertained? He had had nearly a year to do so, and yet he had taken no such action.

Finally, the managers introduced a damning piece of evidence, a letter from Johnson to McCulloch: "In compliance with the requirements of the act entitled 'An act to regulate the tenure of certain civil offices,' you are hereby notified that on the 12th instant [August] Hon. Edwin M. Stanton was suspended from his office as Secretary of War, and General U. S. Grant authorized and empowered to act as Secretary *ad interim*." [64] There can be little doubt, in light of this evidence and other evidence to which the managers had no access, that the "intent" arguments put forward by the defense had no foundation in fact.[65]

After the events leading to impeachment, after a year of presidential obstruction centering upon the Army's role in reconstructing the South, after the President's recent winter offensive, it is difficult to understand how anyone could have accepted at face value the interpretation Johnson's lawyers put on his activities. In explaining why the President had acted in consonance with the requirements of the Tenure of Office Act

64. *Ibid.*, II, 224 (April 27, 1868).
65. According to the notes kept by Johnson's secretary, William Moore, the President consciously rejected the alternative of removing Stanton in August in disregard of the Tenure of Office Act. At the same time, Moore recorded that "it seemed to be well understood that the bill had been passed for the purpose of retaining Mr. Stanton in President Johnson's Cabinet." Moore notes, August 11, 13, 1867, Johnson Mss. Johnson sent his message to the Senate explaining the grounds for Stanton's suspension specifically in compliance with the law. *Ibid.*, December 12, 1867. Shortly before he removed Stanton in February, Johnson expressed to Democrat Jerome B. Stillson his determination to replace Stanton come what may. "He expects to crush his enemies," Stillson wrote S. L. M. Barlow, "and he will." Stillson to Barlow, February 12, 1868, Barlow Mss., Huntington Library.

until February 1868, for instance, Groesbeck told the Senate, "[I]t was an overture from the President . . . to get out of this difficulty, and to conciliate you in the hope you would relieve and let him have a cabinet such as any of you would demand if you were in his place." [66] Given the actual circumstances of Stanton's suspension and the removal of Sheridan and Sickles immediately afterward, Groesbeck's apologia was manifestly false.

Yet it was not easy to disprove the defense counsel's endless affirmations that Johnson had no offensive motives, that he intended no violation of the Reconstruction laws, that he was motivated solely by a desire to preserve intact the powers of the presidency. How could the managers prove all that had happened over a three-year period? How could they prove a feeling, a tension, a universal knowledge that the President and the congressional majority were involved in a death struggle, arrayed in unending hostility? These problems once again put into perspective the question of the Senate's status while trying an impeachment. The managers, insisting that the Senate was not simply a court, urged senators themselves to recall the circumstances in which the alleged crime took place. If they did so, they knew, defense avowals of good faith, honest mistakes, and the like, could not stand.[67]

In arguing the opposite, for the adherence to common-law rules of procedure and standards of evidence, the defense demanded that the managers document all their charges. "[T]he glory and the boast of the English law and of the American Constitution are that we have certain fixed principles of law, fixed principles of evidence that are to guide, to govern, to control in the investigation of causes," Nelson announced. "There sits the judge; there are the jury; here are the witnesses who are called upon to testify; they are not allowed to give in evidence any rumor that may have been afloat in the country; they are compelled to speak of facts within their own knowledge." [68]

66. *Trial of Andrew Johnson,* II, 209 (April 25, 1868).
67. Butler, *ibid.,* I, 121 (March 30, 1868).
68. *Ibid.,* II, 135 (April 23, 1868).

Isolating the violation from its attendant circumstances, the defense counsel ridiculed the seriousness of the crime, an infraction in which "[s]ix cents fine, one day's imprisonment . . . may satisfy the public justice." [69] To counteract these tactics, the managers emphasized the eleventh article, which alleged the violation of the Tenure of Office Act as part of a conspiracy to violate the Reconstruction laws. That set forth the real offense; that put it in context; and that is why the managers and senators felt it was the article on which convicttion was most likely.[70]

The second major point at issue was the President's right, notwithstanding the Tenure of Office Act, to remove an appointee while the Senate was in session and appoint an ad interim replacement. The managers argued that the President could not do this. While the Senate was in session, the only way he could remove an officer was to name another in his place. The incumbent would retain his office until the Senate confirmed his successor. The new appointment and its confirmation worked the removal.[71] To concede the President power to remove an officer and then name an ad interim appointment, which needed no confirmation, nullified the Senate's constitutional power to advise and consent to appointments. Johnson "thus assumes and demands for himself and for all his successors absolute control over the vast and yearly increasing patronage of the government," the managers warned. "If . . . this Senate concede the power arrogated to the President, he is henceforward the government." [72]

Johnson's lawyers answered that the president of the United States possessed an inherent and absolute power of removal. As support, they cited the decision of Congress when it created the executive departments in 1789 to leave the authority to

<hr/>

69. Evarts, *ibid.*, 289 (April 29, 1868).
70. See especially Williams, *ibid.*, 231–34 (April 27, 1868).
71. Boutwell, *ibid.*, 75–77 (April 22, 1868).
72. The first quote is Boutwell's, *ibid.*, 67–68 (April 22, 1868); the second Logan's, *ibid.*, 42 (April 22, 1868).

remove the department heads with the president alone rather than require the Senate's consent, as some congressmen had urged. During that debate, the defense insisted, Congress had fully discussed where the Constitution had vested the removal power and concluded that it lay in the executive department alone.[73] The managers denied that interpretation of the 1789 debate. In the bill creating the Department of State, Boutwell pointed out, the House had stricken language making the head of the department removable by the president. Instead, it substituted detailed prescriptions concerning who should take temporary custody of department property if the president did remove its chief officer. This change, Boutwell argued, left the scope and character of the removal power itself undefined. When Congress, one month later, considered legislation creating the Treasury Department, Boutwell noted, the Senate objected even to this language, striking it and leaving no mention of removal at all. The House insisted on its version, and the Senate, by the casting vote of the Vice-President, receded. "All this shows that the right of removal by the President survived the debate only as a limited and doubtful right at most," Boutwell concluded.[74]

Boutwell's interpretation of the language finally incorporated in these bills was palpably wrong. Contrary to his opinion, the original language had implied that Congress had the power to make such removal provisions as it chose and had simply decided to vest that power in the president alone so far as department heads were concerned. By acknowledging that the president could remove department heads, without specifically granting the power in the bill, the changed language implied that Congress had no power in the premises. Nonetheless, Boutwell's observation that the concession had passed by the narrowest of margins was correct. Moreover, later historical analysis would show that the amended language was passed in the House only after a brilliant parliamentary maneuver that

73. Curtis, *ibid.,* I, 384–85 (April 9, 1868); Groesbeck, *ibid.,* II, 195–96 (April 25, 1868); Stanbery, *ibid.,* 380–82 (May 2, 1868).
74. *Ibid.,* 84–87 (April 22, 1868).

had totally confused the issue. Although his reasons were wrong, Boutwell's statement that the 1789 congressional debates were inconclusive precedents was accurate.[75]

To determine the true scope of the President's power of removal, both sides turned to the actual practice of his predecessors. The managers introduced a list compiled by Secretary of State Seward of all the department heads ever removed while the Senate was in session by means other than the confirmation of a successor. It consisted of one name: Timothy Pickering, removed by President John Adams in 1800. They then introduced a list of all the department heads appointed while the Senate was in session without its advice and consent. That list, giving approximately fifty instances of such appointments, consisted only of men appointed acting secretary or secretary ad interim while the department heads were absent from the capital. Not one had replaced an officer who had been removed.[76]

The President's counsel responded with an immense mass of evidence, consisting of lists from each of the executive departments, ostensibly to prove that removals similar to Stanton's were commonplace, but few examples bore on the question at issue. Besides the Pickering episode, the defense's Treasury Department list disclosed the name of only one man who was dismissed while the Senate was in session apparently (but not certainly) before a replacement was confirmed.[77] The defense offered two lists from the Navy Department. The first disclosed only three instances of dismissals antedating Senate

75. Charles C. Thach, Jr., *The Creation of the Presidency, 1775–1789: A Study in Constitutional History* (Baltimore, 1922), 140–58. Thach says the issue was clear in the Senate, however, where the House language was finally sustained by the vice-presidential casting vote. See also James Hart, *Tenure of Office Under the Constitution: A Study of Law and Public Policy* (Baltimore, 1930), 217–22, and Edward S. Corwin, *The President's Removal Power Under the Constitution* (New York, 1927), 10–23.

76. *Trial of Andrew Johnson,* I, 357–59 (April 4, 1868).

77. The removed Treasury agent was Richard Coe, but there is no indication when his successor was confirmed. I assume Coe was removed independently of the confirmation. *Ibid.,* 560–61 (April 14, 1868).

confirmation of successors. Three Navy agents were involved—
Thomas Eastin, Isaac Henderson, and James S. Chambers—all
accused of defalcation (obviously making their immediate removal necessary). In one of these cases, a successor was nominated the day of the incumbent's removal, but an ad interim
replacement filled the office until his confirmation. The others
could not be checked.[78] The second list ostensibly named thirty
Navy agents removed before the expiration of their four-year
terms. But a tedious search of the *Senate Executive Journal*
discloses that only eight of these removals took place during a
session of the Senate, and of these at most only two had been
removed before the end of their term or by means other than
the confirmation of a successor. The two were Henderson and
Chambers. The other names were included either by mistake or
deliberately to mislead.[79] The list from the Post Office Department was more in point. It disclosed two instances of removals
of Post Office officials during a Senate session by means other
than the confirmation of a successor.[80]

The Interior Department list included all department of-

78. *Ibid.,* 569–72 (April 14, 1868).
79. The list is in *ibid.,* 573 (April 14, 1868). Of the agents claimed
to have been removed during a session of the Senate and before the
expiration of their terms, three were replaced after or at the expiration
of those terms (Amos Binney, James Beatty, and Miles King). See
Senate Executive Journal, III, 419, 424, 442, 445, 469, 473, 531 for
Binney, whose term expired on either February 15 or March 3, 1825.
The Senate refused to confirm his renomination three times. After the
last rejection, President John Quincy Adams dismissed him, on May 6,
1826. Both Beatty and King were refused confirmation for new terms
and left the service at the expiration of the ones they were serving.
Ibid., 635, 645 (Beatty and King). In these cases, Adams renominated
the two men to terms beginning March 3, 1829. The Senate postponed
consideration of the appointments, and when President Andrew Jackson
took office on March 4, he notified the men that he had revoked the
appointments. Three other agents (John Thomas, Charles H. Ladd, and
William Hindman) were removed upon the confirmation of their successors. *Ibid.,* V, 423, 424 (Thomas); VII, 128, 130 (Hindman); 133,
135 (Ladd). Two more cases could not be checked owing to changes
in the format of the *Executive Journal.* They were the removals of
Henderson and Chambers, the same men in the first list. The inac-
curacy of the recounting certainly renders these instances suspect.
80. *Trial of Andrew Johnson,* I, 581–82 (April 14, 1868).

ficers ever removed by presidents, either while the Senate was in session or during recess. A spot check of those removed while the Senate was meeting fails to disclose one case in which officers were removed by means other than the confirmation of a successor.[81]

The second, closely related half of this issue was whether Johnson had authority for naming an ad interim replacement for Stanton after his removal. The President's lawyers cited as his justification a law of 1795:

> In case of vacancy in the office of Secretary of State, the Secretary of the Treasury, or of the Secretary of the Department of War . . . , whereby they cannot perform the duties of their said respective offices, it shall be lawful for the President of the United States . . . to authorize any person or persons, at his discretion, to perform the duties of the said respective offices until a successor be appointed or such vacancy be filled: *Provided,* That no one vacancy shall be supplied, in the manner aforesaid, for a longer term than six months.[82]

The managers pointed to the language, insisting that a "vacancy . . . whereby they cannot perform the duties of their said respective offices" could not refer to vacancies created by removal but only to those that happened naturally in the course of administration—the death of the incumbent, his absence, sickness, or resignation. Furthermore, they argued, the 1795 act was repealed by a new law, passed in 1863 giving the president the same authority to make ad interim appointments "in case of the death, resignation, absence from the seat of government, or sickness of the head of an executive department . . . , whereby they cannot perform the duties of their respective offices . . . ." The case of removal was conspicuously absent from the list.[83]

The defense argued that the 1795 law did apply to vacancies created by removal. Under rules of statutory construction, they insisted, the 1863 law repealed only so much of the 1795 law

81. The Interior Department list is in *ibid.,* 654–60 (April 17, 1868).

82. *U.S. Statutes at Large,* I, 415.

83. *Ibid.,* XII, 656.

as it covered—that is, the cases of death, resignation, sickness, or absence. So far as it related to removal, the 1795 law continued in force. This was a rather weak argument. It pertained, or course, only if the 1795 act *did* authorize ad interim appointments after removal, and a far less strained interpretataion of the 1863 law was that it represented a legislative interpretation of the 1795 law which implied that the law had not covered removals. Finally, the managers pointed out that Johnson had appointed Grant secretary of war ad interim on August 12, 1867, after suspending Stanton. The 1795 law limited the term for which any office could be so filled to six months. Yet Johnson had appointed Thomas secretary ad interim on February 21, 1868, more than six months after the office had become vacant.

From this argument the defense had no escape. If Johnson had suspended Stanton by virtue of his inherent power of removal, as he now insisted, then the vacancy had exceeded the maximum time allowed under the 1795 law. If he changed his ground and argued that he suspended Stanton in consonance with the Tenure of Office Act, then he violated that act by removing Stanton after the Senate refused to agree to his removal. The President's counsel determined to ignore the question completely.[84]

Once again the antagonists turned to the practice of the government to prove their points. The defense again presented long lists of men appointed ad interim under the 1795 law. But of all the names presented, only ten appear to have been in point. Two State Department and two Post Office officials were named ad interim replacements for predecessors removed during a recess of the Senate. Although the Senate was not in session at the time, at least the appointments indicated that on

---

84. Boutwell in *Trial of Andrew Johnson,* II, 89–90 (April 22, 1868); Williams, *ibid.,* 258 (April 27, 1868); Bingham, *ibid.,* 414 (May 2, 1868); Groesbeck, *ibid.,* 210–13 (April 25, 1868); Stanbery, *ibid.,* 385–86 (May 2, 1868). Evarts argued that the Senate did not consider the 1795 law when it passed that of 1863, but this simply depended upon how one interpreted Trumbull's report that "there have been several statutes on the subject." *Ibid.,* 334–35 (April 30, 1868).

these two occasions the 1795 act was construed to apply to vacancies created by removal.[85] Three of the other four ad interim appointees replaced Eastin, Henderson, and Chambers, the Navy agents who had been removed for defalcation. These temporary appointments were made during a session of the Senate and were exactly in point. The Navy Department forwarded one more instance, in which an officer was instructed to assume the duties of yet another fallen Navy agent, pending his resignation. The Post Office Department supplied two more.[86] None of the instances included in the mountains of further evidence offered by the defense appear to have been in point.[87]

85. The two names (John Gardner, appointed September 15, 1839, and August Piexoto, appointed December 7, 1864) were among a list of twenty-one ad interim appointments submitted by the State Department. The others all replaced men who resigned, died, or—in one case—could not meet necessary requirements. *Ibid.,* I, 662–63 (April 17, 1868). The Post Office appointees replaced Samuel F. Marks and [?] Deutzel. *Ibid.,* 581–82 (April 14, 1868).

86. *Ibid.,* 569–72, 581–82 (April 14, 1868). The Post Office cases involved Isaac V. Fowler and Mitchell Steever. Two more ad interim appointees on its list served only while the department head was absent.

87. The defense emphasized the appointment of John Nelson as secretary of state ad interim on February 29, 1844. But the incumbent, A. P. Upshur, had died. *Ibid.,* 557 (April 14, 1868). They also pointed to the ad interim appointment of General Winfield Scott as secretary of war in place of George W. Crawford on July 23, 1850. Crawford had resigned. *Ibid.,* 558 (April 14, 1868). They returned several times to Buchanan's appointment of Joseph Holt as secretary of war ad interim in 1861, replacing John B. Floyd, but Floyd had resigned to join the Rebellion. Curtis, *ibid.,* 385–86 (April 4, 1868); Groesbeck, *ibid.,* II, 211–13 (April 25, 1868). The President's lawyers presented a list of ad interim cabinet appointments on April 14. Of over 150 such appointments listed, only two were for reasons other than the absence or sickness of the incumbent. Incoming President John Quincy Adams named Samuel L. Southard secretary of war ad interim pending the confirmation of his permanent appointee. The incumbent, John C. Calhoun, had resigned to become vice-president. Andrew Jackson appointed Benjamin F. Butler (not the Republican radical) secretary of war ad interim to replace Lewis Cass, who had resigned to become minister to France. So none of the appointees replaced a removed incumbent. *Ibid.,* I, 574–81 (April 14, 1868).

The defense presented a new, even longer list a few moments later. This list offered no explanation of how the vacancy occurred, or whether

It is difficult not to conclude that the President's lawyers presented their massive lists in an effort to obfuscate the weakness of their case. Only fourteen of perhaps a thousand instances of removals and temporary appointments that they presented to the Senate bore on the case, and all but one involved malfeasance in office. Moreover, they presented the evidence in such a way as to bury the facts. Many of the compilations did not indicate whether the removals and appointments listed took place while the Senate was in session or not. The managers and senators were left to compare the dates on the lists with the dates of Senate sessions. Most of the compendia did not indicate how the removals were made, whether by a sort of presidential fiat or by the confirmation of successors; nor did they indicate whether the vacancies that Johnson's predecessors had filled by their ad interim appointments were created by removals or occasioned by other causes. The defense lawyers left it to the managers and senators to sift through this evidence themselves, hoping that the sheer bulk of it would impress them. Only after careful analysis does it become apparent that on this issue the defense fortress was a theatrical prop—externally impressive but without foundation or support.

---

during a session or recess of the Senate. But a second list, offered as a continuation of this one, was more complete. It contained no instance of an ad interim appointment following a removal. It is unlikely that the first did, either. *Ibid.*, 585–88 (April 14, 1868), 590–94 (April 15, 1868).

6

Verdict

AS REPUBLICAN SENATORS voted on the legal issues involved in rejecting and accepting evidence, it became apparent that a large number of them would not vote guilty on all the articles. Many concluded that impeachment lay only for a positive violation of law and dismissed Butler's tenth article, which alleged no such violation. A large number decided that Johnson had never intended to use force to remove Stanton and would therefore vote against Article IX and probably Articles VI and VII as well. The Senate had refused to accept evidence the managers offered to prove Article VIII, and that too would probably fall.[1] Moreover, a number of Republicans had shown signs of accepting the defense argument that the President should not be removed if he violated the Tenure of Office Act only to raise a court case. Combined with Democrats and Johnson Conservatives, these were more than enough to prevent the President's removal. Senator Samuel C. Pomeroy carefully canvassed the Senate and determined that only about twenty-five of the forty-two Republican senators intended to convict on all the articles.[2]

By mid-April, Republicans suspected that impeachment might fail. Senator Joseph S. Fowler clearly signified his intention of voting not guilty, leaving his seat each day as the Senate resolved into a quasi-court to try the impeachment and taking a new place among the Democrats. Grimes, too, freely ac-

1. *Trial of Andrew Johnson,* I, 257–68 (April 2, 1868).
2. Sumner to Edward L. Pierce, July 20, 1868, Sumner Mss.

knowledged his intention to vote against conviction. Four senators were voting to accept all testimony and evidence offered by either side—Ross, William Sprague, Henry B. Anthony, and Sumner. Republicans feared that all but Sumner might vote to acquit. Peter G. Van Winkle, Trumbull, and Fessenden were considered doubtful.[3] As Republican gloom developed, the hopes of Johnson's cabinet and lawyers rose. By May 5, Evarts, Secretary of State Seward, and McCulloch were confident of acquittal, Evarts—who it must be remembered, had been negotiating with conservative Republicans and had arranged Schofield's appointment as secretary of war—being especially certain.[4]

As the trial drew to a close, wavering Republicans urged delay of the final decision. Having won Schofield's appointment as secretary of war, they were now confident they could force the President to appoint a new, Republican cabinet. On May 7, in a closed meeting of the Senate, Fessenden urged the postponement of the final vote to allow him to study the case and especially Bingham's closing argument. Radicals suspected he had motives beyond those he announced and demanded that the Senate open its doors and proceed to a final vote on the impeachment immediately. "[T]his trial of impeachment, after that of Warren Hastings," Sumner complained, "ha[s] occupied more time than any other, more days and a shorter time each day. There ha[s] been postponement after postponement, and it [is] . . . now proposed to postpone the final question . . . ," But his motion to vote immediately was defeated, garnering the support of only sixteen members, and the Senate agreed to delay the final decision until the following week. Overcoming radical objections once more, the Senate decided

3. Colfax to Jonathan Russell Young, April 16, 1868, Young Mss.; Benjamin Perley Poore to William W. Clapp, April 24, 1868, Clapp Mss., Library of Congress; Julian to Mrs. Laura Giddings Julian, May 5, 1868, Julian Mss.
4. Edwards Pierrepont to Stanton, May 3, 1868, Stanton Mss.; Welles, *Diary*, III, 345–46 (May 5, 1868), 349–50 (May 9, 1868); Moore notes, May 1, 3, 6, 1868, Johnson Mss.

to set aside May 11 for closed-door discussion of the articles and delivery of opinions.[5]

On that day, the seriousness of the Republican situation became apparent. Howe and Sherman declared their opinions that the Tenure of Office bill as finally amended did not cover Stanton. Ignoring the managers' argument that in that case Stanton was protected under the law's general provisions, they announced that they would vote not guilty on the first article and all articles that relied on a violation of the Tenure of Office Act. Since Sherman had been the chairman of the conference committee that had framed the amendment, his words carried great weight. Van Winkle, Fowler, Fessenden, and Grimes announced that they would sustain none of the articles, while Trumbull, without finally committing himself, indicated the same. Henderson declared against all but the eleventh. Nonetheless, the well-informed Poore believed Johnson would be convicted on the second article, which alleged that he had violated the law by removing Stanton during a session of the Senate and appointing an ad inteim replacement. Those senators who believed Stanton unprotected by the 1867 law would find Johnson guilty on this, Poore believed. Since the eleventh and third articles included this charge, senators hoped they could muster two-thirds of their number to convict on these also. But the other articles were lost. Of the forty-two Republicans, at least seven would acquit on the seventh and eighth, eight on the first and fifth, nine on the fourth and sixth, ten on the tenth, and twelve on the ninth. And the doubtful senators, Anthony, Ross, Sprague, and Waitman T. Willey, had said nothing at all.[6]

As the vote neared, both sides turned their attention to the

5. Boston *Evening Journal*, May 8, 1868, p. 4; *Trial of Andrew Johnson*, II, 475–79 (May 7, 1868).

6. Boston *Evening Journal*, May 12, 1868, p. 4; Edmund G. Ross, *History of the Impeachment of Andrew Johnson, President of the United States, by the House of Representatives, and His Trial by the Senate, for High Crimes and Misdemeanors in Office, 1868* (Santa Fe, 1896), 131–33.

wavering senators. Grimes won the President's promise not to take drastic action and used it to firm anti-removal sentiment. Chase's daughter Katherine continued to put pressure on her husband, Senator Sprague. Henderson was assured the support of Missouri Democrats in his campaign for reelection to the Senate if the state's Republicans should shunt him aside for voting not guilty. Pro-Johnson lobbyists and politicians touted a proposal to nominate Chase for the presidency in an effort to give conservative Republicans an alternative to the regular party and the Democrats.[7]

Republicans brought political pressure to bear upon the wavering senators. "Great danger to the peace of the country and the Republican cause if impeachment fails," Schenck telegraphed leaders as chairman of the Republican Congressional Campaign Committee. "Send to your Senators before Saturday public opinion by resolutions, letters and delegations." [8] Letters, some of them harsh, poured in upon the recalcitrants. Fessenden's friend, Senator Justin Morrill of Vermont, urged, "[T]he best legal learning of the Senate will sustain the 1st, 2d, & 3d article of Impeachment. My opinion is of no value but with a very close attention to the subject for two months I think there is no doubt about it." Morrill reminded Fessenden that, like himself, he was "[n]ot much in favor of this act nor of Impeachment as original questions, but I must do my duty at all hazards." Finally, he warned his friend of the consequences. "[Y]ou could do nothing which would fulfill the ancient grudge of a certain clique of your foes sooner than a vote on your part in favor of Andrew Johnson." Within six

7. Cox, *Three Decades of Federal Legislation,* 592–94; Thomas Graham Belden and Marva Robins Belden, *So Fell the Angels* (Boston, 1956), 187–94; *House Report No. 75,* 40th Congress, 2nd Session, 1–5, 16–17. Butler argued that the "Chase movement" was really the cover for operations to bribe senators into voting against conviction, but his evidence is scanty, although it is clear a bribe was offered to Senator Pomeroy and that he was very tempted to accept it. *Ibid.,* 8–12; Moore notes, March 18, 1868, Johnson Mss.

8. Schenck to [?], May 12, 1868, Schenck Mss., Rutherford B. Hayes Library.

months, Sumner, Chandler, Wade, and Fessenden's other enemies would drive him into the Johnson camp, Morrill predicted.
But Fessenden would not budge.[9]

To understand the urgency with which Republicans pres-
sured their hesitating colleagues, one must examine the legal
agruments acquittal would endorse. The question of whether the
1867 law covered Stanton was rather unimportant. But at minimum Johnson's lawyers had also argued that the President
could refuse to execute a law he believed unconstitutional if in
his opinion it restricted his rightful powers. Second, they had
argued that he might replace officials appointed by the consent of the Senate and replace them with his own ad interim
appointees without going to the Senate for confirmation. If
these doctrines were sustained, Johnson would be free to remove all Republican officeholders the Senate had forced upon
him through the Tenure of Office Act and replace them with
his own devotees ad interim, with a presidential election only
a few months away. As a practical matter, this would force
government officers to endorse the President and work for the
candidate he favored or face immediate removal.

At worst, the President's lawyers had argued thet he might
violate any statute his cabinet advised him was unconstitutional.
If Johnson acted on that doctrine, he might overthrow the Reconstruction Acts and restore complete authority to his state
governments. Not only would that be disastrous to the rights of
freedmen and southern white loyalists, but in 1869 Congress
would be faced with Democratic electoral votes from all those
states, and the decision about whether to count them would
involve a real possibility of violence.[10]

As the date set for the final vote, May 16, approached, the
dissident senators wavered and urged delay. On May 12 and 13,
Ross told his colleague, Pomeroy, that he would vote to convict

9. Morrill to Fessenden, May 10, 1868, Fessenden Mss., Bowdoin
College Library. The letter is quoted in Fessenden, *Fessenden,* II, 205–7.
10. See, for instance, the fears of the New York *Tribune,* May 13,
1868, p. 4, and (as always, with more restraint) the New York *Nation,*
April 30, 1868, pp. 344–45.

on the first three articles and the eleventh. Anthony, Willey, and Frederick T. Frelinghuysen finally assured colleagues they would sustain the key articles. Henderson indicated that he would resign rather than cast the deciding vote for acquittal and held out the possibility that he would convict on the eleventh article. On May 12, the Missouri congressional delegation assured him that they did not want his resignation and suggested that he abstain on the articles on which he could not vote guilty. The Senator seemed to agree but added that he would speak to Sprague, Van Winkle, Anthony, and Willey. If they intended to convict on the eleventh article, the President would be removed regardless of Henderson's vote.

On May 14, Ross, Henderson, Van Winkle, Willey, and Trumbull met in Van Winkle's rooms. When Pomeroy found them there, they urged another delay in the vote, assuring him it would bring a reorganization of the cabinet, with Massachusetts Republican Representative Samuel Hooper named secretary of the treasury, Evarts secretary of state, and Reverdy Johnson and Groesbeck in other positions. Republicans still believed that, despite their reluctance, Willey and Ross ultimately would cooperate with the party.[11]

The result, of course, is well known. Ross voted with Fessenden, Fowler, Grimes, Henderson, Trumbull, and Van Winkle against conviction, and the seven recusants were recorded in history as the seven martyrs. Of the seven, Fessenden, Fowler, Grimes, Henderson, Trumbull, and Van Winkle formally filed their opinions. All averred that impeachment lay only for positive violations of law. With the exception of Van Winkle, each of the senators began with the affirmation that before the passage of the Tenure of Office Act, the president of

11. *House Report No. 75,* 40th Congress, 2nd Session, 15–16, 30–32; William S. King to E. B. Washburne, May 12, 1868, Washburne Mss.; [?] to Butler, May 12, 1868, Butler Mss.; Boston *Evening Journal,* May 13, 1868, p. 4; May 16, 1868, p. 4. The Cincinnati *Commercial's* correspondent reported that the changed cabinet would include Groesbeck as secretary of the treasury, Evarts secretary of state, Jacob D. Cox as secretary of war, and John D. Catron as secretary of the interior. Reported in the New York *Tribune,* May 20, 1868, p. 4.

the United States had the power to remove government appointees in the manner in which Johnson had removed Stanton. For support, Fowler, Grimes, and Henderson relied on the erroneous but widely held understanding of the debates of the 1st Congress on the subject (see pp. 160–62). Only Henderson acknowledged that the accuracy of that understanding had been questioned (by the time Henderson filed his opinion, several senators had pointed out the true circumstances of that debate), but he simply said, "I think otherwise." [12] Fessenden bolstered his argument with the assertion, which he did not support with proof, that "instances have not infrequently occurred during the session where the president thought it proper to remove an officer at once, before sending the name of his successor to the Senate." [13] Since the defense had been able to produce only seven such instances, it is clear that Fessenden's conclusion was inaccurate. Trumbull made the same assertion, offering three examples from the defense evidence.[14]

Having concluded that Johnson could remove Stanton as the law stood before the passage of the Tenure of Office Act, Fessenden, Fowler, Grimes, Henderson, and Trumbull each decided that, by the terms of the proviso governing the tenure of department heads, Stanton's term had expired. This involved several points that could have been decided either way; the dissidents decided them for the President. But none of them answered the prosecution argument that he was protected under the general provisions of the bill if his term as department head had ended.[15]

Finally, all but Van Winkle determined that after he had removed Stanton, Johnson had the authority to appoint Thomas secretary of war ad interim under the 1795 law governing ad interim appointments. In arriving at this conclusion, each asserted

12. Henderson opinion, *Trial of Andrew Johnson,* III, 296; Grimes opinion, *ibid.,* 329–31; Fowler opinion, *ibid.,* 194–95.

13. Fessenden opinion, *ibid.,* 18.

14. Trumbull opinion, *ibid.,* 320–21.

15. Fessenden opinion, *ibid.,* 18–22; Fowler opinion, *ibid.,* 195–98; Grimes opinion, *ibid.,* 331–33; Henderson opinion, 301–2; Trumbull opinion, *ibid.,* 321–23.

that the word "vacancy" in the law included vacancies created by removal, and each argued that the 1795 law had not been completely repealed by that of 1863 (see pp. 164–65). Trumbull argued that even if Johnson had not had the power to appoint Thomas, the appointment was not an impeachable offense because Congress had not enacted a law making it a crime. None but Fessenden attempted to reconcile their justification of Johnson's act under the 1795 law with the provision of that law limiting to six months the length of time any vacancy could be filled by an ad interim appointment. To solve that problem, Fessenden argued that Johnson had suspended Stanton in August 1867 under the Tenure of Office Act. When the Senate refused to acquiesce, Stanton was legally restored to the office and therefore could not be held ever to have been actually removed. Therefore six months had not elapsed before Johnson made his ad interim appointment of Thomas.[16]

It is evident that Fessenden was straining the law. The 1795 law limited to six months the time any *vacancy* could be filled by an ad interim appointment. Granting that Stanton's suspension did not work a removal, it had vacated the office. The President never revoked that suspension. On the contrary, Johnson had specifically reaffirmed it when he notified the Senate of Stanton's removal on February 21: "On the 12th day of August, 1867, by virtue of the power and authority vested in the President by the Constitution and laws of the United States, I suspended Edwin M. Stanton from the office of Secretary of War. *In further exercise* of the power and authority so vested in the President, I have this day removed Mr. Stanton from the office. . . ."[17] That suspension had ceased only if the Senate's vote had legally restored Stanton to office. That it could not do—despite Fessenden's insistence that it had—unless Stanton was covered by the Tenure of Office Act. Fessenden was interpreting the law both ways. To acquit Johnson of its violation, the Tenure of Office Act did not

16. Fessenden opinion, *ibid.,* 25.
17. Quoted in Richardson, ed., *Messages and Papers of the Presidents,* VI, 621; italics mine.

cover Stanton. To acquit him of a violation of the 1795 statute, it did.

Van Winkle's opinion was truly remarkable in its reasoning. Unlike his fellow dissenters, the portly West Virginia senator conceded that the Tenure of Office Act did protect Stanton from replacement. But, he argued, Johnson had not violated the act. The only evidence that Johnson had attempted to remove Stanton was the written order to that effect. That order could not effect a removal of itself. "There is not even an allegation that the order in writing was ever delivered to, or served on, Mr. Stanton, or ever directed to be so delivered or served, or that any attempt was made to deliver or serve it; or, in fact, that Mr. Stanton ever saw or heard it." This was the pettifogging the managers had feared when they argued against considering the Senate a court; this was the legal quibble in its ultimate degree. All knew Stanton had received the removal order. He had sent a copy of it to the House and that very copy had precipitated the impeachment. The President's answer to the articles admitted the delivery of the order. "To this I reply that the answer cannot confess what is not charged," Van Winkle riposted.[18]

The articles did allege that Johnson had actually delivered a letter of ad interim appointment in violation of the Tenure of Office Act. But Van Winkle denied that the delivery of that letter of appointment violated the act. The penal section of that law made a crime "every . . . appointment, or employment made, had, or exercised contrary to the provisions of this act, and the making, signing, sealing, countersigning, or issuing of any commission or letter of authority, for . . . any such appointment or employment . . . ." The question, therefore, was not whether Johnson had issued a letter of authority to Thomas but whether the appointment that letter embodied was contrary to the Tenure of Office Act.[19] Van Winkle decided it was not;

18. Van Winkle opinion, *Trial of Andrew Johnson,* III, 147–48.
19. Van Winkle also made the uncontroversial observation that Johnson's employment of Thomas and his appointment involved the

it was not an *appointment* at all. "The letter . . . simply empowers and authorizes him to act, and does not use the word appoint, or any equivalent term." The Tenure of Office Act forbade only such appointments contrary to the act as required the advice and consent of the Senate, Van Winkle held. Thomas's was not such an appointment.[20]

Finally, Van Winkle had to consider the problem of whether the President had the right to make such a non-appointment, to authorize a man to fill a position without sending his name to the Senate for confirmation. Although he might have relied on the 1795 law as had Fessenden, Trumbull, and the other recusants, Van Winkle chose not to. He conceded that an ordinary appointment, if not sent to the Senate for confirmation, violated the Constitution. But the letter purported to make the appointment only ad interim, and as "the Constitution makes no mention of such appointments, it does not appear that it can be such a violation." [21] This argument denied one of the fundamental tenets of mid-nineteenth-century constitutional law, that the president had only such powers as were enumerated or implied in the Constitution. Van Winkle held that "it can hardly be intended to assert that every act for which a special or general permission of law is not shown is unlawful and a misdemeanor." This might be true of the conduct of private individuals, who in the United States retain the right to do what they wish as long as they do not violate statutory or com-

---

same question, in a sentence that should be regarded as one of the classics of legal literature: "[T]he section includes only appointments and employments made, had, or exercised, contrary to the provisions of the tenure-of-office act, and certain acts relating to such appointments and employments. As the latter are a consequence of the former, and as if the former was legal, the latter, in the same case, would be legal also; and, in fact, there could be no employment without a previous appointment—the former may be considered as included in the latter—so that if the appointment of General Thomas was legal, or the reverse, his employment would bear the same character." Van Winkle opinon, *ibid.,* 149.

20. *Ibid.*
21. *Ibid.,* 150.

mon law. But it is a more doubtful proposition when applied to public officials, whose public trusts involve not rights but duties and powers granted by the people.

In framing his opinion, Van Winkle demonstrated almost a perverseness, a compulsion to arrive at his conclusions by a route different from that of his colleagues, and one requiring a far more strained interpretation of the law, which at times appears to be almost a parody of the legal dissertations prepared so painstakingly by his peers.[22]

Essentially, the seven recusant senators (with the exception of Van Winkle) had decided every doubtful point in favor of the President. In some cases, especially Van Winkle's, they had adopted a rigidly legalistic approach to a question that in many ways transcended legalism—"narrow special pleading worthy of an Old Bailey lawyer," the Massachusetts jurist George S. Sewall complained.[23]

Republicans realized that there had been great leeway in the case. They knew that the seven Republicans who voted not guilty had decided doubtful points in favor of Johnson in the same way those who voted for conviction had decided them against him. Totally convinced of the President's guilt, most Republicans could only view the recusants' defections as political rather than legal acts. As Blaine observed shortly before the vote, "The class of men who hold the whole thing in their hands are men who take a position deliberately; counting the cost, and then maintain it. . . . "[24]

But actually another consideration impelled the recusant senators to decide as they did. They were not reluctant to acknowledge it in their opinions.

In the case of an elective Chief Magistrate of a great and powerful people, living under a written Constitution [wrote Fessenden], there is much more at stake in such a proceeding than the fate of

22. Van Winkle's entire opinion, *ibid.,* 147–52.
23. Sewall to Sumner, June 4, 1868, Sumner Mss.
24. Blaine to Washburn, May 13, 1868, quoted in Hunt, *Washburn,* 122–23; William Johnston to Hayes, May 28, 1868, Hayes Mss., Rutherford B. Hayes Library; Boston *Commonwealth,* May 23, 1868, p. 2; July 25, 1868, p. 2.

the individual. The office of President is one of the great co-ordinate branches of the government. . . . Anything which con-duces to weaken its hold upon the respect of the people, to break down the barriers which surround it, to make it the mere sport of temporary majorities, tends to the great injury of our government, and inflicts a wound upon constitutional liberty. It is evident, then, . . . that the offence for which a Chief Magistrate is removed from office, and the power intrusted to him by the people transferred to other hands . . . should be of such a character to commend itself at once to the minds of all right thinking men as, beyond all ques-tion, an adequate cause. It should be free from the taint of party; leave no reasonable ground of suspicion upon the motives of those who inflict the penalty, and address itself to the country and the civilized world as a measure justly called for by the gravity of the crime and the necessity for its punishment. Anything less than this . . . would . . . shake the faith of the friends of constitutional liberty in the permanency of our free institutions and the capacity of man for self-government.[25]

James Dixon, the Johnsonite senator from Connecticut, put it more simply in a letter of thanks he wrote Fessenden a few months later. "Whether Andrew Johnson should be removed from office, justly or unjustly, was comparatively of little con-sequence—but whether our government should be Mexicanized, and an example set which would surely, in the end, utterly overthrow our institutions, was a matter of vast consequence. To you and Mr. Grimes it is mainly due that impeachment has not become an ordinary means of changing the policy of the government by a violent removal of the Executive." [26] With senators committed to those considerations, it is clear that im-peachment never could have won their votes.

But if Fessenden and other conservative senators sincerely feared the consequences of successful impeachment, radical senators were just as frightened of the consequences of failure where a president appeared so manifestly guilty. If Andrew Johnson could not be convicted for his actions, for what crimes

25. Fessenden opinion, *Trial of Andrew Johnson,* III, 30; see also Trumbull's opinion, *ibid.,* 328.
26. Dixon to Fessenden, August 9, 1868; see also Grimes to Fes-senden, June 16, 1868, Fessenden Mss., Bowdoin College Library.

would a president ever be removed? How could a chief executive who threatened the well-being of the nation be checked? And, more immediately, how could Johnson be checked? So deep was the gloom that enveloped radicals, who firmly believed Johnson would now wreak havoc upon Republican Reconstruction policy, that Thaddeus Stevens despaired. "My life has been a failure," he mourned. "With all this great struggle of years in Washington, and the fearful sacrifice of life and treasure, I see little hope for the Republic." [27]

Of course, as it turned out, Johnson for once honored his pledge to conservative Republicans. He served out his term without renewing the intensive strife he had precipitated. But the unquestionable fact remains that it is almost inconceivable that a future president will be impeached and removed.

Historians have often interpreted the impeachment movement as part of a drive for congressional supremacy. Had it succeeded, some suggest, the government of the United States might have evolved into a parliamentary system. But in fact it had not been Congress but the President who had been claiming broad new powers. It was Andrew Johnson who had appointed provisional governors of vast territories without the advice and consent of the Senate, who had nullified congressional legislation, who claimed inherent quasi-legislative powers over Reconstruction. In many ways, Johnson was a very modern president, holding a view of presidential authority that has only recently been established. Impeachment was Congress's defensive weapon; it proved a dull blade, and the end result is that the only effective recourse against a president who ignores the will of Congress or exceeds his powers is democratic removal at the polls.

27. A. K. McClure, *Abraham Lincoln and Men of War-Times: Some Personal Recollections of War and Politics During the Lincoln Administration,* 3rd ed. (Philadelphia, 1892), 264; Detroit *Post and Tribune, Zachariah Chandler: An Outline Sketch of His Life and Public Services* (Detroit, 1880), 297.

Epilogue

〰〰〰〰〰〰〰〰〰〰〰〰〰〰〰〰〰〰〰〰〰〰〰

THE SEVEN Republican senators who joined Democrats to defeat Johnson's removal were viciously attacked by many Republicans, as nearly everyone who has taken a course in American history or has read John F. Kennedy's *Profiles in Courage* knows.[1] But ever since Ralph Roske's debunking article, "The Seven Martyrs?," was published, historians have recognized that the legend has been exaggerated.[2] In fact, considering the stakes involved, Republican anger at the recusants was remarkably short-lived. Radicals continued to demand the dissidents' scalps, but Republican nonradicals immediately warned of the dangerous consequences of following such a policy with a presidential election approaching and the Democrats considering the nomination of Chase. "The impeachment trial is a failure," the conservative Cincinnati *Commercial* observed, "it need not be a disaster."[3] At the Republican National Convention, meeting in Chicago on May 19 and 20, only a few days after the failure of impeachment, the efforts of radicals to persuade delegates to issue a formal repudiation of

1. Kennedy, *Profiles in Courage* (New York, 1956), 126–51.
2. Ralph J. Roske, "The Seven Martyrs?," *American Historical Review*, LXIV (January 1959), 323–30.
3. Cincinnati *Commercial*, May 16, 1868, p. 6; May 13, 1868, p. 4; May 21, 1868, p. 4; Chicago *Tribune*, May 11, 1868, p. 2; New York *Nation*, May 14, 1868, pp. 384–85; John Murray Forbes to Fessenden, May 23, 1868, quoted in Sarah F. Hughes, ed., *Letters and Recollections of John Murray Forbes*, 2 vols. (Boston, 1899), II, 164–65; Henry J. Bowditch to Sumner, May 18, 1868; F. V. Balch to Sumner, May 18, 1868; Edward Atkinson to Sumner, June 1, 1868, Sumner Mss.

the seven recusants failed dismally.[4] As Republicans swung into the campaign, the Boston *Evening Journal* noted, "It is surprising to see how far the whole subject of impeachment seems to have been thrown into the background and dwarfed in importance . . . ." In the dissidents' states, Republicans quickly ceased their attacks on their senators and concentrated upon the canvass.[5] Each of the seven endorsed and campaigned for the Republican presidential nominee, Grant, and when Congress next met, all retained their committee assignments and Trumbull, Fessenden, and Grimes retained their immense prestige and power. "I am satisfied that I am stronger in the Senate in every respect . . . than I ever was before I was tried in the furnace of impeachment," Grimes wrote.[6]

Nonetheless, the bitterness of impeachment cut the seven recusants from their Republican moorings. By 1870, each of the active Republican acquitters (Fessenden died in 1869; Grimes had a debilitating stroke the same year) was out of sympathy with the Republican administration and the mainstream of his party. Most participated actively in the Liberal Republican movement. They had not been driven out of the party, however. Undoubtedly their positions on impeachment weakened the dissidents' ability to resist challenges from intra-party rivals, but to a large extent they abandoned their party voluntarily. Ross and Trumbull enjoyed long, respected careers as Democrats. Henderson returned to the Republican party after his

4. New York *Nation,* May 28, 1868, p. 421; Cincinnati *Commercial,* May 19, 1868, p. 1; May 22, 1868, pp. 1, 4; Chicago *Tribune,* May 20, 1868, p. 1; Horace White to Charles Eliot Norton, May 20, 1868, Norton Mss., Houghton Library, Harvard University.

5. Boston *Evening Journal,* May 23, 1868, p. 4; New York *Nation,* May 21, 1868, p. 402; William Frank Zornow, *Kansas: A History of the Jayhawk State* (Norman, Okla., 1957), 120; George A. Boeck, "Senator Grimes and the Iowa Press, 1867–1868," *Mid-America,* XLVIII (July 1966), 159, 161; R. W. Bayles, "Peter G. Van Winkle and Waitman T. Willey in the Impeachment Trial of Andrew Johnson," *West Virginia History,* XIII (January 1952), 86–87; Jellison, *Fessenden,* 250–51; Mark Krug, *Lyman Trumbull: Conservative Radical* (New York, 1965), 269–72.

6. Grimes to Henry W. Starr, March 18, 1869, quoted in Salter, *Life of James W. Grimes,* 367.

flirtation with the Liberals and in 1884 served as the presiding officer of the Republican National Convention. Fowler and Van Winkle, Republicans in Democratic Border states, retired from politics at the end of their terms.[7]

And what of Andrew Johnson? He hoped for the Democratic presidential nomination after his acquittal. Bitter at his failure to receive it (the Democrats turned to former Governor Horatio Seymour of New York instead), he returned to his home state to rebuild his eastern Tennessee, hill-country machine. Once again he assailed the planter and Confederate-dominated regular Democratic organization. In 1874, he succeeded in winning election once more to the United States Senate, combining his Democratic support with that of the Republicans, who won his promise not to attack the Grant administration. They should have known better; there were great constitutional questions involved. Johnson's first address in the august chamber after his thirteen-year absence denounced President Grant's violations of the principles of federalism.

7. Roske, "The Seven Martryrs?," *passim.*

Appendix

〰〰〰〰〰〰〰〰〰〰〰〰〰〰〰〰〰〰〰〰〰〰〰〰〰〰

Currency Question in the 40th Congress

MAIN SCALE

GROUP 0 Those representatives, CONTRACTIONISTS, who voted against the expansionist position on all roll calls in the following groups.

GROUP 1 Those representatives, SUSPENSIONISTS, who voted for the expansionist position on more than one-half of the roll calls in this group, but against the expansionist position on roll calls in the following group. *Congressional Globe*, 40th Congress, 3rd Session, 1325 (February 17, 1869; expansionist vote, nay; final vote, 65–107–50), 1816 (March 2, 1869; nay; 70–108–44), 1333 (February 18, 1869; yea; 106–77–39), 1331 (February 18, 1869; yea; 97–76–49), 1325 (February 17, 1869; yea; 93–86–43), 2nd Session, 1761 (March 9, 1868; nay; 56–65–68), 3rd Session, 1327 (February 17, 1869; nay; 92–78–52), in order of marginal frequency.

—*Currency bill (redistributing bank reserves and expanding currency).*

GROUP 2 Those representatives, EXPANSIONISTS, who voted for the expansionist position on more than one-half of the roll calls in this group. *Congressional Globe*, 40th Congress, 3rd Session, 1883 (March 3, 1869; nay; 118–57–48), 1538 (February 24, 1869; nay; 120–60–42), 1471 (March 3, 1869; yea; 53–119–51), 1538 (February 24, 1869; yea; 54–133–35).

—*Bill to strengthen public credit.*

SUBSCALE

GROUP 0   Those representatives, CONTRACTIONISTS, who voted against the expansionist position on all roll calls in the following groups.

GROUP 1   Those representatives, SUSPENSIONISTS, who voted for the expansionist position on more than one-half of the roll calls in this group, but against the expansionist position on roll calls in the following group. *Congressional Globe,* 40th Congress, 2nd Session, 70 (December 7, 1867; yea; 127–32–28), 4310 (July 21, 1868; yea; 86–49–80).

—*Resolution to issue greenbacks, resolution to end contraction.*

GROUP 2   Those representatives, EXPANSIONISTS, who voted for the expansionist position on more than one-half of the roll calls in this group. *Congressional Globe,* 40th Congress, 3rd Session, 1538 (February 24, 1869; yea; 72–100–50).

—*Amendment to the public credit bill to strike provisions permitting contracts specifically requiring payment in gold.*

NOTE: Only those representatives who ranked consistently on both the main scale and the subscale were included in the comparisons in Chart 2 through Chart 4.

Radicalism in the 39th Congress, Second Session

GROUP 0   Those representatives, DEMOCRATS and JOHNSON CONSERVATIVES, who voted against the radical position on roll calls in all the following groups.

GROUP 1   Those representatives, CONSERVATIVE REPUBLICANS, who voted for the radical position on more than one-half of the following roll calls. *Congressional Globe,* 39th Congress, 2nd Session, 324 (January 7, 1867; radical vote, yea; final vote, 111–26–54), 30 (December 6, 1866; nay; 30–124–36), 322–23 (January 7, 1866; yea; 107–26–58), 11 (December 4, 1866; nay; 32–119–40), 319 (January 7, 1867; yea; 107–

30–54), 1739 (March 2, 1867; yea; 133–37–21), 1535
(February 23, 1867; yea; 96–27–67), 1661 (February 28,
1867; yea; 97–30–63), 447 (January 14, 1867; yea; 107–
36–48), 619 (January 21, 1867; yea; 109–37–45), 646
(January 22, 1867; yea; 109–37–45), 320 (January 7, 1867;
nay; 39–105–47), 616 (January 21, 1867; yea; 94–33–74),
321 (January 7, 1867; yea; 107–39–45), 11 (December 4,
1867; yea; 107–37–47), 970 (February 2, 1867; yea; 111–
38–41), 1733 (March 2, 1867; yea; 135–48–9), 1340
(February 19, 1867; yea; 111–41–38), 1400 (February 20,
1867; yea; 126–46–18), 994 (February 4, 1867; yea; 96–
36–48), 685 (January 23, 1867; yea; 108–42–41), 320
(January 7, 1867; nay; 40–104–47), 1175 (February 12,
1867; yea; 113–47–30), 1215 (February 13, 1867; yea;
109–55–26), 321 (January 7, 1867; yea; 94–47–50), 1280
(February 16, 1867; yea; 80–40–70), in order of marginal
frequency.

*—Repeal of the President's amnesty power, bill to suspend
payment for slaves taken into the Army, resolution reaffirm-
ing the necessity for southern states to ratify the Fourteenth
Amendment before admission, bill prohibiting the President
for one year from reappointing a man rejected by the Senate,
bill to require the test oath of those seeking public lands,
Indemnity bill, resolution instructing the Committee on
Territories to prepare a territorial government bill for the
South, passage of the Reconstruction bill, concurring in conference committee report on the Tenure of Office bill, passage
of the Louisiana Reconstruction bill.*

GROUP 2 Those representatives, CONSERVATIVE CENTER REPUB-
LICANS, who voted for the radical position on more than one-
half of the roll calls in this group, but against the radical
position on roll calls in the following groups. *Congressional
Globe,* 39th Congress, 2nd Session, 115 (December 13, 1866;
yea; 80–55–56), 1133 (February 11, 1867; yea; 84–59–47),
1399–1400 (February 15, 1867; yea; 99–70–21), 970
(February 2, 1867; yea; 82–63–55).

*—Ordering the main question on the Louisiana Reconstruc-
tion bill, amendment to the Reconstruction bill that military
commanders may remove officers of the provisional southern*

governments, reconsideration of the amendment to the Tenure of Office bill to include the department heads in its operation.

GROUP 3   Those representatives, RADICAL CENTER REPUBLICANS, who voted for the radical position on more than one-half of the roll calls in this group, but against the radical position on roll calls in the following groups. *Congressional Globe,* 39th Congress, 2nd Session, 969–70 (February 2, 1867; yea; 75–66–49), 94 (December 12, 1866; yea; 77–81–33), 93–94 (December 12, 1866; nay; 77–78–36), 943–44 (February 1, 1867; yea; 76–78–36), 1215 (February 13, 1867; nay; 69–94–27),* 993 (February 4, 1867; yea; 60–82–48), 817 (January 28, 1867; nay; 88–65–38).

—Amendment to the Tenure of Office bill to include the department heads, motion to recommit the Military Government bill to the Judiciary Committee with instructions to add the "Blaine amendment," resolution that it is Congress's duty to establish new governments in the southern states, motion to refer Stevens's Reconstruction bill to the Reconstruction Committee.

GROUP 4   Those representatives, RADICAL REPUBLICANS, who voted for the radical position on more than one-half of the roll calls in this group. *Congressional Globe,* 39th Congress, 2nd Session, 1340 (February 19, 1867; nay; 73–98–19),* 1213 (February 13, 1867; nay; 85–78–27),* 75 (December 11, 1866; yea; 18–132–41), 1321 (February 18, 1867; nay; 103–60–27).*

—Ordering the main question on the motion to recommit the Military Government bill with instructions to add the "Blaine amendment," motion to concur in Senate amendments to the Military Government bill, amendment to the Tenure of Office bill that any person rejected by the Senate for confirmation shall be ineligible to hold office for three years thereafter, amendment that no person so rejected may be renominated for one year.

GROUP 5   Those representatives, ULTRA RADICAL REPUBLICANS,

* Democratic and Conservative votes changed from positive to negative.

who voted with Democrats, Johnson Conservatives, and conservative Republicans to recommit the Military Government bill to the Judiciary Committee, and to order the main question on non-concurring in Senate amendments to the Military Government bill. *Congressional Globe,* 39th Congress, 2nd Session, 1213 (February 13, 1867; nay; 85–78–27),† 1321 (February 18, 1867; nay; 103–60–27)†.

Impeachment in the Senate
40th Congress, Second Session

MAIN SCALE

GROUP 0   These senators, DEMOCRATS and JOHNSON CONSERVATIVES, supported the defense position on roll calls in all the following groups.

GROUP 1   These senators, REPUBLICANS, voted against conviction and/or sustained the defense position on most questions, but supported the prosecution position on at least one-half of the roll calls in this group. *Trial of Andrew Johnson,* I, 487 (April 11, 1868; pro–conviction vote, nay; final vote, 2–49–3), 1503 (March 2, 1868; nay; 8–22–23), 325 (April 3, 1868; yea; 35–11–8), *Congressional Globe,* 40th Congress, 2nd Session, 1531 (February 29, 1868; nay; 13–27–13), *Trial,* II, 476 (May 7, 1868; nay; 13–37–4), 497 (May 26, 1868; yea; 34–16–4), in order of marginal frequency.

GROUP 2   These senators, REPUBLICANS, were apparently uncommitted to conviction at the beginning of the trial, favored delay and were not strongly committed to conviction by the end of the trial, but supported the prosecution on at least one-half of the roll calls in this group. *Trial of Andrew Johnson,* II, 495 (May 26, 1868; nay; 15–39–0), 494 (May 26, 1868; yea; 35–18–1), I, 507 (April 13, 1868; nay; 15–35–4), II, 487 (May 16, 1868; yea; 35–19–0), 496 (May 26, 1868; yea; 35–19–0), 497 (May 26, 1868; yea; 35–19–0), 435 (May 16, 1868; yea; 34–19–1), I, 633

† Democratic, Conservative, and conservative Republican votes changed from positive to negative.

(April 17, 1868; yea; 29–14–11), *Congressional Globe,*
40th Congress, 2nd Session, 1533 (February 29, 1868; nay;
12–23–18), *Trial,* II, 488 (May 16, 1866; nay; 20–34–0),
I, 336 (April 3, 1868; nay; 16–29–9), 693 (April 18, 1868;
nay; 19–30–5), II, 489 (May 16, 1868; yea; 32–21–1), 474
(May 6, 1868; yea; 28–20–6), I, 693 (April 18, 1868; nay;
20–29–5), 276 (April 2, 1868; yea; 27–17–10), 508 (April
13, 1868; nay; 18–32–4), 716 (April 18, 1868; nay; 20–26–
8), 35 (March 13, 1868; yea; 28–20–6), 247 (April 2, 1868;
nay; 20–29–5), 701 (April 18, 1868; nay; 18–26–10), 85
(March 24, 1868; yea; 28–24–2), 214 (April 2, 1868; yea;
28–22–4), II, 494 (May 26, 1868; nay; 24–30–0), I, 697
(April 18, 1868; nay; 22–26–6), 481 (April 11, 1868; nay;
23–28–3), II, 488 (May 16, 1868; nay; 24–30–0), 491
(May 26, 1868; yea; 29–25–0), *Congressional Globe,* 40th
Congress, 2nd Session, 1578 (March 2, 1868; nay; 20–24–
9).

GROUP 3   These senators, REPUBLICANS, were apparently uncommitted to conviction as the trial began but opposed delay
and were committed to conviction by the end of the trial.
They supported the prosecution position on at least one-half
of the roll calls in this group. *Trial of Andrew Johnson,* II,
491 (May 26, 1868; nay; 26–28–0), 495 (May 26, 1868; yea;
27–27–0), I, 485 (April 11, 1868; nay; 23–29–2), 25
(March 13, 1868; yea; 25–26–3), 521 (April 13, 1868;
nay; 26–25–3), 536 (April 15, 1868; yea; 24–26–4), 609
(April 16, 1868; nay; 27–23–4), 612 (April 16, 1868; nay;
27–23–4), 185 (March 31, 1868; yea; 22–26–6), 518
(April 13, 1868; nay; 26–22–6), 35 (March 13, 1868; nay;
27–23–4), 85 (March 24, 1868; nay; 29–23–2), 187 (April
1, 1868; yea; 21–27–6), 605 (April 16, 1868; nay; 29–21–
4), II, 141 (April 24, 1868; nay; 21–13–20).

GROUP 4   These senators, REPUBLICANS, were strongly committed
to conviction and supported the prosecution position on at
least one-half of the roll calls in this group. *Congressional
Globe,* 40th Congress, 2nd Session, 2598 (May 27, 1868;
nay; 23–14–17), *Trial of Andrew Johnson,* I, 185 (March
31, 1868; nay; 32–18–4), II, 485 (May 16, 1868; yea; 34–
19–1), I, 515 (April 13, 1868; nay; 34–17–3), II, 477

(May 7, 1868; yea; 16–36–2), I, 568 (April 15, 1868; nay; 36–15–3), II, 477 (May 7, 1868; yea; 15–38–1).

GROUP 5 These senators, REPUBLICANS, were more strongly committed to conviction and supported the prosecution position on at least one-half of the roll calls in this group. *Trial of Andrew Johnson,* I, 489 (April 11, 1868; yea; 12–38–4), II, 307 (April 30, 1868; nay; 35–10–9), I, 426 (April 10, 1868; nay; 42–10–2), II, 476 (May 7, 1868; yea; 6–42–6).

SUBSCALE

GROUP 0 These senators, DEMOCRATS, JOHNSON CONSERVATIVES, and REPUBLICANS, either opposed or were not strongly committed to conviction and supported the defense position on roll calls in all the following groups.

GROUP 1 These senators, REPUBLICANS, were relatively committed to conviction, supporting the prosecution position on more than one–half of the roll calls in this group. *Trial of Andrew Johnson,* I, 489 (April 11, 1868; nay; 25–27–2), 489 (April 11, 1868; nay; 25–27–2), 268 (April 2, 1868; yea; 22–27–5), *Congressional Globe,* 40th Congress, 2nd Session, 1698 (March 6, 1868; nay; 24–20–9), *Trial,* I, 186 (March 31, 1868; yea; 20–30–4), 186 (March 31, 1868; nay; 31–19–4), II, 478 (May 7, 1868; nay; 22–15–17), *Congressional Globe,* 40th Congress, 2nd Session, 1531 (February 29, 1868; nay; 25–15–13).

GROUP 2 These senators, REPUBLICANS, were committed to a speedy trial and conviction, supporting the prosecution position on more than one-half of the roll calls in this group. *Trial of Andrew Johnson,* I, 633 (April 17, 1868; yea; 13–30–11).

GROUP 3 These senators, REPUBLICANS, were even more strongly committed to a speedy trial and conviction, supporting the prosecution position on more than one-half of the roll calls in this group. *Trial of Andrew Johnson,* I, 371 (April 4, 1868; nay; 37–10–7).

A
Bibliographical
Review

Reconstruction

One cannot assess the impeachment and trial of Andrew Johnson without a full understanding of the controversy over Reconstruction that precipitated it. Historians' evalutions of that controversy have differed widely since the 1890s, when the first studies appeared. Bernard Weisberger traces these scholarly disagreements through the 1950s in "The Dark and Bloody Ground of Reconstruction Historiography," *Journal of Southern History*, XXV (November 1957), 427–47; Harold M. Hyman and Larry George Kincaid have covered some of the same ground and brought the discussion up to date in their respective studies, *The Radical Republicans and Reconstruction, 1861–1870* (Indianapolis and New York, 1967), xvii–lxviii, and "Victims of Circumstance: An Interpretation of Changing Attitudes Toward Republican Policy Makers and Reconstruction," *Journal of American History*, LVII (June 1970), 48–66.

The first scholarly assessments of Reconstruction appeared at the turn of the century. James Ford Rhodes, in his *History of the United States from the Compromise of 1850 to the Final Restoration of Home Rule at the South in 1877*, 7 vols. (New York, 1893–1906), offered a thoroughly nationalistic interpretation of the Civil War era but condemned Republicans' Reconstruction policies in light of "modern" proofs of Negro racial inferiority. William A. Dunning, in his *Essays on the Civil War and Reconstruction, and*

Related Topics (New York, 1898) and *Reconstruction, Political and Economic, 1865–1877* (New York and London, 1907), also questioned the wisdom of Congress's policy, especially the decision to impose black suffrage in the South, but was not as critical of Republican Reconstruction as many later historians have believed. John W. Burgess, who combined a career in history and political science, shared Dunning's distaste for the Republican program, manifesting his feelings in his *Reconstruction and the Constitution, 1866–1876* (New York, 1902). A firm nationalist, Burgess sympathized with Republican opposition to Johnson's interpretation of national power over Reconstruction. But Republicans' post–1867 legislation, imposing black suffrage upon the South and protecting blacks from southern violence, transcended constitutional limits in Burgess's opinion, and his study contributed to the growing public and scholarly conviction that Northerners had perpetrated serious wrongs upon the South after the war.

By the 1930s, as Dunning's students one after another brought forward their studies of Reconstruction in each of the southern states, historians almost unanimously depicted Republican policy as a monstrous blunder. The special pleading of a black Marxist, W. E. B. Du Bois, in his *Black Reconstruction: An Essay Toward a History of the Part Which Black Folk Played in the Attempt to Reconstruct Democracy in America, 1860–1880* (New York, 1935), could not shake the conviction, so eloquently popularized in the pseudo-scholarship of Paul G. Bowers, that Reconstruction was *The Tragic Era* (sub-titled *The Revolution After Lincoln* [Cambridge, Massachusetts, 1929]).

By 1930, the insights and axioms of the Progressive historians began to influence Reconstruction history. Sharing the economic determinism that marked the Progressive school, Howard K. Beale assumed in *The Critical Year: A Study of Andrew Johnson and Reconstruction* (New York, 1930) that the radical Republicans spoke for the new, industrial capitalists of the Northeast, who used Civil War issues to deflect possible opposition from southern and western agrarians to their new economic order. Sympathizing with the anticapitalists, Beale shared President Andrew Johnson's hostility to the Republicans, but the President still emerged as the inept politician who could not frame the issues in such a way as to win the allegiance of agrarian Northerners. By the 1940s, Beale's revisionist interpretation had become the new orthodoxy, but it was

Beale himself who called for the reassessment of Reconstruction, especially in the South, which has culminated in recent histories that emphasize the justice and humanitarianism of Republican goals. His article, "On Rewriting Reconstruction History," *American Historical Review*, XLV (July 1940), 807–27, and Francis B. Simkins's "New Viewpoints of Southern Reconstruction," *Journal of Southern History*, V (February 1939), 49–61, mark the real beginnings of modern Reconstruction revisionism, which has in the 1970s become an orthodoxy in its own right.

The general understanding of Reconstruction upon which my assessment of impeachment proceeds emerged from my own re-search, but it clearly fits within the mainstream of recent writing. Most recent analysts agree that the Republican insistence on a settlement of Civil War issues that would eradicate as far as possible the causes of the Civil War was hardly a product of vindictiveness or undue radicalism. The Republicans demanded legal and later political equality for the freedmen both to gain security for the Union and from moral considerations. When Andrew Johnson's policy promised neither, they enacted legislation that led him to break with the party. Firmly committed to racial equality in the twentieth century, the historians who have developed this new in-terpretation clearly sympathize with the long-maligned radicals.

For a more thorough background in the Reconstruction issues that precipitated the impeachment crisis, the student should read the key works that established the pro-Republican viewpoint: William R. Brock's, *An American Crisis: Congress and Reconstruc-tion, 1865–1867* (New York, 1963); LaWanda and John H. Cox's, *Politics, Principle, and Prejudice, 1865–1866: Dilemma of Recon-struction America* (New York, 1963); John Hope Franklin, *Reconstruction: After the Civil War* (Chicago, 1961); Eric L. Mc-Kitrick, *Andrew Johnson and Reconstruction* (Chicago, 1960); Kenneth M. Stampp, *The Era of Reconstruction, 1865–1877* (New York, 1965); and Hans L. Trefousse, *The Radical Republicans: Lincoln's Vanguard for Racial Justice* (New York, 1968).

For those readers who desire to investigate the Reconstruction era in more detail, primary sources are ample. Of these the most important is, of course, the *Congressional Globe,* in which the great debates on the critical issues of Reconstruction are recorded. Many of the participants kept diaries or shared reminiscences. Among the most important is the *Diary of Gideon Welles—Secretary of the*

Navy Under Lincoln and Johnson, 3 vols. (Boston and New York, 1911), which offers an acerbic account of Johnson's troubled administration. Welles was a bitter partisan whose political hostilities determined his assessment of contemporaries. The appearance of his diary at the turn of the century greatly influenced the development of the anti-radical interpretation of Reconstruction history. The diary is of value for establishing developments within Johnson's political circle, but the opinions expressed in it should be treated with caution. Less complete is the diary of another member of Johnson's cabinet: James G. Randall, ed., *Diary of Orville Hickman Browning,* 2 vols. (Springfield, Illinois, 1938). Johnson's secretary of the treasury, Hugh McCulloch, penned his memoirs in the 1880s: *Men and Measures of Half a Century* (New York, 1888).

In his *Twenty Years of Congress: From Lincoln to Garfield . . . ,* 2 vols. (Norwich, Connecticut, 1884–86), Republican leader James G. Blaine displayed an admirable historical sense. Although Blaine wrote with great detachment, the opinions and personality of this conservative Republican leader become clear to the sensitive reader. George Washington Julian, one of the most radical Republicans, left a more avowedly personal account of Reconstruction in his *Political Recollections, 1840–1872* (Chicago, 1884). Among the more useful reminiscences (but by no means the only ones) are Representative George S. Boutwell's *Reminiscences of Sixty Years in Public Affairs* (New York, 1902); Democratic Representative Samuel S. Cox's *Union—Disunion—Reunion. Three Decades of Federal Legislation, 1855 to 1885* (Providence, 1886); and Senator John Sherman's *Recollections of Forty Years in the House, Senate, and Cabinet: An Autobiography,* 2 vols. (New York, 1895). Other leading politicians also published memoirs, but most are anecdotal, vague, and useful only in understanding some specific event or aspect of Reconstruction.

Many of the leading actors in the Reconstruction drama carefully preserved their correspondence. The letters to and from some of the most important have been published, sometimes as parts of semi-official biographies. For example: Edward L. Pierce, *Memoir and Letters of Charles Sumner,* 4 vols. (Boston, 1893); Jacob William Schuckers, *The Life and Public Services of Salmon P. Chase, U.S. Senator and Governor of Ohio* (New York, 1874); Robert Bruce Warden, *An Account of the Private Life and Public Services of Salmon P. Chase* (Cincinnati, 1874); Francis Fessenden,

Life and Public Services of William Pitt Fessenden, 2 vols, (Boston and New York, 1907); William Salter, *The Life of James W. Grimes, Governor of Iowa, 1854–1858; Senator of the United States, 1859–1869* (New York, 1876); Mary L. Hinsdale, ed., *Garfield-Hinsdale Letters: Correspondence Between James Abram Garfield and Burke Aaron Hinsdale* (Ann Arbor, Michigan, 1949); Frederic Bancroft, ed., *Speeches, Correspondence, and Political Papers of Carl Schurz*, 3 vols. (New York, 1913); and Rachel Sherman Thorndike, ed., *The Sherman Letters: Correspondence Between General and Senator Sherman from 1837–1891* (New York, 1894). Unpublished correspondence and papers of numerous leaders of the Reconstruction era may be found in the Manuscript Division of the Library of Congress in Washington, D.C. Among the largest and most important collections are those of Carl Schurz, Salmon P. Chase, Henry L. Dawes, William Pitt Fessenden, Edward McPherson, John Sherman, and Lyman Trumbull. Andrew Johnson's papers are also located in the Library of Congress but are more conveniently available on microfilm. Other repositories also have important collections: The voluminous correspondence of Charles Sumner is in the Houghton Library of Harvard University in Cambridge, Massachusetts. Important letters of James R. Doolittle and interesting accounts of Reconstruction events by Timothy Otis Howe are held by the Wisconsin Historical Society, Madison, Wisconsin. The papers of William Henry Seward and Thurlow Weed are in the Rush Rhees Library of the University of Rochester, Rochester, New York, and the extremely revealing letters from William Pitt Fessenden to his family may be found at the Bowdoin College Library, Brunswick, Maine.

Also essential, for both opinions and facts, are the newspapers published during the Reconstruction crisis. The reader should remember, however, that the nineteenth-century press was partisan and reflected the opinions of the political parties and the factions of those parties the various journals represented. The two wings of the New York Republican party were represented by the New York *Times* (the organ of the conservative Seward-Weed faction) and the New York *Tribune* (Horace Greeley's radical newspaper). The self-consciously ex-Democratic wing of the Republican party spoke through William Cullen Bryant's New York *Evening Post*. The New York *Herald* voiced the opinions of War and Union Democrats during Reconstruction, while the extreme, pro-southern (formerly

Peace) Democrats expressed their views through the New York *World*. The more extreme Republicans of the Midwest no doubt found the Chicago *Tribune* more congenial than the more conservative Cincinnati *Commercial*. Former abolitionists and extreme radical antislavery men spoke through the weekly New York *Independent* and New York *National Anti-Slavery Standard,* while more moderate Republicans no doubt favored the sophisticated New York *Nation*. Local papers throughout the country often reprinted the opinions or information carried in the larger dailies, but some of the smaller papers are important because of their connection with leading politicians; for example, the Centreville *Indiana True Republican,* edited by George Julian's brother, Isaac, featured a weekly letter from the great radical Representative himself.

Finally, historians have published numerous biographies of the men who made—and tried to unmake—Reconstruction. Among the most important are David Donald, *Charles Sumner and the Rights of Man* (New York, 1970); Fawn Brodie, *Thaddeus Stevens: Scourge of the South* (New York, 1959); Richard N. Current, *Old Thad Stevens: A Story of Ambition* (Madison, Wisconsin, 1942); Charles A. Jellison, *Fessenden of Maine, Civil War Senator* (Syracuse, New York, 1962); Mark Krug, *Lyman Trumbull: Conservative Radical* (New York, 1965); William S. McFeely, *Yankee Stepfather: General O. O. Howard and the Freedmen* (New Haven and London, 1968); Patrick Riddleberger, *George Washington Julian, Radical Republican: A Study in Nineteenth Century Politics and Reform* (Indianapolis, 1966); Benjamin P. Thomas and Harold M. Hyman, *Stanton: The Life and Times of Lincoln's Secretary of War* (New York, 1962); Hans L. Trefousse, *Benjamin Franklin Wade: Radical Republican from Ohio* (New York, 1963); Trefousse, *Ben Butler: The South Called Him Beast!* (New York, 1957); and Glyndon G. Van Deusen's trilogy, *Thurlow Weed: Wizard of the Lobby* (Boston, 1947), *Horace Greeley: Nineteenth Century Crusader* (New York, 1964), and *William Henry Seward* (New York, 1967).

Andrew Johnson

The historical reputation of no other president has risen so suddenly or fallen so precipitately as that of Andrew Johnson—from historical "goat" in the 1890s to hero in the 1920s and 1930s and back to "goat," and in some cases even villain, in the 1960s and

1970s. The details of these metamorphoses have been recorded by Albert Castel in "Andrew Johnson: His Historiographical Rise and Fall," *Mid-America*, XLV (July 1963), 175–84, a good starting point for the reader who wants to learn more of the life of this stubborn, courageous, self-righteous, principled champion of what he conceived to be the common man. Eric L. McKitrick has prepared a useful collection of contemporary and historical assessments of Johnson, in *Andrew Johnson: A Profile* (New York, 1969), which offers excerpts from many of the studies of this controversial president.

In the opinions of the earliest historians of Reconstruction—Rhodes, Dunning, Burgess, and others—Johnson was in large part responsible for the evils they perceived in Radical Reconstruction. An inept politician who thoroughly misjudged the temper of the North, a stump speaker who degraded the presidency with his harangues, Johnson may have had the right instincts, but his incapacity for leadership and stubborn refusal to accommodate even justified northern concerns played into the hands of the radicals and fixed "Black Reconstruction" upon the South.

In the 1920s, however, a new appreciation of Johnson developed. A series of studies depicted him as the battling champion of the common man, valiantly resisting cynical radicals bent on the vindictive destruction of southern society and the subjugation of southern whites before ignorant and venal blacks led by corrupt, white "Carpetbaggers." As the economic determinist axioms of the Progressive historians won acceptance in the profession, these apologists for the President added antipathy toward developing industrial capitalism to his collection of virtues. First apparent in Robert W. Winston's *Andrew Johnson: Plebeian and Patriot* (New York, 1928), Johnson-worship continued with Lloyd Paul Stryker's *Andrew Johnson: Profile in Courage* (New York, 1929) and George Fort Milton's *The Age of Hate: Andrew Johnson and the Radicals* (New York, 1930). The scholarly Beale and the popularizer Bowers continued the trend, depicting Johnson sympathetically in their works on Reconstruction (*The Critical Year* and *The Tragic Era*, respectively). Pro-Johnson sentiment was well established among historians through the 1940s, and echoes of it continued into the 1960s, in Milton Lomask, *Andrew Johnson: President on Trial* (New York, 1960), and Lately Thomas, *The First President Johnson* (New York, 1968), which is not quite so uncritical of its hero as its predecessors.

Naturally, Andrew Johnson's star fell as that of the Republicans rose. In *Andrew Johnson and Reconstruction,* among the first of the "new wave" studies of Reconstruction, McKitrick portrayed Johnson as the political "outsider," a "loner" most comfortable in bitter opposition to those in power, unable to wield power effectively himself. LaWanda and John H. Cox painted Johnson as an ambitious politician, as concerned with reelection in 1868 as with principle, and a thoroughgoing bigot besides, in their *Politics, Principle, and Prejudice.* And Benjamin Thomas and Harold Hyman in their biography, *Stanton,* concluded that Johnson tried to subvert the Army and threatened the disruption of American democratic process in his reckless effort to subdue the Republicans. The President's reputation has not yet recovered, and may never recover, from this historiographical barrage.

Impeachment

The only monographic study of the Johnson impeachment is David Miller DeWitt's *The Impeachment and Trial of Andrew Johnson, Seventeenth President of the United States: A History* (New York and London, 1903). Fully agreeing with the then developing anti-Republican interpretation of Reconstruction, DeWitt regarded impeachment as simply another element of the misguided radical Republican program. Superficial in analysis and interpretation, DeWitt's work serves best as a digest of the events and arguments of the great trial. The pro-Johnson histories—Bowers's *Tragic Era,* Milton's *Age of Hate,* Winston's *Andrew Johnson: Plebeian and Patriot,* Stryker's *Andrew Johnson: Profile in Courage,* and Lomask's *Andrew Johnson: President on Trial*—went further than DeWitt, establishing virtually a "devil" theory of impeachment, with the radical Republicans cast as the devils. The only historian to offer a more considered view of impeachment among the early writers was Dunning. His "The Impeachment and Trial of President Johnson," in his *Essays on the Civil War and Reconstruction,* remains the best essay upon the subject. Without judging the case, Dunning clearly recognized the weakness of many of the arguments presented by Johnson's lawyers and discussed the points of law with a fuller understanding and deeper insight than any historian since.

As historians have become more sympathetic to the radical Republicans in recent decades, they have tempered their judgments of the barely aborted attempt to remove the president. David

Donald, Eric L. McKitrick, and Hans L. Trefousse have all pointed out the mitigating circumstances surrounding impeachment, but they still argue the flimsiness of the case and disparage its political motivation. Only Harold M. Hyman has implied that the events that preceded impeachment may have justified it. For Donald's and McKitrick's analyses, the student should see Donald, "Why They Impeached Andrew Johnson," *American Heritage,* VIII (December 1956), 21–25, and McKitrick, *Andrew Johnson and Reconstruction.* Trefousse articulated his opinions in a paper delivered at the 1968 convention of the American Historical Association—"Radical Republicans, Reconstruction, and the Executive and the Impeachment of Andrew Johnson." Hyman's article "Johnson, Stanton and Grant: A Reconsideration of the Army's Role in the Events Leading to Impeachment," is in the *American Historical Review,* LXVI (October 1960), 85–100. He carried his suggestions further in *Stanton,* co-authored with Benjamin Thomas. For a more complete historiography of impeachment, the reader should see James E. Sefton, "The Impeachment of Andrew Johnson: A Century of Writing," *Civil War History,* XIV (June 1968), 120–47.

To a large extent, the prejudicial view of impeachment most historians have adopted is based on the mistaken notion that government officials can be impeached only for actual criminal offenses indictable in regular courts. However, numerous studies of impeachment have contradicted this widely held conviction, sustaining the position adopted by the more radical Republicans during the crisis. Among analyses of impeachment published by lawyers and political scientists are David Y. Thomas, "The Law of Impeachment in the United States," *American Political Science Review,* II (May 1908), 378–95; Paul S. Fenton, "The Scope of the Impeachment Power," *Northwestern University Law Review,* LXV (November-December 1970), 719–47; and Raoul Berger, "Impeachment for 'High Crimes and Misdemeanors,'" *Southern California Law Review,* XLIV (1971), 395–460. A book-length study of impeachment by Berger will shortly be published by Harvard University Press. Irving Brant's book, *Impeachment: Trials and Errors* (New York, 1972), has just appeared. In it Brant argues that the framers of the Constitution intended impeachment as a remedy only for criminal acts and violations of the oath of office. In arriving at this conclusion, Brant rejects English precedents and precedents from American impeachments that do not agree with his position. I do not believe his arguments will convince scholars who have studied the question closely. (Brant devotes a chapter to the Johnson impeachment; it is rather superficial and manifests little familiarity with the political circumstances in which the proceedings took place.)

For the student who wishes to delve into the primary materials, the most important source is, of course, the published record of the impeachment trial, *The Trial of Andrew Johnson, President of the United States, Before the Senate of the United States, on Impeachment by the House of Representatives, for High Crimes and Misdemeanors,* 3 vols. (Washington, 1868). The *Congressional Globe* offers the record of congressional infighting over the impeachment-connected issue of adjournment as well as both the December 1867 and February 1868 battles over impeachment itself. Representative William Lawrence's analysis of impeachment, "The Law of Impeachment," which represented the views of the more radical Republicans, was published in the *American Law Register,* XV, o.s. (September 1867), 641–80. Theodore Dwight defended the more conservative view that the President could be removed only for indictable crime in "Trial by Impeachment," *American Law Register,* XV, o.s. (March 1867), 257–83. The majority and minority reports on impeachment by the House Judiciary Committee and testimony given to the committee are published in *House Report No. 7,* 40th Congress, 1st Session.

Several of the participants in the impeachment and trial later assessed the proceedings. The most famous account is that offered by Edmund G. Ross, the doubtful senator who cast the crucial vote against conviction. His *History of the Impeachment of Andrew Johnson . . .* (Santa Fe, 1896) was written after he had become a Democrat, glorifies his own role, and should be used with caution. Senator John B. Henderson offered his view in "Emancipation and Impeachment," published in *Century Magazine,* LXXXV (December 1912), 196–209. Like Ross, Hendeson voted against the removal of the President and offered a dissident's view of the proceedings. Senator George F. Edmunds challenged part of Henderson's account in a letter the magazine published as "Ex-Senator Edmunds on Reconstruction and Impeachment," *Century Magazine,* LXXXV (April 1913), 863–64. Representative George S. Boutwell, the leader of the pro-impeachment forces in the House Judiciary Committee and later one of the managers of impeachment, recalled the great events in "The Impeachment of Andrew Johnson: From the Standpoint of One of the Managers of the Impeachment Trial," *McClure's Magazine,* XIV (December 1899), 171–82. A Democratic view, recorded in Representative John V. L. Pruyn's journal, has been edited by Jerome Mushkat and appears as "The Impeachment of Andrew Johnson: A Contemporary View" in *New York History,* XLVIII (July 1967), 275–86.

The foregoing review of sources is by no means complete. The student who wishes to undertake primary research into this fascinating era will have to pay the price in the form of the "literature search," that frustrating, exhausting, and tedious job that nonetheless unlocks the gates of the gardens of history.

Index